American Indian Literatures

AN INTROD

BIBLIOGRAPHI

AND SELECTED BIBLIOGRAPHY

A. LaVonne Brown Ruoff

The Modern Language Association of America
New York, NY   1990

Library of Congress Cataloging-in-Publication Data

Ruoff, A. LaVonne Brown.
     American Indian literature : an introduction, bibliographic review, and selected bibliography / A. LaVonne Brown Ruoff.
        p.   cm.
     ISBN 0- 87352-191-9   ISBN 0-87352-192-7 (pbk)
     1. Indian literature—United States—History and criticism.
2. Indian literature—United States—Bibliography. 3. American literature—Indian authors—History and criticism. 4. American literature—Indian authors—Bibliography. I. Title.
     PM155. R86   1990
     897—dc20   90-13438

Third printing 1993

Published by The Modern Language Association of America
10 Astor Place, New York, New York 10003-6981

Printed on recycled paper

For my family—Gene, Stephen, and Sharon—
and for Carol Hunter (1937–87),
an Osage friend and scholar who died too soon.

Contents

Preface

This volume focuses primarily on the literature of the native peoples of what is now the United States. However, the literatures of specific tribal groups cross national boundaries. Among the many tribal groups split between the United States and other countries are the Yaqui (Mexico) and the Ojibwas and the Iroquois tribes (Canada). Consequently, when specific works or authors from the Arctic, Canada, Mexico, or Central America are important to understanding the development of native literature in the United States, these are included. One such author is Emily Pauline Johnson (Mohawk), a proud Canadian. Most of her short stories appeared in magazines published in the Chicago area and were widely read in the United States. Because of her popularity here and her importance to the development of literature written by American Indian women, she is included.

This volume uses as its basic definition of *American Indian identity* that given by N. Scott Momaday in "The Man Made of Words": "an idea which a given man has of himself" (96–97). The complex issue involved in defining *American Indian* is made clear in the following statement from the Bylaws of the National Indian Education Association:

> For purposes of the NIE Constitution the term American Indian shall mean any person who: (1) is a member of a tribe, band, or other organized group of Indians, including those tribes, bands, or groups terminated since 1940 and those recognized now or in the future by the state in which they reside, or who is a descendent, in the first or second degree, of any such member, or (2) is considered by the Secretary of the Interior to be an Indian for any purpose, (3) is an Eskimo or Aleut or other Alaska Native, or (4) is recognized as an Indian by his community. (Membership, art. 3)

In conformity with this definition, Eskimos and other Alaskan Natives are included in the term *American Indian* as used in this volume. Although I have generally accepted writers' designations of themselves as American Indian, I have respected the wishes of those who have indicated that their Indian ancestry was so marginal that they did not feel it appropriate to so define themselves. For lack of space, this volume will not include a discussion of the very important work of the many non-Indian authors influenced by American Indian literatures and traditions.

In this book, the term *literature* refers to both oral and written works. Although the origins of the term *literature* have led some to apply it only to what has been written, such a strict interpretation ignores the oral basis of our literary heritage, Indian and non-Indian. A more useful definition is the one suggested by William Bright in *American Indian Linguistics and Literature*: "that body of discourses or texts which, within any society, is considered worthy of dissemination, transmission, and preservation in essentially constant form" (80). Other terms frequently used to designate oral literature are *verbal art, folklore, oral poetry and narrative,* and *myth.* Most of the literature of Native North America before contact was transmitted orally and aurally. Oral literature remained the dominant form until the twentieth century. Since 1772, however, American Indian authors have published their written work. In the twentieth century, particularly since 1968, increasing numbers of American Indians have become highly accomplished and prolific writers.

Although American Indian literatures are the oldest literatures on this continent, they have not generally been included in American literature courses. In 1917, Mary Hunter Austin, in her chapter "Aboriginal" literature in *The Cambridge History of American Literature*, decried this exclusion:

> Probably never before has a people risen to need a history of its national literature with so little conscious relation to its own aboriginal literature. Yet if we extend the term American to include the geographical and racial continuity of the continent, unbroken at its discovery, we have here the richest field of unexploited aboriginal literature it is possible to discover anywhere in the world. (610)

More needs to be done to redress this neglect. Undoubtedly, one reason for the exclusion of American Indian literatures from American literature curricula is the fact that few teachers are trained in this field. The Modern Language Association has been in the forefront of encouraging scholars and teachers to study and teach American Indian literatures. In 1977, the MLA and the National Endowment for the Humanities jointly sponsored a Seminar on Contemporary Native American Literature, which was instrumental in establishing a group of scholars dedicated to this field. One important result of this seminar was the MLA's publication of *Studies in American Indian Literature* (1983), edited by Paula Gunn Allen (Laguna/Sioux), a volume of essays and course designs. Also crucial to the development of the field have been the MLA's Committee (formerly Commission) on the Literatures and Languages of America and the earlier Commission on Minority Literature, which have sponsored forums and workshops including scholarly papers on the field. The MLA has supported the development of the field through its approval of the Discussion Group on American Indian Literatures and of allied-organization status for the Association for Study of American Indian Literatures. The NEH has also made important contributions to training faculty members to teach the literatures of native America through offering summer seminars on the subject for high school, community college, and college and university teachers. Recently, editors of major anthologies have become sensitive to the importance of including the literatures of native America in their textbooks, although some anthologies still include only token selections. Despite these efforts, many teachers and students are unaware of the contributions of Native Americans to our national literary history. This volume is designed to assist them in beginning their study of the literatures of peoples native to what is now the United States.

American Indian Literatures is divided into three parts: part 1—"Introduction to American Indian Literatures," part 2—"Bibliographic Review," and part 3—"A Selected Bibliography of American Indian Literatures." The introduction in part 1 discusses types of oral literatures, life histories and autobiographies (both oral and written), and the history of written literature. The bibliographic essay in part 2 contains the following sections: "Bibliographies and Research Guides," "Anthologies, Collections, and Recreations," and "Scholarship and Criticism" (oral literature, oral and written life histories and autobiographies, general literary studies, studies of Native American writers, the teaching of American Indian literatures, and backgrounds—biography, demography, ethnohistory, languages, philosophy, women's studies, and image of the Indian). Part 3 is an extensive selected bibliography that includes works mentioned in parts 1 and 2 as well as additional references. Besides the works discussed in part 2, part 3 includes additional works by Indian authors. When chapbooks of poetry have been incorporated into collected works, these are not listed separately. The "Selected Bibliography" generally follows the structure of the "Bibliographic Review"; however, in the section entitled "Backgrounds," items have been combined into one alphabetized list instead of being separated into subcategories.

Spellings of tribal names are those currently in use either in the most recent editions of the *Handbook of North American Indians* or adopted by tribes: for example, *Mashpee* rather than *Marshpee*, *Navajo* rather than *Navaho*, *Nez Perce* rather than *Nez Percé*, and *Paiute* rather than *Piute*.

I am grateful for the encouragement of Paula Gunn Allen, Michael A. Dorris, Karl Kroeber, and Andrew O. Wiget, at whose insistence I first began the historical and bibliographic work that has resulted in the present volume. I also am grateful for the guidance of Larry Evers, who was generous with his help.

Earlier versions of portions of this volume have appeared in *Studies in American Indian Literature*, edited by Paula Gunn Allen (New York: MLA, 1983); *Critical Essays on Native American Literature*, edited by Andrew O. Wiget; and in the Bibliography Issue of *American Studies International* (Fall 1986). Research was done under grants from the Native American Studies Program, Dartmouth College, and the Research Division of the National Endowment for the Humanities.

Part One

Introduction to American Indian Literatures

They carried dreams in their voices;
They were the elders, the old ones.
They told us the old stories,
And they sang the spirit songs.
　　　　　　　　Big Tree (Kiowa)

American literature begins with the first human perception of the American
landscape expressed and preserved in language.
　　　　　　　　N. Scott Momaday (Kiowa)

Backgrounds

The literature of this nation originated with the native peoples who migrated to North America over twenty-eight thousand years ago, not with the Western Europeans who began to immigrate in the late sixteenth and early seventeenth centuries. When Western Europeans arrived, 18 million people inhabited North America and 5 million lived in what is now the United States. After contact, the population of the native peoples of North America greatly diminished—primarily as a result of diseases brought by whites. According to the United States Census Bureau, there were only 210,000 left in this country by 1910. In the twentieth century, however, the Indian population in the United States has greatly increased. The 1980 census, which Indians feel gives a very low count, indicated that the native population of the United States (including Alaska) was 1,418,195. Of these, 681,213 lived on reservations and 736,982 lived off reservations. Thus over half of the Indian population now lives in towns or cities rather than on reservations.

At the time of contact, the native peoples of North America were divided into more than three hundred cultural groups and spoke two hundred different languages, plus many dialects, derived from seven basic language families. By 1940, 149 of these languages were still in use (Spencer, Jennings, et al. 38–39). Divided into numerous cultural and language groups, native North Americans practiced many different religions and customs. However, there are some perspectives on their place in the universe that many native American groups shared and continue to share. Among these are an emphasis on the importance of living in harmony with the physical and spiritual universe, the power of thought and word to maintain this balance, a deep reverence for the land, and a strong sense of community. Although individual Indians today vary in the extent to which they follow tribal traditions, their worldviews and values continue to reflect those of their ancestors.

The history of American Indian literature reflects not only tribal cultures and the experience and imagination of its authors but Indian-white relations as well. Although a detailed discussion of Indian-white relations is beyond the scope of this volume, a brief overview of some of the major events is important to understanding the interrelationship between Indian history and literature. Whites' settlement in Indian territory was inevitably followed by attempts to expand their land holdings and Indians' determined efforts to retain their ancestral land. During the seventeenth century, Indians rose up against white domination in the Pequot War in New England (1637), King Philip's War (1672–76) against the British, and the Pueblo Revolt of 1680 against the Spanish. As the fur trade expanded into Indian territories, Indians became increasingly dependent on whites for firearms, metal traps, and other trade goods. So important did trade become to Indians that from the late seventeenth century through the War of 1812, tribal relations were frequently dictated by trapping and trade opportunities. For example, between 1644 and 1680, the Iroquois, whose lands were depleted of fur-bearing game, defeated Indian tribes from the Hudson to Illinois in their westward invasion to gain new trapping territory in order to meet whites' demands for fur. Before the end of the War of 1812, the British, Americans, and French enlisted Indian tribes to help secure their claims to various territories or to defeat their enemies, Indian and non-Indian. Controversies over trade and Indian land helped precipitate the American Revolution. After the conclusion of the Revolutionary War, there was considerable racial animosity against Indians because of accusations about their wartime atrocities, the allegiance of most of the Iroquois to the British, and the demand by whites for Indian land. Settlers' westward migration into the Ohio Valley brought new conflicts. After the defeat of England in the War of 1812 essentially ended that nation's threat to American interests on the continent, the United States no longer felt it necessary to placate Indians to ensure that they would fight the British. Increasingly, legislators and settlers advocated the relocation of the Indians. During the debate on removal, the federal government negotiated numerous treaties between 1815 and 1830 arranging for immediate or ultimate resettlement. The death knell of Indian hopes for retaining tribal lands east of the Mississippi free from white encroachment was sounded in 1830, when Congress passed the Indian Removal Bill, which authorized the federal government to move Indians from these areas to Indian Territory, now Oklahoma, and other locations deemed suitable. Some tribes were forced to move several times. No sooner had the Removal Bill been implemented than whites violated it by migrating westward into Indian territories.

In 1848, the Treaty of Guadalupe Hidalgo with Mexico brought new territory and numerous tribes under the jurisdiction of the United States. The discovery of gold in California in 1849 stimulated new encroachments on Indian land as hordes of emigrants passed through Indian land on their way to the California gold fields, Idaho ore deposits, or Oregon timber. What began as a stream of settlers in the 1830s became a flood by the 1850s.

The 1862 rebellion of the Santee Sioux in Minnesota and the allegiance of the Five Civilized Tribes in Oklahoma (Cherokee, Chickasaw, Creek, Choctaw, Seminole) to the Confederacy during the Civil War provided new excuses for removal of the Santee and drastic reductions in land holdings of the Five Civilized Tribes after the Civil War. In the Southwest, the withdrawal of federal troops led to attacks by Navajos and Apaches, who were then rounded up onto reservations by Kit Carson and others. Conflicts between Colorado Indians and whites resulted in the Sand Creek Massacre of 1864, in which Colonel J. M. Chivington and his men brutally murdered Cheyennes, primarily old men, women, and children. The opening of the Bozeman Trail through Indian land during the Civil War resulted in fierce retaliations by the Teton Sioux. Western migration, slowed during the Civil War, greatly increased when the end of the war brought renewed demand for land. As a result, the government was determined to pacify the Indians once and for all. To do so, they forced Indians onto reservations by destroying their food supplies—the buffalo and stored winter food. Public outrage over the Indians' victory over General George A. Custer and his men in 1876 brought swift retribution to defiant tribes. By the end of the 1880s, the buffalo had been exterminated from the Plains and the last of the tribes had been forced onto reservations.

As part of its policy of assimilationism, the government passed the General Allotment Act of 1887, which had been sponsored by Senator Henry L. Dawes. Popularly called the Dawes Act, it allotted in severalty land previously owned by tribes. This bill was supported by liberals, who felt the Indians could survive only by becoming independent farmers, and by land grabbers, who plotted to gain Indian territory by legal and illegal means. It was also supported by Indians like Sarah Winnemucca (Paiute) and Charles A. Eastman (Sioux), who felt it offered Indians independence and citizenship. The Allotment Act resulted in enormous losses of Indian land, however. Wilcomb E. Washburn estimates that by 1934, Indians had lost over sixty percent of the land they owned in 1887 (*The Indian in America* 242–43).

The last gasp of Indian resistance was the Ghost Dance religion, a messianic movement that swept across the Plains in the late 1880s and 1890.

Its leader was Wovoka, or Jack Wilson (Paiute), who predicted that the Plains would again support millions of buffalo and that whites would disappear. By 1890, his words roused the Plains tribes and frightened whites before it died out. One tragic result was the massacre at Wounded Knee, South Dakota, in 1890, when Big Foot's band of Sioux Ghost Dancers was slaughtered after a dispute about turning in their weapons. This incident ended the Indian wars.

One dimension of the government's assimilationist policy was the education of Indian children in English and in Western European traditions. Many Indian children were shipped off to boarding schools in such faraway places as Carlisle, Pennsylvania, and Riverside, California, where they were separated for years from their families and forbidden to speak their native languages or practice their tribal customs and religions. The isolation of Indian children eroded strong family bonds and ancient tribal traditions.

Although official policy was to assimilate Indians into the dominant society, the government did not grant Indians citizenship until 1924. Because Indians volunteered, were wounded, and died in World War I far out of proportion to their numbers in the society, Congress awarded them citizenship out of gratitude for their service. Another major gain for Indians in the first half of the twentieth century was the passage of the Wheeler-Howard Indian Reorganization Act in 1934, which its advocates called the Indian Magna Carta. The act ended allotment in severalty, continued the trust period indefinitely, confirmed cultural pluralism, and reestablished tribal government. After World War II such policies came under increasing criticism, as politicians sought ways to end the "Indian problem." In 1953, House Concurrent Resolution 108 was passed, which began the campaign to terminate the federal government's role in Indian affairs. Under this policy, tribes such as the Klamath and Menominee lost their reservation status and the government actively encouraged Indians to move to cities. As a result, urban Indian populations greatly increased during this period, but termination was disastrous for the tribes. After fighting for years to regain reservation status for their land, the Menominee finally won their in battle in 1973, when they again became wards of the government.

The battle for justice for Indians has increasingly been fought in Congress, state legislatures, and courts. Many Indian organizations—such as the Indian Rights Association, National Association of Indian Affairs, National Indian Education Association, and National Congress of American Indians—emerged to serve as effective advocates for Indian causes. Indian activism was stimulated by the American Indian Chicago Conference of 1961, after which many young Indian activists formed the National Indian Youth Council to mobilize "Red Power." Other groups that developed during the 1960s include the American Indian Civil Rights Council, National Tribal Chairmen's Association, the American Indian Movement, and the National Council of Indian Opportunity. The revitalism of Indian identity during the 1960s led to renewed interest in tribal languages, customs, and religions. Increased Indian militancy resulted in the occupation of Alcatraz Island (1969); the Bureau of Indian Affairs office in Washington, D.C. (1972); and Wounded Knee, South Dakota (1973).

Strong Indian advocacy resulted in the passage of several bills that ensured Indian rights. The Indian Civil Rights Act (1968) provides for free exercise of religion, speech, press, and right of assembly; protection against the taking of property without just compensation; and tribal consent before the state can assume civil and criminal jurisdiction over Indian reservations within its borders. In 1971 the Alaska Native Claims Settlement Act was passed. The Indian Self-Determination and Education Assistance Act, which became law in 1974, allows tribes to contract with the government to provide educational and other services to tribal members. Two measures passed in 1978 were the American Indian Religious Freedom Act and Indian Child Welfare Act, which guarantee the exercise of native religion and ensure a tribal role in the adoption of Indian children.

Indian tribes continue to fight many crucial battles over such issues as control over their water, mineral, and wildlife resources; retention of rights guaranteed by treaties; just compensation for land; self-determination; and tribal legal jurisdiction over crimes committed on Indian land. The history of the native peoples of America is one of endurance despite adversity. Through the diversity of their cultures, significant achievements as tribes and individuals, and the richness of their literatures, American Indians remind us of their important contributions to the mosaic of American culture.

Oral Literatures

Indian oral literatures are a vibrant force that tribal peoples continue to create and perform and that strongly influence the written works of Indian authors, as Simon Ortiz (Acoma) makes clear:

> The oral tradition is not just speaking and listening, because what it means to me and to other people who have grown up in that tradition is that whole process, . . . of that society in terms of its history, its culture, its language, its values, and subsequently, its literature. So it's not merely a simple matter of speaking and listening, but living that process. ("Interview" 104)

Because the oral literatures of Native Americans reflect the diversity of their religious beliefs, social structures, customs, languages, and lifestyles, these literatures should be studied within the contexts of both the cultural groups that produced them and the influences on these groups resulting from their interactions with other tribes and with non-Indians.

Central to American Indians' traditional way of life is the belief that human beings must live in harmony with the physical and spiritual universe, a state of balance vital to an individual and communal sense of wholeness or beauty; this theme pervades American Indian oral and written literatures as well. In traditional Indian societies, all aspects of life are conducted according to the religious beliefs and rituals deemed essential to the survival and well-being of the group. Breath, speech, and verbal art are so closely linked to each other that in many oral cultures they are often signified by the same word. The reverence for the power of thought and the word that is an integral part of American Indian religions is exemplified in Navajo culture. In *Language and Art in the Navajo Universe*, Gary Witherspoon points out that the Navajo world was brought into being by the gods, who entered the sweathouse and thought the world into existence. The thoughts of the gods were realized through human speech, song, and prayer (16). The following excerpt from Witherspoon's translation of the "Beginning of the World Song" illustrates the interrelation among knowledge, thought, and speech in Navajo culture:

> The earth will be, from ancient
> times with me there is knowledge of it.
> The mountains will be, from ancient
> times with me there is knowledge of it.
> [and so on, mentioning other things to be]
>
> The earth will be, from the very
> beginning I have thought it.
> The mountains will be, from the very
> beginning I have thought it.
> [and so on]
>
> The earth will be, from ancient times
> I speak it.
> The mountains will be, from ancient times
> I speak it.
> [And so on]   (16)

According to Witherspoon, the language of the Navajo emergence myth indicates "that in the beginning were the word and the thing, the symbol, and the object." For the Navajos, the awareness of symbol is knowledge. "Symbol is word, and word is the means by which substance is organized and transformed" (46).

Such emphasis on word as symbol and the power of symbols to structure the universe is common among American Indian societies. Jack Frederick Kilpatrick and Anna Gritts Kilpatrick (Cherokee) stress in *Run toward the Nightland* that in "any magical ritual all generative power resides in thought" and that the songs which focus and direct the thought are alone inviolate. The singer or medicine man merely augments the authority of thoughts, applies or disseminates it more effectively (6). Lame Deer emphasizes that the Sioux live "in a world of symbols and images where the spiritual and the commonplace are one":

> To us they are part of nature, part of ourselves—the earth, the sun, the wind and the rain, stones, trees, animals, even little insects like ants and grasshoppers. We try to understand them not with the head but with the heart, and we need no more than a hint to give us the meaning.
> (*Lame Deer: Seeker of Visions* 109)

The power of thought and word to create and the continuum of the oral tradition from the mythic past of the Lagunas to the present are beautifully demonstrated by Leslie Marmon Silko (Laguna) in her introduction to her novel *Ceremony*. In the following passage, Silko describes how the Laguna creator thought the universe into existence:

> Ts'its'tsi'nako, Thought-Woman
> is sitting in her room
> and whatever she thinks about
> appears.
> . . . .
> Thought-Woman, the spider,
> named things and
> as she named them
> they appeared.
>
> She is sitting in her room
> thinking of a story now
> I am telling you the story
> she is thinking.   (1)

American Indians hold thought and word in great reverence because of their symbolic power to alter the universe for good and evil. The power of thought and word enables native people to achieve harmony with the physical and spiritual universe: to bring rain, enrich the harvest, provide good hunting, heal physical and mental sickness, maintain good relations within the group, bring victory against an enemy, win a loved one, or ward off evil spirits. Thought and word can also be used for evil against one's enemies. Because of their power and because words spoken can turn back on the speaker, for good or evil, thought and word should be used with great care. The power of the word to help the individual fit into the universe is exemplified in the Yokuts prayer below:

> My words are tied in one
> With the great mountains,
> With the great rocks,
> With the great trees,
> In one with my body

> And my heart.
> Do you all help me
> With supernatural power,
> And you, Day
> And you, Night!
> All of you see me
> One with this world!
> (Kroeber, *Handbook of*
> *Indians of California* 511)

Coupled with the power of the word is the power of silence. Momaday, in "The Native Voice," calls silence "the dimension in which ordinary and extraordinary events take their proper places." In the American Indian oral tradition, "silence is the sanctuary of sound. Words are wholly alive in the hold of silence; there they are sacred" (7). The Mescalero Apache express this reverence for the power of silence. In "Singing for Life," Clare R. Farrer indicates that the Apache believe that the Creator God communicates through the power of thought in dream. People can utilize this channel through "communicating without words." To think a thought during this state is often all that is necessary for action to occur (151). Keith H. Basso concludes in " 'To Give Up on Words' " that the critical factor in a Western Apache's decision to speak or keep silent was the nature of his or her relationships to other people. Apaches "give up on words" in such diverse situations as a meeting with strangers, the initial stages of courting, verbal attack, and the presence of someone for whom they sing a ceremony (153–58). Although attitudes toward silence vary from tribe to tribe, those outlined by Basso emphasize the importance of understanding the social customs governing the use of silence in individual Indian communities.

American Indians' desire for harmony is also reflected in their deep reverence for the land, another recurrent theme in their oral and written literatures. Because the earth nurtured them and because their tribal origins and histories are associated with specific places, Native North Americans have a strong sense of the sacredness of these places. In "Native Oral Traditions," Larry Evers and Paul Pavich say this sense of place is made possible by the "cultural landscape," which is created "whenever communities of people join words to place" (11). The words of a Havasupai Medicine Song, sung by Dan Hanna, illustrate tribal identification with the land:

> The land we were given
> The land we were given
>
> It is right here
> It is right here
>
> Red rock
> Red rock

Streaked with brown
Streaked with brown

Shooting up high
Shooting up high

All around our home
All around our home
    (Hinton and Watahomigie,
    Spirit Mountain 108–09)

American Indian authors continue to emphasize in their writings the importance of place, as Momaday movingly does in *The Way to Rainy Mountain*:

> Once in his life a man ought to concentrate his mind upon the remembered earth, I believe. He ought to give himself up to a particular landscape in his experience, to look at it from as many angles as he can, to wonder about it, to dwell upon it. He ought to imagine that he touches it with his hands at every season and listens to the sounds that are made upon it. He ought to imagine the creatures that are there and all the faintest motions of the wind. He ought to recollect the glare of noon and all the colors of the dawn and dusk. (83)

In an interview, Silko reveals the importance of cultural landscape when she describes how the river that runs through Laguna pueblo influenced tribal stories and her own work. Though muddy and shallow, the river was "the one place where things can happen that can't in the middle of the village." It was a special place where all sorts of things could go on. As an adolescent, Silko realized that the river was a place to meet boyfriends and lovers: "I used to wander around down there and try to imagine walking around the bend and just happening to stumble upon some beautiful man." Later she understood that these fantasies were exactly the kind of thing that happened in the Laguna Yellow Woman stories, a series of abduction/seduction myths, as well as in the pueblo's stories about those who used the river as a meeting place:

> These stories about goings-on, about what people are up to, give identity to a place. There's things about the river you can see with your own eyes, of course, but the feeling of the place, the whole identity of it was established for me by the stories I'd hear, all the stories. . . . (Evers and Carr, "A Conversation with Silko" 29)

Linked to reverence for the land is the emphasis on directionality and circularity that occurs frequently in American Indian oral and written literatures. Following the natural order of the universe, humankind moves in a circle from east to south to west to north to east. For many tribes, the numeral four, representing the cardinal directions, seasons, and stages of human life, is a sacred number often incorporated into the content and form of their literatures. Multiples of four and the number six, representing the cardinal directions plus the directions above and below the earth, are also common.

The circle symbolizes the sun and its circuit. It also represents the cycle and continuum of human life as it passes through infancy, childhood, adulthood, old age. Black Elk explains the significance of the circle to the Sioux:

> You have noticed that everything an Indian does is in a circle, and that is because the Power of the World always works in circles, and everything tries to be round. In the old days when we were a strong and happy people, all our power came to us from the sacred hoop of the nation, and so long as the hoop was unbroken, the people flourished. The flowering tree was the living center of the hoop, and the circle of the four quarters nourished it. The east gave peace and light, the south gave warmth, the west gave rain, and the north with its cold and mighty wind gave strength and endurance. This knowledge came to us from the outer world with our religion. Everything the Power of the World does is done in a circle. The sky is round, and I have heard that the earth is round like a ball, and so are the stars. The wind, in its greatest power, whirls. Birds make their nests in circles, for theirs is the same religion as ours. The sun comes forth and goes down again in a circle. The moon does the same, and both are round. Even the seasons form a great circle in their changing, and always come back again to where they were. The life of a man is a circle from childhood to childhood, and so it is in everything where power moves. Our tepees were round like the nests of birds, and these were always set in a circle, the nation's hoop, a nest of many nests, where the Great Spirit meant for us to hatch our children. (*Black Elk Speaks* 198–200)

The circle is also reflected in many American Indian ceremonies and dances. Among the Mescalero Apache, for example, the girls performing the puberty ceremony provide a visual reminder of the circularity of time and the cycles of life by running around a basket four times (Farrer 150). In addition, circularity and cycles are often incorporated into the structure of narratives. For instance, mythic culture heroes or heroines may leave the community only to return after many trials and adventures.

A strong sense of communality and cooperativeness, reflecting Native Americans' belief in the importance of harmony, is another recurrent theme in American Indian literatures. Tribes often stress cooperation and good relations within the group, demonstrated in communal rituals, work and play, and decision making. Among many tribes, generosity, helpfulness to others, and respect for age and experience are highly valued virtues that enabled them to survive. Ella C. Deloria comments in *Speaking of Indians*

(1944) that her people, "the Dakotas, understand the meaning of self-sacrifice, perhaps because their legends taught them that the buffalo, on which their very life depended, gave itself voluntarily that they might live" (14). In *The Life, Letters and Speeches of Kah-ge-ga-gah-bowh* (1850), George Copway describes how his Ojibwa father taught him the importance of generosity to the aged:

> *If you reverence the aged, many will be glad to hear of your name. . . .* The poor man will say to his children, "my children, let us go to him, for he is a great hunter, and is kind to the poor, he will not turn us away empty." The Great Spirit, who has given the aged a long life, will bless you. (24)

The following Keres song, which Paula Gunn Allen learned from her cousin, exemplifies this sense of oneness with the community and with the land:

> I add my breath to your breath
> That our days may be long on the Earth
> That the days of our people may be long
> That we may be one person
> That we may finish our roads together
> May our mother bless you with life
> May our Life Paths be fulfilled.
> (Qtd. in *The Sacred Hoop* 56)

Some themes are more culturally specific. For example, the narratives of the pueblo-dwelling Hopis tend to stress hard work, while those of the nomadic Navajos tend to emphasize movement (Courlander, *Hopi Voices* xxvii–xxix; Astrov, "Concept of Motion as the Psychological Leitmotif of Navaho Life and Literature").

American Indian oral literatures were most often transmitted aurally. However, some groups did record portions of their literatures. The Ojibwa, for example, used pictographic symbols to preserve their Midé (Grand Medicine) rituals on birchbark scrolls and other materials; other tribes, such as those on the Plains and Northwest Coast, also kept pictographic accounts. One of the few tribes to record their literature in books was the Quiche Maya of the Guatemala highlands, who preserved the stories of the origin of their culture in a work called the *Popol Vuh*, or *Council Book*. Their scribes continued to create books before the arrival of Western Europeans, who subsequently burned hundreds of hieroglyphic volumes. According to Dennis Tedlock, only four have survived, three in Europe and one recently discovered in Guatemala (*Popol Vuh* 23–27).

Native American oral literatures include both the works performed by American Indians within the communities that produced them and performances preserved in written transcriptions. These literatures reflect the mythology and history of the past as well as the experiences of the present. Although traditional ceremonies, myths, and songs follow general patterns established within the group over time, ceremonialists, storytellers, and singers create their own performances within those patterns. So long as the interpretations are accepted by the group as true to the spirit and content of the original, are performed appropriately, and achieve the desired result, many tribes may consider each performer's version as valid. The Iroquois follow this approach in their ceremonies, according to Michael K. Foster. After studying four Iroquois Longhouse speech events performed by seven speakers, Foster concludes in *From the Earth to Beyond the Sky* that their rituals are not memorized verbatim but are composed, or "literally built anew," each time a performer rises to speak:

> What speakers share, and what gives continuity to the tradition across longhouse and reserve lines, is a set of composition rules for each ritual type (rules governing the statement, development and resolution of themes) and a common repertoire of conventionalized formulas. (vi)

Foster emphasizes that flexibility is the key resource for the speaker, who uses what works at the moment.

However, the degree to which improvisation is permissible may vary from one form of literature to another within the tribe. Discussing the magical rituals of the Cherokee in *Run toward the Nightland*, Kilpatrick and Kilpatrick state that master singers of rituals are "at perfect liberty to improvise a text if the spirit moves" them to do so. While the singers will not knowingly alter a text that has descended to them through tradition, they may occasionally elect to use only part of it (7). In *Singing for Power*, Ruth Murray Underhill comments that among the Papago, the storytellers work years to memorize the complicated mass of prose and verse that constitutes that tribe's bible. When the sun stands still, the storytellers recite this bible over four winter nights to those gathered in the ceremonial house. Although the storytellers may elaborate the prose with their own illustrations and explanations, they cannot do so with the verse. The words and tune of every song and the point at which they enter the story were given by Elder Brother, their culture hero. Nevertheless, as Underhill notes, some variations have crept in (12).

In *Kinaaldá*, Charlotte Johnson Frisbie indicates that improvisation is restricted in this Navajo girl's puberty rite and that an essential core exists in both myth and ceremony. Songs can be lengthened or shortened and verses within them ordered differently or even omitted, although the details of ceremonial songs per se may not be changed. Characters must retain their original names, costumes, and habitats; they must pursue their established journeys and perform determined acts. However, Frisbie also states that the timing and performances of the ceremony can vary not only for reasons inherent in Navajo customs and religion but also for more immediate, observable causes—available material, economic welfare, personal preference, environmental conditions, death of relatives, school restrictions, and regional customs and beliefs (82–84, 91–92). While tribal custom determines the degree to which improvisation is acceptable in communal rites as well as in traditional songs and narratives, American Indian artists also create oral literature that reflects their personal experience and imagination.

Even if verbatim memorization is not essential, the performance of oral literatures can sometimes demand great feats of recall. For example, the Navajo Night Chant, or Nightway, a healing ceremony, begins at sunset and ends eight and a half days later at sunrise. Because each ceremony, story, and song survived through time immemorial only in tribal memory, every generation faced the danger of losing its ancestral oral traditions if tribal members did not preserve them in their memories and encourage their performance. In *Indian Boyhood* Charles Eastman describes how his people, the Sioux, trained their young boys from an early age to assume the task of preserving and transmitting tribal and ancestral legends:

> Almost every evening a myth, or a true story of some deed done in the past, was narrated by one of the parents or grandparents, while the boy listened with parted lips and glistening eyes. On the following evening, he was usually required to repeat it. If he was not an apt scholar, he struggled long with his task; but, as a rule, the Indian boy was a good listener and has a good memory, so that the stories were tolerably well mastered. The household became his audience, by which he was alternately criticized and applauded. (42-43)

Many American Indians consider religious ceremonies, myths, and songs as too sacred to be discussed or collected for study by those outside the tribe. In an interview with Joseph Bruchac, Ray A. Young Bear (Mesquakie) describes his family's opposition to collecting the tribe's oral narratives:

> I have been consulting my Grandmother as well as other people, and I am afraid that it is simply impossible. The first and only stories we could have picked from Mesquakie people were published by William Jones, who was a protégé of Franz Boaz [sic], in the early 1900s. I tried to tell my relatives that there had been previously published material on Mesquakie people by our forefathers. I thought it would still be possible to, at least, try and share some stories now before they are forgotten. But this idea of trying to keep a culture free of what would be called cultural contamination is still very prevalent among the Mesquakie. It would be easier just to forget the stories and not publish them at all. If one attempts to do that, they are risking their lives. As my grandmother [sic] told me, "I used to hear stories about William Jones being here on the Settlement when I was young. He must have

gone around with a bag over his shoulder, collecting these stories. But what happened to him? He went overseas and was killed by the Philip[p]ines or some tribe in those islands in the Pacific." She uses that as a reference and I think it is reference that must be heeded. (*Survival This Way* 348)

Some Indians and non-Indians believe that printing oral literature dooms it as oral performance; others feel that because stories and songs are fast-vanishing relics, performed only for anthropologists and folklorists, they must be captured in books in order to survive. In *Yaqui Deer Songs*, Larry Evers and Felipe S. Molina emphasize that their experience suggests the contrary: "that Yaqui deer songs and the traditions which surround them are very much alive and that more than sixty years of recording and printing versions of them has complemented and reinforced more traditional oral modes of continuance, rather than contributing to their disappearance" (14).

Because the verbal arts are performed arts, the recordings and transcriptions of them should incorporate as much of the performance as possible. Elizabeth C. Fine comments in *The Folklore Text* that although the literary model of the text is the most widespread format for folklore publications, it ignores recording performance context and style. As Fine makes clear, the ethnolinguistic text, developed by early anthropologists and continued by modern linguistic anthropologists, is primarily an accurate verbatim transcript of "connected discourse to aid linguistic analysis and to preserve vanishing cultural traditions." Early ethnolinguistic texts preserved little, if any, information about "the informant, setting, or cultural significance of the tale." Many of the published folklore texts may be reports or summaries rather than records of authentic performances (55, 61).

In addition, many of those who recorded oral literatures sometimes abbreviated or revised the texts to suit the tastes of the time. Aspects of style and performance that are part of the total verbal art of a given work include choice of ritual or ordinary language, repetition, structure of the work, revisions of the text to incorporate relevant allusions to the present, appeals to the audience, and use of the voice and body to dramatize the content. As Andrew O. Wiget emphasizes in "Telling the Tale," performance theory sees stories as "storytelling events." Performance is simply one of many ways of providing a "frame" for communication, which Barbara Babcock-Abrahams defines in "The Story in the Story" as "an interpretative context or alternative point of view within which the content of the story is to be understood and judged" (66). According to Wiget, "a frame signals to the receiver, through a variety of verbal and nonverbal markers, that a particular kind of message is being sent" that must be interpreted in a specific way to be intelligible (314).

In "The Poetics of Verisimilitude," Dennis Tedlock notes that Zuni narrators use a variety of the techniques of style and performance described above to create the appearance of reality. According to Tedlock, a few gestures seem to be standard usages in tale telling:

> A sweeping motion of a partially outstretched arm and hand may indicate the horizontal or vertical motion of a tale actor; a completely outstretched arm and hand, accompanied by the words, 'It was at this time,' may indicate the height of the sun at a particular point in the stories; the forefingers or palms may be held a certain distance apart to indicate the size of an object; and so forth. (166)

In keeping with the fact that tales take place "long ago," the Zuni narrators exclude modernisms from quotations and insert archaisms (167). Tedlock states that the narrators break the story out of its frame set in the "long ago" by alluding to the present, by such phrases as "It was about this time of year," centering the story action in the narrator's own house or alluding to members of the audience or their actions (168–69).

Whereas Tedlock bases his analysis of the storyteller's art on performances he attended and tape-recorded, Wiget bases his, in "Telling the Tale," on a videotaped performance by Helen Sekaquaptewa. Using photographs to illustrate his discussion, Wiget examines Sekaquaptewa's skill as a storyteller through her choice of words, the way she expresses the words, and the way she augments her tale with gestures and facial expressions. Discussing the kinesthetic features of her performance, Wiget notes, for example, that Sekaquaptewa basically sits in a neutral body position, erect and a bit forward on her sofa, hands in her lap and eyes slightly lowered. Though she varies this position, she always returns to it. Her most engrossing movements are those that reach into what is exclusively audience space, including actually touching the audience. Wiget concludes that gestures create suspense and climax (320–25).

The audience also plays a role in the performance of American Indian verbal arts. In *Verbal Art as Performance* Richard Bauman suggests that there is a "heightened intensity of communicative interaction which binds the audience to the performer in a way that is specific to performance as a mode of communication." The performers elicit the participative attention and energy of their audience. To the extent that audience members value the performance, "they will allow themselves to be caught up in it" (43).

Proper etiquette in many Indian cultures requires the audience to give the storyteller a gift, usually tobacco. Often the audience is expected to give a ritual response during the course of the story, to encourage the storyteller either to begin or to continue. If such encouragement is not forthcoming, the storyteller may stop. Audience participation becomes part of some ceremonies. Foster notes in *From the Earth to Beyond the Sky* that in the Iroquois Longhouse, the speaker for the men of the leading side begins the day's events with the Thanksgiving Address. At the end of each section, the men of the opposite moiety utter a term of assent. The speaker for the nonleading side then takes the floor (28–29). In *Yaqui Deer Songs*, Evers and Molina point out that in the Yaqui ceremonies the old men serve as ceremonial hosts and clowns. They are always interacting with the audience, which is drawn to them. "During their joking and repartee, they constantly play to their audience and expect laughter and verbal response." Even when the eldest member delivers the opening and closing sermons, he expects the audience to respond with the formulaic affirmative *"heewi"* (78). Another example of audience participation in ritual is described by Joann W. Kealiinohomoku in "The Drama of the Hopi Ogres." Kealiinohomoku indicates that the "ogre" ritual is unique because it is one of the few Hopi ceremonies totally performed in public and because its dramatis personae include members of the audience—Hopi children and some of their adult relatives. Those depicting orges interact with audience members by incorporating them into highly structured, improvised scenes (38).

Accurate and appropriate translation is crucial to the preservation in English of American Indian verbal arts. Unfortunately, all too often translations have not been true to the original texts. In the past, translations were rendered in the Victorian or pseudo-biblical styles considered by non-Indians to be appropriate for literature and incorporated elements common to Western European literature but not present in the literature of native North America. In "On the Translation of Style in Oral Narrative," Tedlock reveals how Frank Cushing, whose translations of Zuni literature were widely praised in the past, interjected such oaths as "Souls of my ancestors" and "By the bones of the dead" into his translations. According to Tedlock, the Zunis themselves have no such oaths and never make profane use of words denoting death, souls, ancestors, corpses, "Powers," and gods (35). He also points out that Cushing incorporated devices, lines, and whole passages of his own invention. At the opposite extreme were the highly literal and often graceless translations of Zuni literature made by the followers of the great anthropologist Franz Boas, whose work and disciples dominated the field of American Indian anthropology early in the twentieth century (36–37).

Other translations molded individual songs to fit the translators' or retranslators' interpretations of what the texts were about. Recently, poets and critics have reworked some of the early translations to produce their own versions. Evers and Molina illustrate in *Yaqui Deer Songs* what can happen to the beauty of the original Yaqui text. Working in 1982 from Juan Ariware's original performance of a Yaqui song recorded on phonographic cylinder by Frances Densmore in 1922, Molina transcribed the following song:

> Sikili . . .
>   kaita va vemu weamakasu
>   hakun kukupopoti hiusakai

Sikili . . .
   kaita va vemu weamakasu
     hakun kukupopoti hiusakai

lyiminsu seyewailo
   huya nainsasukuni
     kaita va vemu weamakasu
       hakun kukupopoti hiusaka

Sikili . . .
   kaita va vemu weamakasu
     hakun kukupopoti hiusaki. (26)

Densmore, one of the earliest and most prolific recorders and translators of American Indian music, translates this simply as "The quail in the bush is making his sound (whirring)" (song 84, *Yuman and Yaqui Music* 157). Molina's translation demonstrates how much is lost in Densmore's paraphrase:

Little red [quail],
   walking afar where there is no water,
     where do they make the kukupopoti sound?
Little red [quail],
   walking afar where there is no water,
     where do they make the kukupopoti sound?

Over here, in the center
   of the flower-covered wilderness,
     walking afar where there is no water,
       where do they make the kukupopoti sound?
Little red [quail],
   walking afar where there is no water,
     where do they make the kukupopoti sound?   (26)

As Evers and Molina make clear, Densmore's paraphrase omits the line, stanza structure, rhetorical structure, action, onomatopoeic representation of the sound of the quail, and other features that contribute to the song's aesthetic effect in Yaqui (26–27). They also demonstrate the dangers of generalizing about American Indian songs on the basis of faulty translations. This danger is exemplified by Kenneth Rexroth's comments in "American Indian Songs." Using Densmore's abbreviated translations, Rexroth erroneously concludes not only that "the texts of almost all these songs are . . . extremely simple, but that most of them are pure poems of sensibility resembling nothing so much as classical Japanese poetry or Mallarmé and certain other modern French and American poets" (282). Although Densmore may sometimes provide paraphrases rather than translations, she nevertheless made invaluable contributions to the history of American Indian song. Indefatigable, she moved from tribe to tribe recording, transcribing, and translating or paraphrasing a voluminous collection of songs.

The history of the collection of oral literatures of native America begins in Mesoamerica in the books of the Maya. After contact, some of the Spanish priests helped to preserve the literature. In his *General History of the Things of New Spain*, Fray Bernardino de Sahagun included considerable native literature, which he translated into Spanish. His example was followed by other priests, who encouraged their Indian converts to record their cultural heritage. Tedlock notes in *Popol Vuh* that although the priests' primary concern was to prepare grammars and dictionaries, their interest encouraged their pupils to preserve their Indian literary legacy (28). In North America, some myths were incorporated into the accounts of Jesuits and other early explorers of the continent. However, the systematic collection of the oral literature of what is now the United States was stimulated by the publication of Henry Rowe Schoolcraft's *Algic Researches* (1839), which focused on Ojibwa culture and literature. Presses responded to the public's subsequent interest in the culture of the supposedly vanished "noble savages" and in their literature by publishing a number of life histories and autobiographies, most of which included selected examples of oral literature.

The scholarly collection of oral literatures did not flourish until the development of the anthropological and linguistic study of American Indian cultures in the late nineteenth and early twentieth centuries. In *The Folklore Text*, Fine credits John Wesley Powell, founding director of the Bureau of American Ethnology from 1879–1902, and Boas with establishing the ethnolinguistic approach that dominated the collection of American Indian verbal arts during this period. One of Powell's main reasons for collecting oral literatures was to provide samples of connected discourse to aid in learning the structure of Indian languages. The verbal arts also provided insights into Indian culture. Boas had a deeper interest in the literature itself. Fine concludes that his rejection of cultural evolutionism, respect for American Indian culture, and appreciation of the aesthetic values and important cultural functions of Indian folklore strongly influenced other anthropologists and linguists (19–22).

Tribes and individual scholars vary considerably in their categorization of oral literatures. Native Americans have their own distinctive terms to identify particular genres, which often do not correspond to Euroamerican genres. Dan Ben-Amos's history of the attempts to categorize oral literatures, in the introduction to *Folklore Genres*, demonstrates the complexity of the task. Ben-Amos stresses that ethnic-particular and cross-cultural systems may use different concepts of genre. Forms of oral tradition are not merely analytical constructs but "distinct modes of communication which exist in the lore of peoples" (xxv, xxi). However, despite the perils of categorizing oral literature, the following genres will be used in this volume to discuss Indian oral literatures: ritual dramas—chants, ceremonies, and rituals; songs; narratives. Oratory and speeches are discussed in a fourth section.

Ritual Dramas: Chants, Ceremonies, Rituals

Ritual drama is a very sacred form of oral literature that contains both song and narrative and sometimes includes oratory as well. Although *ritual drama* is the current term most commonly used by scholars to denote ceremonial complexes, tribes usually use the terms *chants* or *chantways, ceremonies*, or *rituals*. Specific terms are sometimes used to indicate particular kinds of ceremonial complexes. For example, Leland C. Wyman indicates in *Blessingway* that most of the Navajo chantways, whose primary purpose is to cure illness, require the use of the rattle. Father Berard Haile, who did much of the pioneering study of Navajo ceremonial complexes, suggests in "Navajo Chantways and Ceremonies," that other ceremonies that do not use the rattle be called "rites" (3–4).

Religious ceremonies express a tribe's attempts to order its spiritual and physical world through the power of the word, whether chanted, spoken, or sung. Ceremonies, and the songs, narratives, and orations included in them, may be expressed in special forms of language. Evers and Molina emphasize that the Yaqui use a variety of ways of speaking for talking, praying, giving a sermon, storytelling, and singing. In addition, there are many special ways to sing in Yaqui tradition, each with its own subject matter, style of performance, and performance setting: "All Yaqui songs are not the same. One who wishes to sing a deer song cannot come out with just any words, rhythm, or melody. He, almost always the singer is a he, must express himself in Yaqui within the conventions which Yaqui audiences have come to expect of *maso bwikam* deer songs" (28).

Frances Densmore points out in *Chippewa Music* that a special archaic language is used in the Midé songs. The words serve as a key to the idea of the song, without fully expressing it. Sometimes only one or two words occur in a song. Although their literal translation is meaningless, they convey an "occult significance" to the knowledgeable (1: 14–15). In *Sacred Language*, William K. Powers states that the Sioux have two types of sacred language: the generic *wakan iye* (sacred language) and the *hanbloglaka* (vision talk). *Wakan iye* is the form of language used between medicine men, "the language of philosophical commentary on the nature of religious things." *Hanbloglaka* is used in sacred discourse between individual medicine men and their spirit helpers. Both types are incomprehensible to the common people when used in their ritual context. Outside that context, *wakan iye* is translatable by the uninitiated, whereas *hanbloglaka* is not (25). The processes by which Sioux transform common language into sacred language include abbreviating common words; affixing the radical element *kan*, which refers to anything old, accepted because it has been so in former times, or wonderful or incomprehensible; reduplication of common words; inversion; and the use of a variety of stylistic features. Powers notes that from the standpoint of verbal stylistics, most terms employed in sacred language are generated out of familiar words assigned occult meanings or other kinds of verbal ornamentations (28–34).

In "Zuni Ritual Poetry," Ruth L. Bunzel comments that Zuni prayers must be formally learned. Each kiva, an underground house in which communal rituals are conducted, has a Ca'lako wo'le, who keeps the prayers. Members of the Saiyataca group, whose ritual is the most elaborate, meet every night to master the "long talk," the litany declaimed in the house of the host on the night of their final ceremonies. The "long talk" and the "morning talk" are chanted aloud in unison and must be letter-perfect (616). Bunzel also states that the Zuni use regular stereotyped phrases for all items commonly alluded to in prayer:

> The sun always "comes out standing to his sacred place," "night priests draw their dark curtain," the corn plants "stretch out their hands to all directions calling for rain," the meal painting on an altar is always "our house of massed clouds," prayer sticks are "clothed in our grandfather, turkey's, robe of cloud." (618)

Further, events are always described in terms of these stereotypes, which are often highly imaginative and poetic. Bunzel stresses that these fixed metaphors are the outstanding feature of Zuni poetic style (618).

Participation in ritual dramas unites tribal members with one another and enables them to communicate with and attempt to control natural and supernatural forces. Such rituals emphasize structure and order as the parts of the ritual are performed in sequence to achieve the desired result. Ceremonies are used for many communal and personal purposes. While some are performed seasonally as part of rituals assuring renewal of the earth or fertile crops, others mark communal events, such as entrance into a tribal society. Still others, such as purification ceremonies performed for those held captive by other tribes or for war veterans, protect the group from possible contamination. Many pertain to special occasions in one's life, such as receiving a name, the onset of puberty, marriage, death, and honoring the dead after the passage of time.

Ritual dramas are performed by priests or singers, shamans, and special societies. As Underhill indicates in *Red Man's Religion*, ceremonies in the Southwest were conducted by those of "more or less priestly status," which meant that they were proprietors of ritual passed down by inheritance. Acolytes apprenticed themselves to such priests or singers for periods of time in order to learn the complexities of the ritual they wanted to master. Priests, who differ from shamans because they do not need to be inspired by a vision in order to perform ceremonies, are most frequently found among organized planters and medicine men; shamans, among hunter-gatherers (93, 92, 81). The duties of shamans vary. Among the Eskimo, they perform the spirit flight, find lost souls, and foretell the future. On the Northwest Coast, their chief function is to cure illness. Ceremonies are also performed by religious cult societies. Åke Hultkrantz points out in *The Religions of the American Indians* that such religious cult societies are centered in California, the Northwest Coast, and the Great Lakes (117). For example, among the Ojibwa, Menominee, and Winnebago of the Great Lakes, the Midéwiwin, or Grand Medicine Society, carried out healing ceremonies. Hultkrantz feels that such societies represent a collective transformation of the institution of the medicine man, with an accompanying weakening of the visionary and a strengthening of the dramatic elements (119).

The Navajo Night Chant, or Nightway, exemplifies a healing ritual designed to cure an individual's illness in mind and body. The ceremony begins at sunset and closes eight and a half days later at sunrise. Accompanied by song, the patient purifies himself or herself for the first four days and prays to the gods. The gods awake at midnight of the fourth day and descend to appear in the sand paintings created on the fifth through the eighth days. The gods then "touch" their bodies to the patient's body so that he or she may absorb their power. At the beginning of the ninth day, thunder is summoned and the ceremony breaks free. The songs of the previous eight days now burst forth and last through the whole night. At sunrise, the healed patient faces east and begins life anew. The following, often-quoted prayer is from the morning of the third day—the day of the west. The prayer illustrates the emphasis on physical and spiritual harmony and on the sacredness of place so much a part of American Indian oral literatures. Among the elements of the prayer that are common in these literatures are the following: repetition, movement in time and location, progression from physical well-being to spiritual peace to ability to speak, and the comprehensiveness of the allusions to aspects of nature.

> Tsegihi!
> House made of dawn.
> House made of evening light.
> House made of the dark cloud.
> House made of male rain.
> House made of dark mist.
> House made of female rain.
> House made of pollen.
> House made of grasshoppers.
> Dark cloud is at the door.
> The trail out of it is dark cloud.
> The zigzag lightning stands high up on it.
> Male deity!
> Your offering I make.
> I have prepared a smoke for you.
> Restore my feet for me.

Restore my legs for me.
Restore my body for me.
Restore my mind for me.
Restore my voice for me.
This very day take out your spell for me.
Your spell remove for me.
You have taken it away for me.
Far off it has gone.
Happily I recover.
Happily my interior becomes cool.
Happily I go forth.
My interior feeling cold, may I walk.
No longer sore, may I walk.
Impervious to pain, may I walk.
With lively feelings, may I walk.
As it used to be long ago, may I walk.
Happily may I walk.
Happily with abundant dark clouds may I walk.
Happily with abundant showers may I walk.
Happily with abundant plants may I walk.
Happily on a trail of pollen may I walk.
Happily may I walk.
Being as it used to be long ago, may I walk.
May it be beautiful before me.
May it be beautiful behind me.
May it be beautiful below me.
May it be beautiful above me.
May it be beautiful all around me.
In beauty it is finished.
In beauty it is finished.[1]

Navajo ceremonials have been reprinted more often than those of any other tribe. Authoritative texts have been prepared by such scholars as Frisbie; Haile; Karl W. Luckert; Washington Matthews; and Wyman.

The Iroquois version of the Ritual of Condolence illustrates a ritual drama designed to heal the group as a whole. The Iroquois were divided into a senior moiety (Mohawk, Onondaga, and Seneca) and a junior (Oneida, Cayuga). To integrate the two sides, as John Bierhorst notes, women ideally married "across the fire" by taking husbands from the opposite moiety (*Four Masterworks* 109). The ceremony is conducted to repair the breach in Iroquois society caused by the death of one of the chiefs of the council of fifty representing the League of Five Nations. Here society is conceived of as a grieving widow whose eyes are filled with tears and whose throat and ears are clogged with ashes as she hovers among the cold coals of her darkened house. In Bierhorst's words, "death has stamped out her fire and scattered the firebrands who were her chiefs" (109). The enemy of society, however, is both death itself and the cult of death, which leads to depression and possible insanity. The Iroquois had attempted to achieve peace between tribes and thus thwart this cult of death by forming the confederated Five Nations, conceived by Hiawatha, who lived around 1500. In 1715, the league was expanded to six to include the Tuscaroras (109–111).

In his version, prepared from several texts, Bierhorst follows William N. Fenton's division of this ritual drama into five sections: "The Eulogy or Roll Call of the Founders," "At the Wood's Edge" (the coming together of the two moieties), the "Requickening" (restoration of the senses and mind from the destruction of grief), the "Hymn" in praise of the League, "Over the Great Forest" (preparation for the day when yet another death shall occur and final dispensation of the corpse) (Fenton, "Horatio Hale" xxiii–xxiv). The following oration, called "Within His Breast," is the fourth article of the "Requickening" section and was delivered by the "Cleareyed Orator." This ritual, and many other Iroquois ceremonies, places great emphasis on oratory. Like the excerpt from the Night Chant, it stresses the progressive nature of healing:

> Oh, my offspring, now there is still another thing that ever occurs wherever and whenever a great calamity has befallen a person; verily, this affliction comes when the being demonic of itself, the Faceless One, the lineaments of whose face our ancestors failed to discern, the Great Destroyer, puts forth excessive ferocity against one. . . .
>
> Is not what has befallen thee then so dreadful that it must not be neglected? For, at the present time, there are wrenchings without ceasing within thy breast, and also within thy mind. Now truly, the disorder now among the organs within thy breast is such that nothing can be clearly discerned. So great has been the affliction that has befallen thee that yellow spots have developed within thy body, and truly thy life forces have become greatly weakened thereby; truly thou dost now suffer.
>
> It is that, therefore, that in ancient times it thus came to pass that the hodiyaanehshon, *the Federal Chiefs*, our grandsires, made a formal rule, saying "Let us unite our affairs; let us formulate regulations; let us ordain this among others that what we shall prepare we will designate by the name Water-of-pity, which shall be the essential thing to be used where Death has caused this dreadful affliction, inducing bitter grief."
>
> And so, in whatever place it may be that such a tragedy will befall a person, it shall be the duty of him whose mind is left unscathed by it to take up and make use of the Water-of-pity, so denominated by us, by taking it in hand, and then pouring it down the throat of the one on whom the great affliction has fallen; and, it shall be that when the Water-of-pity shall have permeated the inside of his body, it will at once begin the work of reorganizing all the many things there which have been disarranged and disordered by the shock of the death, not only in his body but also in his mind; and it will also remove utterly all the yellow *gall* spots from his throat and from the inside of his body. (*Four Masterworks* 144–46)

Through the participation in ritual dramas or ceremonies, American Indians renew themselves in the rich culture that has sustained tribal life for centuries.

Songs

Because they are central to all aspects of ceremonial and nonceremonial life, songs constitute the largest part of the American Indian oral literatures. Songs that are part of ceremonies are sometimes sung outside that context or used for other purposes. In *Chippewa Music* (1910) Densmore describes music as one of the greatest pleasures of the Ojibwa and emphasizes that every phase of their life is expressed in music: "If an Indian visits another reservation one of the first questions asked on his return is: 'What new songs did you learn?' " (1: 1). Song is equally important to the Papago, who, according to Underhill, regard song as far more than simply self-expression. As she points out in *Singing for Power*, song is "a magic which called upon the powers of Nature and constrained them to man's will." Song is not only the practical basis of communal life but also "the most precious possession of the people" (5, 6). In *Prayer: The Compulsive Word*, Gladys A. Reichard comments that among the Navajo, song is a form of prayer. To the demands of "verbal sound and of words arranged in order are added musical values: notes, melody, beat, rhythm, phrasing, and the like." She concludes that it is most likely that "ritualistically singers do not consider song and prayer independently" (10, 11). The Eskimo share this respect for the power of song. Tom Lowenstein, in *Eskimo Poems from Canada and Greenland*, notes that their word *anerca* has the double meaning of "breath" and "poetry." Orpingalik (Netsilik Eskimo) describes his songs as "thoughts, sung out with the breath when people are moved by great forces and ordinary speech no longer suffices." Orpingalik calls his death-bed song "My Breath" because "it is as important to me to sing as to draw breath" (Lowenstein xxiii, 38).

The performance of songs is often accompanied by some form of percussion, usually the drum or rattle. Marcia Herndon indicates in *Native American Music* that a musical bow and wind instruments, such as whistles, vertical open flutes, and flageolets, were also used (20–22). However, the voice of the singer is the basic instrument and provides the variety of melodic line. For example, Densmore notes in *Chippewa Music* (1910) that singers of that tribe used a vibrato, a technique that is difficult to acquire and considered a sign of musical proficiency (1: 4). In *Papago Music* (1929), Densmore points out that the Papago use a prescribed manner of singing certain classes of songs. They frequently use a *glissando* in songs connected with the ceremony for bringing rain and with the ceremony called Limo, held for successful warriors after their return from battle (13). When Alan P. Merriam questioned a Flathead Indian about the criteria for a good singer, he replied, "If his lungs and throat are strong, and he can remember

the songs, he would be a good singer," a description other Flatheads suggested as well. Merriam also notes that a high-pitched voice is considered
good because it is loud and penetrating but that it should not be so high-
pitched as to make it difficult for others to sing as well (*Ethnomusicology of
the Flathead Indians* 40, 41). In *Yaqui Deer Songs*, Evers and Molina indicate
that a deer singer, who is male, should not call attention to himself by
singing too well; at the same time, he should not be sloppy or slovenly
about his singing either. According to Don Jesús, their Yaqui collaborator,
a good singer concentrates on his songs, sings with a high voice, and carries
his voice at a high pitch through the longest song lines without pausing
(78, 79). In *Songprints*, Judith Vander notes that Emily Hill (Shoshone)
described her mother as a good singer because she possessed a high voice
and large repertoire. According to Hill, those who performed the women's
singing role in the Sun Dance should have a "strong, clear sound" (34).

Songs are composed both communally, and individually. Barbara Tedlock provides an interesting insight into the composing process among the
Zuni in her description of how new songs are introduced in their Kachina
Societies. In "Songs of the Zuni Kachina Society," she indicates that each
kiva group in this society has two or three song composers in its member-
ship. Someone may offer a song after the dance chief asks, "What is he
holding?" The composer will then sing a shortened version. Although sometimes a song is accepted the way the composer presents it, more often it is
revised by the group (21, 27). Mando Sevillano notes in "Interpreting Native
American Literature" that among the Hopi some of the ceremonial songs
are personal, having been freely composed by an individual. Yet they are
not purely personal expressions because they embody, articulate, and share
the personal reality of the composer in an attempt to bring all the individuals of the tribal community into harmony and balance with the universe.
Indeed, the songs are never ascribed to individuals (2–3). Vander emphasizes the communal nature of Shoshone music in *Songprints*. Angelina Wagon,
a Shoshone singer, and her sisters always supported their father when he
sang, which Vander sees as part of a broader sociomusical ethic:

> This, in turn, springs from music's essential function at all communal
> occasions, social and religious. A powwow is, in part, judged by the
> number of dancers out on the dance floor. Good singers arouse and
> inspire the dancers to dance. Sun Dance singers lend critical assistance
> to Sun Dancers in their quest for health and power. (57)

Vander concludes that Shoshone songs do not express individual feelings
and that singers do not "seek personal recognition and admiration for their
public performances." Singers "help" one another and contribute to the
success of each occasion through their participation and presence (57–58).

Among some tribes, however, ownership of particular songs and dances
is the prerogative of a particular individual or family. Herndon indicates

in *Native American Music* that the tribes of British Columbia and Washington acknowledge individual composition as a means of producing music. She cites another example of ownership described by a Hupa from northern California:

> I have made two songs for the White Deer Dance. When I made them, I would go out by myself and sing them low so nobody could hear them. Then I sang them the next time there was a White Deer Dance. Then people knew them; they were my songs. I would sing them again and again, when there was a White Deer Dance. People could learn them because they heard them a few times. But they could not sing them. If there was a White Deer Dance and I was not there, a relative of mine could sing them. If somebody else wanted to sing them he would have to ask me for permission, whether I am there for the dance or not. (Qtd. in Herndon 18)

In *Blackfoot Musical Thought*, Bruno Nettl delineates three types of ownership: (1) songs belonging to the tribe at large and thus to be performed by anyone at any time; (2) songs owned by individuals that may be transferred (given or sold); and (3) songs owned by individuals but not transferable (140–41). One of Nettl's Blackfeet consultants commented that owning songs was almost as good as owning horses because one could buy and sell them like horses. Nettl notes that in the 1960s the Blackfeet still gave songs but he had not heard of selling them. When asked what it meant to own songs, a Blackfeet consultant gave this reply:

> It makes me feel very proud to be a Blackfoot. I have songs that belong to my tribe, but they are songs that I can give to somebody, or I can sing them, and everybody knows they belong to me, and if somebody else sings them, they know these are my songs. (142)

In contrast, Densmore comments in *Chippewa Music* (1910) that the Ojibwa have no songs that are the exclusive property of families or clans. A young man may learn his father's songs by giving him the customary gift of tobacco, "but he does not inherit the right to sing such songs, nor does his father force him to learn them" (1: 2).

Underhill notes in *Singing for Power* that Papago songs are handed down from singer to singer: "A man dreams his own songs, and he gives them to his son" (11). According to Underhill, the power of song is an honor to be earned and cannot be assumed lightly at the "mere whim" of an individual. Song magic is "given" by supernatural powers: "A man who desired a song did not put his mind on words and tunes: he put it on pleasing the supernaturals" (6). The Papago ask the would-be singer to perform an act of heroism, the greatest of which is going to war, because they believe that one who has performed an act of heroism has placed himself in contact with the supernatural. After the heroic act has been performed, the would-be singer fasts and waits for a vision, which comes only to the worthy. Such a vision always contains a song (7). Evers and Molina indicate that Don Jesús learned all his songs from other deer singers. He did not compose any deer songs and did not know anyone who did (64–65). Reichard states in *Prayer: The Compulsive Word* that among the Navajo, songs are "plentiful and purchasable just as any commodity, although some are more precious than others" (11). Their value depends on the number of people who know them and the purposes to which they are put:

> A chanter does not think of teaching a chant without communicating many of the songs; indeed, he would not think a person knew anything important about a chant if he did not know the songs. On the other hand, a few short, general prayers go with the chant, but most of them are stipulated by agreement between the patient's intermediary and the chanter for each ceremony, and often they are bargained for one by one. (11–12)

Customs as to the amount of innovation permitted in traditional songs also vary among tribes. In *Songs and Dances of the Lakota* Ben Black Bear and Ron D. Theisz comment that like oral literature, Sioux music allows for some personal creativity and variety as long as core elements are present and the final product is accepted as "valid." Less deviation is acceptable in religious songs (11). Densmore indicates in *Teton Sioux Music* that among both the Sioux and the Ojibwa, variations in time and intonation are found more often in unimportant than in important parts of a song (10). In *Chippewa Music* (1910) she notes that Ojibwa songs emphasize melody rather than words: the musical idea is more important than the words. It is permissible and customary to compose new words for old tunes, but the innovations are always similar in general character to the words previously used (1: 2). The songs of the Midéwiwin (Grand Medicine Society), the native religion of the Ojibwa, are the exception to this rule. Merriam comments that although individual composition must be of growing importance among the Flatheads, it is not a valued means of creating new musical material. Consequently, few Flatheads are willing to admit to having composed. He did not observe any Flatheads composing songs (*Ethnomusicology of the Flathead Indians* 21).

According to Viola E. Garfield, the Tsimshian Indians honor talented composers who can supply new songs for feasts, potlatches, and secret society initiations. In "The Tsimshian and Their Neighbors," she states that a host, planning an affair, engages the services of a composer to arrange melodies and words and to teach them to his group. This is done secretly so that the guests do know know what they will hear. The host requests not only songs of praise for his achievements and the glorification of his ancestors but also cleverly worded and subtle comments on the weaknesses and defects of selected guests. Because it is not polite or safe to insult guests directly, these derisive songs use double meanings and wordplay that leave little doubt about the identity of the intended victims (56–57).

Although tribes vary in their descriptions of the origins of songs, they usually include songs from three sources: the supernatural, the individual, and other tribes. According to Herndon, the Pima believe that many of their songs were sung in the beginning by the Creator or other mythical personages and then handed down by teachers. These songs are embedded in their origin myths and major ceremonies. Other songs are those created by individuals whose power is derived from their contact with the supernatural, primarily through dreams (*Native American Music* 14). Merriam emphasizes that the Flathead Indians believe that while some songs are individually composed by human beings and others are borrowed from neighboring peoples, all true and proper songs, particularly from the past, owe their origin to a variety of contacts experienced by humans with superhuman beings who are the source of individual and tribal powers and skills (3). According to Merriam, songs learned through contact with the supernatural contain a pattern in which the distance between the human novice and the spirit is gradually closed: the song that the individual later learns is first heard from far away; the being who sings it comes gradually closer and closer, singing constantly (9). The number of times the spirit being has to repeat the song for the novice seems to reflect the creativity of the hearer: the more times the song is repeated, the less creative the hearer.

Merriam notes that Flathead songs derived from the supernatural lead to two types of power for the individual who receives them: shamanistic power and individual power that enables a person with special capabilities to do or effect special things (3–4). Merriam's comments generally describe the perspectives of other tribes toward the origins and power of song. As both Merriam (4–9) and Herndon (14) point out, contact with the supernatural occurs primarily in dreams, which are usually regarded as a supernatural experience.

Song categories within a tribe are often based on how the songs are used. In *Blackfoot Musical Thought*, Bruno Nettl illustrates the complexity of that tribe's categorization of songs: (1) religious; (2) religious with significant social components; (3) religious narrative—songs sung as part of the telling of myths; (4) ceremonial and partially religious—songs associated with warfare and death; (5) secular ceremonial, with religious aspects, such as songs of societies; (6) secular, performed at secular ceremonies—social dance songs; (7) secular and formally recreational—music associated with games; (8) informally recreational—children's and game songs; (9) informal without audience—occasional songs, such as "walking" or "riding" songs (34-35).

As indicated earlier, Indian tribes frequently include songs within a ceremonial context. Densmore, for instance, estimates in *Chippewa Music* (1910) that there are several hundred songs connected with the Midéwiwin religion of the Ojibwa; many of these have direct ceremonial use. Some are sung in initiation ceremonies, others are used in medicine, and still others are performed in dances. These songs preserve the ancient teachings and beliefs of the Midé. The words often provide the texts for discourses by the Midé shamans (1: 15). The following song affirms the power of the Midé religion on a participant. Midé songs were customarily accompanied by mnemonic drawings, exemplified below:

Song Picture No. 97. The arch represents the sky from which rain is falling. The two ovals represent quiet lakes. In his left hand the man holds a Midé drum and in his right hand a stick for beating the drum.

The Sky Clears

Verily
The Sky clears
When my Midé drum
Sounds
For me
Verily
The waters are smooth
When my Midé drum
Sounds
For me. (*Chippewa Music* 1 [1910]: 112; Day 107)

Expressing the religious rites and supplications of the group, sacred songs, like other genres of oral literature, utilize repetition, enumeration, and incremental development. The following "Flower Wilderness World" song, which is part of the Yaqui Deer songs, describes the freshness of the world which the deer sees as the sun rises:

> You are an enchanted flower wilderness world,
>   you are an enchanted wilderness world,
>   you lie with see-through freshness.
> You are an enchanted wilderness world,
>   you lie with see-through freshness,
>   wilderness world.
>
> You are an enchanted flower wilderness world,
>   you are an enchanted wilderness world,
>   you lie with see-through freshness.
> You are an enchanted wilderness world,
>   you lie with see-through freshness,
>   wilderness world.
>
> You are an enchanted flower wilderness world,
>   you are an enchanted wilderness world,
>   you lie with see-through freshness.
> You are an enchanted wilderness world,
>   you lie with see-through freshness,
>   wilderness world.

Over there, in the center
  of the flower-covered wilderness,
    in the enchanted wilderness world,
      beautiful with the dawn wind,
        beautifully you lie with see-through freshness,
          wilderness world.
You are an enchanted wilderness world,
  you lie with see-through freshness,
    wilderness world.   (Evers and Molina 104)

Directions and locations are delineated with great care, as is the enumeration of the parts of the body to be healed in curing songs, exemplified in the excerpt from the Navajo Night Chant. The following Tewa prayer illustrates incremental development of the metaphor of the sky loom:

Song of the Sky Loom

Oh our Mother the Earth, oh our Father the Sky,
Your children are we, and with tired backs
We bring you the gifts that you love.
Then weave for us a garment of brightness;
May the warp be the white light of morning,
May the weft be the red light of evening,
May the fringes be the falling rain,
May the border be the standing rainbow.
Thus weave for us a garment of brightness
That we may walk fittingly where birds sing,
That we may walk fittingly where grass is green,
Oh our Mother the Earth, oh our Father the Sky!
(Spinden, *Songs of the Tewa* 94)

Alice Fletcher's interpretative and rhythmic translation of a song from the Pawnee Hako ceremony, ritual 4, part 3, illustrates enumeration and directionality. This portion of the ceremony occurs outside the lodge, where the preceding parts of the ceremony have occurred. The participants move along symbolically numbered steps to face the localities where these powers are believed to live:

The Hako Party Presented to the Powers

Look down, West gods, look upon us! We gaze afar on your dwelling.
Look down while here we are standing, look down upon us, ye mighty!
Ye thunder gods, now behold us!
Ye lightning gods, now behold us!
Ye that bring life, now behold us!
Ye that bring death, now behold us!
Look down, South gods, look upon us! We gaze afar on your dwelling.
Look down while here we are standing, look down upon us, ye mighty!
Ye daylight gods, now behold us!

Ye sunshine gods, now behold us!
Ye increase gods, now behold us!
Ye plenty gods, now behold us!
Look down North gods, look upon us! We gaze afar on your dwelling.
Look down while here we are standing, look down upon us, ye mighty!
Ye darkness gods, now behold us!
Ye moonlight gods, now behold us!
Ye that direct, now behold us!
Ye that discern, now behold us! ("Hako" 298–99; Day 102–03)

Like ritual dramas, sacred songs often celebrate the major events in human life: birth or naming, arrival of puberty, healing or purification, death and burial. Francis La Flesche gives the following naming song of the Bow People in "The Osage Tribe, Part 3: Two Versions of the Child-Naming Rite." In this song, the expression "make of me their bodies" means "make of me an ideal for the formation of character." In this portion of the ceremony, the clan chief touches the symbols that will guide his life: everflowing waters, red cedar (an everlasting tree), and life-giving corn.

I am a person who is fitted for use as a symbol.
Verily, in the midst of the rushing waters
Abides my being.
Verily, I am a person who has made of the waters his body.
Behold the right side of the river,
Of which I have made the right side of my body.
When the little ones make of me their bodies
And use the right side of the river
To make their bodies,
The right side of their bodies shall be free from all causes of death.
Behold the left side of the river,
Of which I have made the left side of my body.
When the little ones also make of it the left side of their bodies,
The left side of their bodies shall always be free from all causes of
    death.
Behold the channel of the river,
Of which I have made the hollow of my body.
When the little ones make of me their bodies,
The hollow of their bodies shall always be free from all causes of
    death. (47–48; Day 107)

Songs are also part of fertility rituals that ensure the survival of the group. Underhill states in *Singing for Power* that Papago planters sing as they walk around their fields, night after night, "singing up the corn." The following song is sung by the planters as they sit in a circle in front of effigies of the plants that will nourish them. Corn with kernels of two colors is called "crazy corn"; that with three colors, "laughing corn." Marks between stanzas are Underhill's.

Evening is falling
Pleasantly sounding
Will reverberate
Our songs

———

The corn comes up;
It comes up green;
Here upon our fields
White tassels unfold.

The corn comes up;
It comes up green;
Here upon our fields
Green leaves blow in the breeze.

———

Blue evening falls,
Blue evening falls;
Near by, in every direction,
It sets the corn tassels trembling.

———

The wind smooths well the ground.
Yonder the wind runs
Upon our fields.
The corn leaves tremble.

On Tecolote fields
The corn is growing green.
I came there, saw the tassels waving in the breeze,
And I whistled softly for joy.

———

Blowing in the wind,
Singing,
Am I crazy corn?

Blowing in the wind,
Singing,
Am I laughing corn? (44–45)

A unique use of song in a ceremonial context is the Eskimo tradition of the musical duel, which is used to settle disputes among contestants that could seriously affect the harmony of the group and even lead to homicide. These duels entertain as well. According to E. Adamson Hoebel, song duels among the East Greenlanders may be carried on for years, just for fun. Elsewhere, grudge contests are usually finished in a single season. Traditional songs are used, but special compositions are created for each competition to ridicule opponents and emphasize their weakness ("Song Duels among the Eskimo" 256–57). The following example of a competition between K and E exemplifies their use of innuendo and deprecation to defeat each other. E had married the divorced wife of old man K, who wanted her back:

> K—
> Now shall I split off words—little, sharp words
> Like the wooden splinters which I hack off with my ax.
> A song from ancient times—a breath of the ancestors
> A song of longing—for my wife.
> An impudent, black-skinned oaf has stolen her,
> Has tried to belittle her.
> A miserable wretch who loves human flesh—
> A cannibal from famine days.
> E—
> Insolence that takes the breath away
> Such laughable arrogance and effrontery.
> What a satirical song! Supposed to place the blame on me.
> You would drive fear into my heart!
> I who care not about death.
> Hi! You sing about my woman who was your wench.
> You weren't so loving then—she was much alone.
> You forgot to prize her in song,
> in stout, contest songs.
> Now she is mine.
> And never shall she visit singing, false lovers.
> Betrayer of women in strange households. (257–58)

Songs are a part of the rituals not only of individual tribes or culture areas but also of pan-Indian, nativist religious movements. Around 1890, the Ghost Dance religion swept across the Plains, led by the Paiute medicine man Wovoka, who taught that Indians would be reunited with family and friends in another world where there was no sickness, death, or old age, if they lived in peace and put away the old practices. By performing the Ghost Dance at intervals, each time for five successive days, believers could help bring this prediction to pass. The following Sioux Ghost Dance song, recorded by James Mooney in *The Ghost Dance Religion*, summarizes the whole hope of the Ghost Dance—the return of the buffalo and dead loved ones—as well as the belief that the message was to be brought to the people by the sacred birds, the crow, symbolizing the spirit world, and the eagle, which provided feathers for war bonnets:

> The whole world is coming.
> A nation is coming, a nation is coming,
> The Eagle has brought the message to the tribe.
> The father says so, the father says so.
> Over the whole earth they are coming.
> The buffalo are coming, the buffalo are coming.
> The Crow has brought the message to the tribe,
> The father says so, the father says so. (307)

Another nativist religion that incorporates song in its rituals is the Native American Church, often called the peyote cult. This widespread religion grew up after the decline of the Ghost Dance and combines elements of the vision quest and beliefs in supernatural powers with the Christian Trinity. It teaches that God is a Great Spirit and Jesus, a Guardian Spirit. This cult uses peyote as a means of gaining insight and power through the visions it stimulates. The Kiowa peyote priests begin their ceremony with the following prayer to Sayn-daw-kee, the powerful peyote spirit:

> Sayn-daw-kee, pity us and guard us through the night,
> We who are the eaters of this little herb.
> Let this meeting be successful,
> And may this honored one have blessings throughout life,
> May she become successful and old. (Boyd, *Kiowa Voices* 1:106)

The religious songs of American Indians also include those expressing the power of an individual shaman. As Merriam points out, shamanistic power among the Flathead Indians depends to a considerable extent on song: "The songs of the shaman do not differ in kind from those obtained by any individual through the vision quest or other supernatural contact. The difference between the shaman and the ordinary individual is that the former has more songs and these songs tend to be connected with curing" (17).

As Kilpatrick and Kilpatrick observe, the Cherokee medicine man can trap and kill the evil spirits or night-walkers if he chooses to do so in ceremonies performed at dawn, midday, and dusk on the same day. Essential to such ceremonies is "remade," unadulterated tobacco, which has been interfused with supernatural authority by thinking, saying, or singing a text over it. Early in the evening, the medicine man rings the patient's home with the smoke from his tobacco. Any witch in any guise who tries to cross the smoke line dies:

> Now! No one is to climb over me!
> His soul itself over there will be broken as the Sun rises, this
> Thinker of me; in the very middle of the light of the setting Sun
>   he will be broken, this Thinker of me!
> I will have emerged from the Seven Clans.
> Then I have just come to strike you with Small Arrows. with Small
>   Arrows I have just come to strike you!
> Then I have come to strike you with Lightning!
> Then I have just come to strike you with Thunder!
> Then with Clay your soul will be broken! (158–59)

Songs also express the personal experiences of the individual. The dream song is especially common among the Plains and Algonkian-speaking Woodland tribes, whose young men fasted for the dreams that would reveal their sacred totem. In *Life, Letters and Speeches*, George Copway (Ojibwa) includes this song, which was taught to him in a vision:

> It is I who travel in the winds,
> It is I who whisper in the breeze,
> I shake the trees.
> I shake the earth,
> I trouble the waters on every land.   (40)

While singing, Copway heard the winds whistle, saw the tree waving at its top, the earth heaving, and waters roaring. The spirit told Copway that he would come to see the boy again: "You will not see me often; but you will hear me speak." When told of the dream, Copway's father responded that *"the god of the winds* is kind to you; the aged tree, I hope, may indicate long life; the wind may indicate that you will travel much; the water which you saw, and the winds, will carry your canoe safely through the waves" (40).

Indian songs include personal lyrics created by the individual to express his or her own feelings, such as love, personal sorrow or loss, and one's own death. Here a Chippewa reveals her sadness at parting from her lover:

> A loon
> I thought it was
> But it was
> My love's
> Splashing oar
>
> To Sault Ste. Marie
> He has departed
> My love
> Has gone on before me
> Never again
> Can I see him.
> (Densmore, *Chippewa
> Music* [1910]: 150–51)

Among the Cherokee, there are special spells or chants to remake or repair oneself. According to the Kilpatricks, "a person who has 'remade' himself has surrounded the ego with a spiritual aura through which the light of the old self is brilliantly refracted." This radiance attracts the opposite sex, wealth, success, and good fortune (53). The following "remaking" chant is recited when remaking tobacco to be smoked at any time and place that a desired woman is present. The tobacco is remade early in the morning by saying the spell four times while rolling the tobacco in the usual counterclockwise manner.

I am as beautiful as the Tsugv:tsala:la.
I am as beautiful as the Hummingbird.
I am as beautiful as the Dhla:nuwa.
As the Red Cardinal is beautiful, I am beautiful.
As the Red Dhla:nuwa is beautiful, I am beautiful.
As the Red Redbird is beautiful, I am beautiful.
As the Blue Cardinal is beautiful, I am beautiful.
                    (*Run toward the Nightland* 55)

Special occasions are celebrated in song, such as those describing the exploits of individual warriors, victory, and defeat. Sitting Bull led his warriors into battle with this chant:

Young men, help me, do help me!
I love my country so;
That is why I am fighting.   (Vestal 97)

After his surrender to United States authorities, Sitting Bull composed this moving song that expresses his sense of loss:

A warrior
I have been
now
it is all over
a hard time
I have.
     (Densmore, *Teton*
Sioux Music [1918]: 61.459)

The Kiowas have a category they call wind songs, which are war songs usually created and sung by someone at home who thinks of a distant warrior. Maurice Boyd states in *Kiowa Voices* that these songs derive their generic name from the fact that they describe loneliness and longing on the open prairie, where only the "sweep of the wind broke the silence." The following exemplify this genre:

Maiden's Song

Idlers and cowards are here at home now,
Whenever they wish, they see their loved ones.
O idlers and cowards are here at home now,
O idlers and cowards are here at home now,
But the young man I love has gone to war, far away.
Weary, lonely, he longs for me.

Young Warrior's Song

You young men sitting there
You have wealth and parents, relatives, friends.
But me, I am a poor and lonely boy.
I will remain here and go on another expedition,
I know how to sleep and eat on the prairie away from home.
This kind of life makes me happy and content. (1: 58)

Other kinds of personal songs include lullabies, women's work songs, hunting songs, and elegies. The following Thule Eskimo lullaby illustrates a mother's pride in her baby boy and her feeling of contentment about her motherhood and her son's well-being:

It is my big baby
That I feel in my hood
Oh how heavy he is!
Ya ya! Ya ya!

When I turn
He smiles at me, my little one,
Well hidden in my hood,
Oh how heavy he is!
Ya ya! Ya ya!

How sweet he is when he smiles
With two teeth like a little walrus.
Ah, I like my little one to be heavy
And my hood to be full.
(Lewis, *I Breathe a New Song* 63)

The Zunis sing a special song when presenting their infants to the sun. On the eighth day of life, the head of the infant is washed by the women of his or her father's clan, cornmeal is placed in the infant's hand, and the baby is taken outside, facing the east, at the moment of sunrise. Cornmeal is then sprinkled to the rising sun while the paternal grandmother utters the following prayer:

Now is the day.
Our child,
Into the daylight
You will go out standing.
Preparing for your day,
We have passed our days.
When all your days were at an end,
When eight days were past,
Our sun father

Went in to sit down at his sacred place.
And our night fathers
Having come out standing to their sacred place,
Passing a blessed night
We came to day.
Now this day
Our fathers,
Dawn priests,
Have come out standing to their sacred place.
Our sun father
Having come out standing to his sacred place,
Our child,
It is your day.
This day,
The flesh of the white corn,
Prayer meal,
To our sun father
This prayer meal we offer.
May your road be fulfilled
Reaching to the road of your sun father.
We offer prayer meal.
To this end:
May you help us all to finish our roads.
                    (Bunzel, "Zuni Ritual Poetry" 635–36)

The Tlingit mourning song below uses the metaphor of a drifting log full
of nails that was used to build a house:

I always compare you to a drifting log with iron nails in it. Let my
  brother float in, in that way. Let him float ashore on a good sandy
  beach.
I always compare you, my mother, to the sun passing behind the
  clouds. That is what makes the world dark. (Swanton, "Tlingit
  Myths and Texts" 395)

In addition to the ritual and personal songs are the social songs and
dances that have no connection with personal power in any form. These
are performed primarily for pleasure. A popular form of contemporary
Indian song among young people is the "49 songs" sung in get-togethers
after events, dances, and powwows. One example of the social song is the
Lakota Night Dance, which Ben Black Bear (Sioux) indicates the young
people used to dance all night long. "Black face paint" refers to a victorious
return from war.

1. [Name], stand up!
   You are looking for black face paint.
2. It is said that you said I gave you a ring.
   Give it back to me, you have embarrassed me.

3. I did not have a choice in marrying him, so he has kept me in misery.
   I will leave him and we will live together.

(Black Bear and Theisz 96–97)

NARRATIVES

Storytelling has been one of the major ways of entertaining and educating Indian children in the beliefs and history of the tribe. In *The Traditional History and Characteristic Sketches of the Ojibway Nation* George Copway eloquently describes the importance of storytelling to him and his people:

> There is not a lake or mountain that has not connected with it some story of delight or wonder, and nearly every beast and bird is the subject of the story-teller, being said to have transformed itself at some prior time into some mysterious formation—of men going to live in the stars, and of imaginary beings in the air, whose rushing passage roars in the distant whirlwinds.
>
> I have known some Indians who have commenced to narrate legends and stories in the month of October, and not end until quite late in the spring, sometimes not till the month of May, and on every evening of this long term tell a new story.
>
> Some of these stories are most exciting, and so intensely interesting, that I have seen children during their relation, whose tears would flow most plentifully, and their breasts heave with thoughts too big for utterance.
>
> Night after night for weeks I have sat and eagerly listened to these stories. The days following, the characters would haunt me at every step, and every moving leaf would seem to be a voice of a spirit.   (95–96)

Copway's experience as an Ojibwa boy growing up in the nineteenth century is corroborated, a century later, by Virginia Beavert (Yakima) in *The Way It Was*. She points out that the legends were traditionally told by grandparents to children during the cold months, in a warm house filled with food. It was essential that each child listen attentively to learn the lessons being taught:

> There were times when there was more than one story-teller involved, which made it a more interesting evening. Many questions were answered in the minds of the children; for instance, why did the characters in the legend do things five times? It was explained that this was a part of our lives, the parts of our bodies, the part of the religion, and many other things we take for granted in our everyday living. (xi)

As Copway's and Beavert's comments demonstrate and as Leanne Hinton and Lucille J. Watahomigie (Hualapai) emphasize in *Spirit Mountain*, traditional stories and songs help the tribal members learn about the world and their place in it, how to behave, and how to live harmoniously with nature. Hinton and Watahomigie state that although many of the Yuma tales have morals, few actually condemn specific behavior: "Instead, they are designed to cause people to contemplate their own behavior, to understand something of the consequences of such behavior, and to give them insights that allow them to change their behavior when necessary" (6). Their comments are applicable to many other tribal narratives as well.

Tribal groups use a variety of categories to describe forms of oral narrative. Stories are sometimes divided into those that are true and those that are fictional, into the sacred and nonsacred, or into some combination of these categories. Stories can include aspects of both the true and the fictional or the sacred and the nonsacred. Further, some stories originally categorized as sacred can subsequently be classified as nonsacred. Although the general plot outline of a given story may be found in narratives among several tribes, the details, the categorization, the significance of a specific version, and its performance depend on the cultural context of the tribe in which that version is told. As the following examples illustrate, the precise nature of the literature within these categories and subcategories varies considerably among tribal groups. Paul Radin notes in *The Trickster* that the Winnebago divide their narratives into *waikan* (what is sacred) and *worak* (what is recounted). The Winnebago's sacred stories, which can be told only after the snakes are underground, belong to a past that is irretrievably lost and to the realm of what is no longer attainable by humans or spirits. Such stories have divine heroes and never end tragically. The recounted stories deal with the present and can be told at any time. The heroes of these stories are always either human beings or, rarely, divine beings who had come to live among humans (118). Like the Winnebago, the Ojibwa tell their sacred stories only in the winter. Among some other tribes, the telling of such sacred stories is not limited to winter. Dennis Tedlock indicates in "The Poetics of Verisimilitude" that the Zuni divide their narratives into *chimiky'ana'kowa* (origin) stories, which can be told at any time of day or in any season, and *telapnaawe* (tales), which can be told only at night and during the winter. Both are set in the long-ago past "before the introduction of objects and institutions recognized as belonging to the period of European contact" (159–60).

In *Coyote Was Going There*, Jarold W. Ramsey provides an excellent summary of the distinction between myths and tales or legends in his discussion of the narratives of Oregon Indians. Myths describe a primal world, peopled by animal spirits in more-or-less human form and by monsters and confusions of nature. The myth age flows into the age of transformation, during which a culture hero or transformer orders the world, turning animal people into actual animals and other beings into natural landmarks. The transformation age is followed by the historical age of human memory (xxiv). One of the explanations of the myth age that Archie

Phinney (Nez Perce) offers in *Nez Percé Texts* is similar to Ramsey's. However, he also offers another that on the surface seems contradictory: in the former world all of the creatures we know today were then a human-like people and only through a general transformation, when Indian people arrived, did they assume their present forms. Phinney attributes the Indian ability to accept two contradictory descriptions to the peculiar speculative efforts of Indians, and their readiness, when challenged, to ascribe definite features to propositions that are impossible to describe. According to Phinney, "The Indian does not visualize the characters of a tale as being animal or human. No clear picture is offered or needed. If such tangible features were introduced a tale would lose its overtones of fantasy, its charm" (ix).

The general characteristics of American Indian oral narratives differ from those of the written literary tradition of Western Europe. In his analysis of characteristics present in Lakota oral narratives, *Buckskin Tokens*, Theisz provides a good introduction to those frequently present in the stories of other tribes as well. The plots of Lakota stories are compressed and episodic, settings are simple, and style is terse. The stories have one-dimensional characters, who rarely express thought or emotion, and emphasize only the external aspects of behavior necessary to advance the action. The stories also sometimes contain inconsistencies of time, logic, and detail, which are simply accepted by the listeners as artistic conventions that serve to further the action (7–8).

American Indian oral narratives include considerable humor. Phinney emphasizes in *Nez Percé Texts* that humor is the "deepest and most vivid element" of that tribe's mythology—"the element that animates all the pathos, all the commonplace and the tragic" (ix). However, he also indicates that it is the element most lost in "translation" because of its subtlety: "There is nothing hilarious or comical but there is the droll, the ludicrous and the clever exaggeration" (ix). Theisz's comment that in Lakota oral narrative, frank references to sexual parts and acts and to body functions are not uncommon and are not considered distasteful or out of place is important to understanding this aspect of other Indian oral literatures as well (8). Beavert notes that through the stories, the Yakima child "learned that sex was a part of his life too. This part of his training was not secret, because secrecy creates bad results. They learned about sex early in life, and it was emphasized that the Creator was involved as the important part of it, and without Him the stories probably would be classified as 'dirty' " (xi–xii). However, translations and retellings of stories sometimes omit sexual references or ribald portions of stories considered to be offensive to the delicate sensibilities of non-Indian readers. Much of the rich humor that characterizes Indian culture was eliminated by such censorship, which was exercised by non-Indian editors and occasionally by Indians themselves. For example, Charles Eastman (Sioux) and Elaine Goodale Eastman carefully excluded such material from their version of Sioux stories prepared

for children. Anthropologists and linguists sometimes recorded the titles
and sexual portions of the suggestive narratives in Latin, presumably to be
sure that they were read only by scholars.

A variety of customs accompany the act of storytelling. John Stands
in Timber (Cheyenne) describes in *Cheyenne Memories* the rituals a tribal
elder performed before he told a story:

> An old storyteller would smooth the ground in front of him and make
> two marks in it with his right thumb, two with his left, and a double
> mark with both thumbs together. Then he would rub his hands, and
> pass his right hand up his right leg to his waist, and touch his left hand
> and pass it on up his right arm to his breast. He did the same thing
> with his left and right hands going up the other side. Then he touched
> the marks on the ground with both hands and rubbed them together
> and passed them over his head and all over his body. (12)

Among the Cherokee only those who observed the proper form and
ceremony were permitted to hear sacred myths. James Mooney indicates
in "Myths of the Cherokee" that boys who wanted to learn the sacred
traditions of the tribe met with a tribal priest in a sweat lodge, where they
sat up all night talking. At daybreak, the group would go into a stream.
After the boys stripped themselves, their teacher scratched their skin with
a bone-tooth comb. They then waded out, faced the rising sun, and dipped
themselves seven times under water while the priest recited prayers on the
bank (230). In *Chippewa Customs*, Densmore notes that requests among the
Chippewa for storytelling about the myth age and about their culture hero
were accompanied by a gift, and the performance itself, by a feast (103).
The Chippewas did not reveal the title of the story until the storytelling
was finished (103 n. 56).

In many tribes, storytellers use ritual formulas to open or close stories
or to elicit audience response. Jesse Cornplanter says, in *Legends of the
Longhouse*, that among his people, the Seneca, storytellers introduce origin
stories with the words *Neh nih Che yonh en ja se* ("When the world was new")
(24). According to Dean Saxton and Lucille Saxton, the Pima and Papago
begin fictional stories with a formula such as *sh hab wa chu'i na'ana* ("They
say it happened long ago") or *heki huh* ("long ago"). The stories close with
phrases such as *am o wa'i hug* ("That is the end") or *am o wa'i at hoabdag*
("That's the center of the basket"). The latter suggests that all details woven
into the story have been treated and nothing is left hanging (*O'othham
Hoho'ok A'agitha* 371). In "The Poetics of Verisimilitude," Tedlock indicates
that the fictional Zuni narratives are identified by a formulaic frame. The
narrator says, "*So'nahchi*," which may have meant "Now we are taking it
up." The audience replies with *Eeso* ("Yes, indeed"), a word peculiar to
storytelling. The narrator then says, "*Sonti ino———te*," which may have
once meant "Now it begins to be made." The audience responds with a

second *Eeso* (160–61). Beavert describes a similar audience-response requirement among the Yakima. The storyteller gains the children's attention by saying, "*Awacha nay!*" ("This is the way it was"). The children respond loudly, "*Ii*" ("Yes") (xi).

Tribes sometime use archaic language for myths. For example, Tedlock points out in "The Poetics of Verisimilitude" that when Zuni storytellers narrate tales that take place "long ago," they exclude all modernisms from their quotations and inserts archaisms (167). The Nez Perce also use specialized terms and language in some of their stories. Phinney indicates in *Nez Percé Texts* that some animals have two names, the second of which is peculiar to their roles in mythopoeic life. The two names may not be varied or interchanged at will. According to Phinney, some animals have distinctive speech characteristics. Fox speaks with utmost clarity and directness, Bear slurs consonants, and Skunk nasalizes in a high-pitched voice and changes sound patterns. Coyote, the Nez Perce culture hero, has a separate name when he is presented as the ribald or trickster character (ix).

Some tribal stories follow a specific structure. In *O'othham Hoho'ok A'-agitha*, the Saxtons state that Pima and Papago legends consist of an introduction, one or more episodes, and a conclusion. The introduction gives the major time-place-setting and shows the participants in a harmonious situation. It may begin with a storytelling formula. An episode consists of thesis, which describes a disruption of harmony, and an antithesis, which describes the measures employed to overcome the disruption. The conclusion describes restored harmony: "While stories are complete when harmony is restored, events are complete with a cycle of four, or some power of four. Songs are sung four times, and in a traditional ceremony four songs make a set, four sets a night, and four nights a ceremony, four to the fourth power" (371).

Although American Indian oral literatures differ considerably in content, there are some common themes. Their myths usually include stories about the creation of the world, origins and migrations of the tribe, culture heroes and trickster-transformers. The most extensive creation stories exist in the Southwest. One form is that of world parents, consisting of a Sky Father and Earth Mother. Anna Birgitta Rooth states in "The Creation Myths of the North American Indians" that this form is common in Arizona, New Mexico, and southern California, but is also present as far west as the eastern Mediterranean and in southeastern and southern Asia (500–02). Others, such as the following Papago origin story, describe the miraculous birth of a culture hero, who then creates the universe. The excerpt also illustrates the narrator's successful attempt to humanize his description of the infant culture hero:

> Long ago, they say, when the earth was not yet finished, darkness
> lay upon the water and they rubbed each other. The sound they made
> was like the sound at the edges of a pond.

There, on the water, in the darkness, in the noise, and in a very
strong wind, a child was born. The child lay upon the water and did
as a child does when it is being made to stop crying. (Like when its
mother sings and tosses it up and down and walks back and forth with
it). The wind always blew and carried the child everywhere. Whatever
made the child took care of him, fed him, and raised him.

First Born sent termites to gather lots of algae, which he used to
decide how to make a seat so the wind could not blow it anywhere. The
following is his creation song:

Earth Medicine Man finished the earth.
Come near and see it and do something to it.
He made it round.
Come near and see it and do something to it.

In this way First Born finished the earth and then made all animal
and plant life. (Saxton and Saxton, *O'othham Hoho'ok A'agitha* 1–3)

Emergence myths describe the ascent of beings from under the surface
of the earth to its surface and their subsequent settlement or migration.
Ermine Wheeler-Voegelin and Remedios W. Moore indicate in "The Emergence Myth in Native North America" that the belief in origin from the
underworld is strongly connected with belief in return to the underworld
after death. In the course of the ascent, tribal ways of life and economic
activities are established. The major areas of distribution of this type of
origin myth are along the eastern and southern limits of the United States
and north and south through the middle of the continent (68, 73–74).

Pueblo and Navajo creation stories incorporate emergence and migration myths. In the Zuni emergence myth, recorded and translated by
Tedlock in *Finding the Center*, Awonawilona, an androgynous figure, created
the universe, which was filled with fog. Awonawilona then created two Bow
Priests (Ahayuuta) to bring out people from the fourth room who would
pray to him in the proper way. They descended to the fourth room, where
they found people in darkness. Some versions describe the people as in-
sectlike or lacking human form, who lived in dark, ammonia-filled rooms
or caves far below the earth's surface. The Sun Priest sends the twins to
various priests. After underworld people and the priests are assembled,
the twins lead them on their journey. The elder twin orders prayer sticks
to be made, which turn into trees or plants that enable the people to climb
from one room to the other. When they emerge, they are dazzled by the
sun.

Emergence from a series of underworlds is followed by migration,
during which the tribe wanders from location to location. When it reaches
its special or middle place, the tribe settles there. Such migration myths
are reflected in the origin stories of the Navajo and numerous Pueblo tribes.
The concept of movement through a series of worlds to the point of emergence is not common to tribes outside the Southwest.

The formation of the world through struggle and robbery is the form of creation myth found especially on the Pacific coast as far south as California. Movement from an earlier sky world to a water world, accomplished by means of a fall, characterizes the genesis stories of the Iroquoian tribes of the Northeastern Woodlands. According to the version recorded by Cornplanter in *Legends of the Longhouse*, humankind originally existed in a celestial world, lighted only by the white blossoms of a great celestial tree. The chief's wife became pregnant from inhaling her husband's breath without his knowledge. The jealous chief then had a dream that called for the tree of light to be uprooted. He had this done and thus caused the sun to shine through the opening. After he persuaded his unsuspecting wife to look down the hole, he pushed her through and, in his anger, also threw down the plants and animals that humankind would need to survive. As these fell, he transformed them into their present-day forms and then replaced the tree of light. SkyWoman was rescued by the water animals, who dived beneath the sea to bring up some earth that they placed on Turtle's shell. After she landed on this earth, it grew in size (19–20).

The fortunate-fall creation story is closely related to the earth-diver myth, which usually includes a flood that occurred after the creation of the universe and resulted in the re-creation of the present world out of mud brought up from under the water by the earth-diver, often a muskrat or waterfowl. This is the most common myth type found throughout North America except in the extreme north, northeast, and southwest. It is especially predominant among the Algonkian-speaking tribes originally of the Great Lakes area. The myth is also found in part of South America, the Pacific Islands, Australia, and Eastern Europe.

Also widespread are stories about the culture hero, who is of divine birth, frequently with Sun, Wind, or Stone for a father and a lesser being for a mother. Often an orphan whose mother died or was killed before or at his birth, the culture hero possesses the power to transform various aspects of nature into their final shapes as well as to transform beings into animals and humans. Particularly on the Northwest Coast and as far south as California, the culture hero shapes the world and gives it its character by theft or robbery of sun, fire, or water. These myths are not concerned with the original owners of these substances, but only with the culture hero's acquisition of them (Rooth 506). An example is the Tsimshian story of how Raven brought light into a dark world, which Boas summarizes in his introduction to "The Traditions of the Thompson Indians." Raven's mother was faithless to her husband, a chief, who killed and buried her. Born after her burial, the boy was found and raised by another chief. After making himself a blanket of birdskins, the boy flew up to the sky, where he married the Sun's daughter. Their son accidentally fell down from heaven and was found by an old chief who took him home. At first, the boy would not eat, but when given a special food, he became so voracious that he ate all the tribe's winter provisions. Cast out for his selfish gluttony, which threatened the tribe's survival, the child assumed raven form and flew across the earth looking for food. When he saw some fishermen catching fish in the dark, Raven asked for some. After they refused, he threatened to make the sun shine.

To make good his revenge, Raven flew to the home of the chief who owned daylight and transformed himself into a hemlock spike that was swallowed by the chief's daughter. She subsequently gave birth to Raven in baby form. The old chief so loved his new grandson that he allowed Raven to play with the box containing sunlight. As soon as he got the box, the grandchild transformed himself back into Raven, flew to the spot where the men were fishing, and opened the box to free the sun. Raven then saw that the fishermen were really ghosts. While they sped away, Raven devoured their fish. To quench his thirst from eating so much, Raven took water from an old chief who possessed it. Pursued, Raven spilled the water, thus spreading it all over the world (*Race, Language and Culture* 408–09).

Another common motif related to the power of the culture hero is the theft of fire. According to the version from California recorded by Roland Dixon in "Shasta Myths," the culture hero, Coyote, goes to the house where the Pain people, who posess fire, live. The Pain elders had left their children alone, warning them that Coyote might come. Although the Pain children suspect that their visitor is Coyote, he vehemently denies this. Coyote stretches his long blanket to the flames to make it catch fire. He then runs away and passes the fire to various birds to carry while the Pain children try vainly to catch them. Finally Quail gives the fire to Turtle, who puts it under his armpit and jumps into the water. The Pain people shoot him in the rear, which accounts for Turtle's tail, and then go away. Coyote is furious when he learns that the Turtle dove under water with the fire. However, Turtle still has the burning fire, which he throws all around so that everybody gets some (13–14).

As these stories indicate, the culture hero can be a sly trickster who feels superior to all others and relies on cunning deceptions and mean tricks to reach his goals—often to get food or possess a woman. One example of such a trickster tale that is widespread in the Midwest and Plains is called the "Hoodwinked Ducks." In the Winnebago version, contained in Radin's *The Trickster*, a hungry Trickster persuades some naive ducks to keep their eyes closed and dance while he sings. An accomplished con artist, Trickster gets the ducks to keep their eyes closed by warning that if they disobey, their eyes will become red. While the obedient ducks dance happily with closed eyes, Trickster quickly devours them until one duck secretly opens his eyes and alerts the others. Most of the remaining ducks escape (14–16).

The trickster is also an overreacher who frequently gets his comeuppance after a temporary victory. In a Sioux trickster story in *Buckskin Tokens*, Iktomi (Spider) decides that he wants to be a medicine man after watching some men pray in the high mountains for four days and nights without food. Iktomi prepares himself properly by singing sacred songs in the sweatlodge and wiping himself with sage, all the time thinking, "These Indians, these medicine men don't pray. They just go on the hill, sit around and look around." Iktomi goes up into the mountains, where he just sits and looks around for four days until a herd of buffalo runs him off the mountain. Hiding in some bushes, Iktomi desperately begins to pray: "O Great Spirit, help me. These buffalo are going to kill me!" The Great Spirit takes pity on Iktomi and turns the buffalo away. When Iktomi returns to camp, he vows, "I'll never be a medicine man again, because I haven't the power, I haven't the knowledge and the wisdom to do what they do. I'll just have to do something else." So he returns to his mischief making (Theisz 30).

Although the trickster-transformer figure is usually male, in some cultures, such as the Hopi, it is occasionally female. The culture hero-trickster-transformer takes many forms, most of which are animals: Coyote in the Southwest and Plateau, Raven in the Northwest and Arctic, Hare in the Great Lakes and Southeast, Old Man among the Blackfeet of the Northern Plains, Spider among the Sioux of the Dakotas, and Wolverine and Jay in Canada. Because the trickster's appetites are enormous, incessant, and unrestrained by tribal taboos, myths about the mischievous acts of the culture hero-trickster-transformer provide outlets for socially unacceptable feelings and impulses and teach the consequences of unrestrained or taboo behavior.

Some hero myths are concerned with lesser beings who serve as intermediaries, helping the gods or slaying monsters, either as individuals or as twins. Other themes and motifs often present in Indian myths include star-husband, about an earth woman who yearns to marry a star; Orpheus, concerning the attempts of a spouse or loved one to bring his or her beloved back from the world of the dead; animal husband or wife; abduction; and witches and monsters. The star-husband stories combine thematic elements found in other myths. The earth woman who yearns to marry a star ascends to the sky, where she becomes pregnant. While there, she breaks some form of taboo. She subsequently descends to the earth, frequently by means of a sky rope. She dies either when she lands or in childbirth. Her son lives, and the second part of the story deals with the adventures of her sky son, who is adopted by an old woman and becomes a culture hero.

While myths are true stories of the prehistoric past, tales may be true or fictional and usually are set in the historical period. Many stories describe events significant to the history of the tribe. Over the years, custom in a particular tribe may reassign stories or portions of stories from one category to another.

ORATORY

Oral speeches can be divided into the ceremonial, the nonceremonial, or some combination of these two forms. Oratory has long been a highly regarded skill in many Indian tribes; Theodore J. Balgooyen emphasizes in "The Plains Indian as a Public Speaker" that it was synonymous with good citizenship: "Public speaking was associated with nearly every kind of public ceremony and was an important means of settling political and legal questions. Every respected warrior was expected to speak on matters of policy if he had a strong opinion" (13,15).

Although most Indian orators were men, women sometimes played important roles as speakers. Balgooyen notes that the Plains Indians placed restrictions on the right of women to speak in public, except for an occasional woman warrior or strong medicine woman: "A woman could not speak in public who held no position at all in the tribe, and no woman was seriously listened to unless she was virtuous and chaste according to the standards of the tribe" (21). Among the Paiute, they contributed significantly to the deliberations of the tribal council. In *Life among the Piutes*, Sarah Winnemucca comments that "women know as much as the men do, and their advice is often asked" (53).

Ceremonies, such as the Iroquois Ritual of Condolence, often contain addresses by shamans or priests to the supernatural powers or to the community. The Iroquois particularly emphasize oratory in their ceremonies. Foster indicates in *From the Earth to beyond the Sky* that speakers will shorten orations by cutting them down to essentials and expand them by repeating earlier ideas or restating points in different terms (182–83). An excerpt from the opening speech of a Thanksgiving ritual given by Enos Williams (Mohawk/Cayuga) illustrates Iroquois oratorical style:

The Creator

And now we will speak again,
About him, he who in the sky dwells, Our Creator.
He decided, "Above the world I have created
Will be the ever-living world.
And I will continue to look intently
And to listen intently to the earth, when people direct their voices at me."
And now the speech
That you heard come straight out
As far as it was possible, is becoming difficult
Truly he has been listening intently to us.
And if it happened that we left something out
It would never be diminished for him who in the sky dwells, Our Creator
For it is right in our minds.
Let there be gratitude day and night for the happiness he has given us.
He pities us also.
And he loves us, he who in the sky dwells.
He gave us the means to set right that which divides us. (355–57)

Foster indicates that the oratorical tradition among the Iroquois remains strong and its prospects for survival are reasonably good (252).

The Pima also place great emphasis on oratory in their ceremonies. Donald M. Bahr points out in *Pima and Papago Ritual Oratory* that most Piman rites include oratory, which is distinguished from the preaching that now thrives at fiestas, political meetings, funerals, and in churches. There is little preaching or exhortation in ritual oratory. Instead, it focuses on the hero's journey from one place to another and contains three kinds of words: those related to departure, travel, and arrival. The following prelude describes the death and resurrection of Elder Brother and the recovery of his strength through the use of haze and wind, clouds and snakes, a process necessary to prepare him for his journey:

Gregorio's Oration

Prelude

Thus I did, Elder Brother Shaman, on open ground laid himself
    down, on it lying, on it four days completed, on it really pressed
    and arose, around himself looked and tried to see;
land got put, distantly lay;
mountains stood [formerly by somebody], now rottenly stood;
trees stood, now firewood toppled, and that I tried to see;
and there from the east he caused to run his white winds, by means
    of which his heart got moistened and finished;
there from the north he caused to run his red winds, by means of
    which his heart got moistened and finished;
there from the west he caused to run his black winds, by means of
    which his heart got moistened and finished;
there from the south he caused to run his yellow winds, by means of
    which his heart got moistened and finished. (61)

Speeches can be used to initiate ceremonies in whole or in part. In *Ojibwa Religion and the Midéwiwin*, Ruth Landes cites the following speech given by the Bowman, who serves as proxy for the sacred Bear and is said to "own" the Midéwiwin (Grand Medicine Society). *Bowman* is a canoeist term meaning literally "the foremost one." Landes's explanations of this speech, given as part of the public segment of the healing rite, are in brackets:

    Hail, Colleagues! First and foremost I offer thanks for the tobacco I take now; and for the food prepared by the [other] people, which they will take later. *These* people [patient and family] seek renewed life on this occasion. I salute the midé chief, who will take the tobacco and food. "Oh, thanks," he will say, "surprisingly, they remember what they were taught." I beg the midé people to regard me with indulgence. Soon we will call them in. Soon invitations will be carried from lodge to lodge. I salute them tenderly. And I salute the one [manito] who takes care of them. [Addressing the servitor, waiting at the chief's side for directions:] Now, go about inviting the people. For tobacco smoke spreads over the skies [in ritual invocations] and the food too is known there [so the Supernaturals are prepared to heed Indians' requests]. Indeed, he [collective manitos] is grateful that the Indian remembers how to gain life. Tenderly does he say, "Thank you. From here I am pleased to grant you what you beg for. See me: never do I ail. That is why I was set here, to watch over Indians and listen. And I too gain, receiving tobacco and food. Yes, for this was I set here, from afar to give Indians what they request, from afar to give them strengthened life. That is all I need say."

I will take up a song [Bowman informs the Supranatural] and you will understand why. (150)

In *Sweet Medicine*, Peter J. Powell recorded a brief coups count—commemorating a victory over one's enemies—recited by a member of the Northern Cheyenne military society as part of the Sacred Arrows ceremony performed in 1960:

I was the first Indian boy in service during World War II. I took basic here in the States, and went to North Africa. November 8, 1942, we landed near Casablanca. That morning, they gave me a flag to carry to shore. I carried that flag for three days. When all firing stopped, Captain Roundly took it back and give it to Corporal Garrison. (1: 640)

Nonceremonial speeches can include those made at council meetings, coups counts, formal petitions, addresses of welcome, battle speeches to warriors, and statements of personal feeling or experience. Although Indian oratory is more commonly associated with formal addresses, informal, personal speeches often deeply move the audiences. For instance, a young Crow warrior, Double-face, describes how he regained his courage to battle his enemies after being previously filled with doubts:

I used to think that since my birth I had had many sorrows. It turns out that there was something in store for me. I was grieving, but I did not know that today all manner of sorrow would be coming to a head. The women at my home are miserable, I daresay. "How are the captive Crow faring?" they are thinking to themselves. My poor dear housemates, my distressed kin, the enemy makes them sit under the dripping water, he is ever abusing them, he thinks his men are the only ones to be brave. What can I do to distress him, I wonder?

You Above, if there be one who knows what is going on, repay me today for the distress I have suffered. Inside the Earth, if there be any one there who knows what is going on, repay me for the distress I have suffered. The One Who causes things, Whoever he be, I have now had my fill of life. Grant me death, my sorrows are overabundant. Though children are timid, they die harsh deaths, it is said. Though women are timid, You make them die harsh deaths. I do not want to live long; were I to live long, my sorrows would be overabundant. I do not want it!

Those who heard him all cried. (Qtd. in Balgooyen 20)

A major form of oratory after the coming of whites—and the type most frequently anthologized—consisted of the speeches made at meetings of Indians and settlers. Because our knowledge of the content and form of Indian oratory often derives from versions taken down or remembered by the orator's audience, using such versions to generalize about the genres, content, and style of Indian oratory is problematic at best. In "Chief Seattle's Speech (es)," Rudolf Kaiser demonstrates how greatly the versions of these famous speeches can vary. The two short speeches preserved among the documents of the Port Elliott Treaty negotiations of 1855 bear no resemblance to what is currently publicized as "Seattle's speech" in America and Europe (502–03). According to Kaiser, the first published version of the popular speech was presented to the public by H. A. Smith in 1887, thirty years after Chief Seattle is said to have delivered it. Possibly, Smith based his version on "extended notes" in his diary, written down when Chief Seattle gave his original speech (506). This version was subsequently revised by others.

One of the earliest collected protest speeches is the plea made in 1609 by Wahunsonacock, or King Powhatan, and copied down by Captain James Smith:

> Why should you take by force that from us which you can have by love? Why should you destroy us, who have provided you with food? What can you get by war? We can hide our provisions, and fly into the woods; and then you must consequently famish by wronging your friends. What is the cause of your jealousy? You see us unarmed, and willing to supply your wants, if you come in a friendly manner, and not with swords and guns as to invade an enemy. (Nabokov, *Native American Testimony* 88)

Aware that whites were not going to cease their conquest of Indian lands, the Shawnee Chief Tecumseh attempted in 1811 to persuade Indians to unite in a southern confederation to oppose these invaders:

> Where today are the Pequot? Where are the Narragansett, the Mohican, the Pocanet, and other powerful tribes of our people? They have vanished before the avarice and oppression of the white man, as snow before the summer sun. . . . Will we let ourselves be destroyed in our turn, without making an effort worthy of our race? Shall we, without a struggle, give up our homes, our lands, bequeathed to us by the Great Spirit? The graves of our dead and everything that is dear and sacred to us? . . . I know you will say with me, Never! Never! (Armstrong, *I Have Spoken* 45)

Indians' love of the land and commitment to family is eloquently expressed in the excerpt below from Chief Joseph's speech delivered in 1879 to members of Congress and other officials in Washington, D.C. Unfortunately, Chief Joseph's attempt to persuade the government to allow his people to return to tribal lands was unsuccessful:

> . . . In order to have all people understand how much land we owned, my father planted poles all around it and said:
>
> "Inside is the home of my people—the white man may take the land outside. Inside this boundary all our people were born. It circles around the graves of our fathers, and we will never give up these graves to any man." . . . My father sent for me. I saw he was dying. I took his hand in mine. He said: "My son, my body is returning to my mother earth, and my spirit is going very soon to see the Great Spirit Chief. When I am gone, think of your country. You are chief of these people. They look to you to guide them. Always remember that your father never sold his country. You must stop your ears whenever you are asked to sign a treaty selling your home. A few years more, and white men will be all around you. They have their eyes on this land. My son, never forget my dying words. This country holds your father's body. Never sell the bones of your father and mother." I pressed my father's hand and told him I would protect his grave with my life. My father smiled and passed away to the spirit-land.
>
> I buried him in that beautiful valley of winding waters. I love that land more than all the rest of the world. A man who would not love his father's grave is worse than a wild animal. (Ramsey, *Coyote Was Going There* 38)

The power of American Indian oratory is still a strong tradition, whether practiced as part of a ceremony held on a reservation, testimony at a congressional hearing for Indian legal rights, or a veteran's speech about his wartime exploits that entitle him to carry the Indian flag at the opening ceremonies of the Indian Achievement Award Dinner in Chicago.

Life History and Autobiography

The tide of Indian-white relations influenced the content and popularity of Indian autobiographies, as well as other genres of Indian literature written and narrated during the nineteenth century. Because white desire to abrogate Indian treaty rights and to gain control of Indian land increased during this century, most Indian writers of the period devoted themselves to fighting for the rights of their people. The enactment of the Indian Removal Bill of 1830, the westward migration of settlers onto Indian land, the relocation of the Indian tribes onto reservations by the 1880s, and the passage of the General Allotment Act (1887), which allotted Indian land in severalty, ended the traditionally free Indian life. At the turn of the twentieth century, as Indians from the Plains and Far West were educated in white-run schools, Native Americans in these regions began increasingly to write the stories of their lives.

Personal narratives achieved considerable popularity during the nineteenth and early twentieth centuries. Much of this popularity was the result of the great interest in the lives of the "vanishing Americans" as well as in the slave narratives and traditional autobiographies of the period. The personal narrative spans both oral and written literatures, incorporating elements of oral storytelling and personal statement as well as written autobiography. Most of the life histories were narrated to translators or collaborators. As Indians became educated in the white man's language and literature, they began to write autobiographies that frequently combined oral history, myths and tales, and personal experience. However, the publication of written Indian autobiographies preceded that of oral life histories.

The first autobiography to be published was *A Son of the Forest* (1829) by William Apes (Pequot, b. 1798); he included a briefer autobiography in his *Experience of Five Christian Indians of the Pequod Tribe* (1833). Apes, who claimed to be descended from King Philip, was one-quarter white. In his autobiographies, he gives a moving account of the abuse he suffered as a child at the hands of his alcoholic grandparents. (He uses the experience to introduce an attack on Indian alcoholism, a condition for which he holds whites responsible.) After a severe beating, Apes was taken in by a white family and bound out from age five to a series of masters, a common practice in dealing with orphans and foster children. He later converted to Methodism, ran away to join the army during the War of 1812, and was ordained in 1829. Apes, who was influenced by the spiritual confessions of the period, describes in his autobiographies his perilous journey to salvation, fall from grace, and subsequent rededication to Christianity. He also strongly criticizes whites' treatment of Indians. The whites with whom Apes lived as a child taught him to be terrified of his own people. If he disobeyed, they threatened to punish him by sending him to the forest. As a result, he became frightened when he encountered a group of Indians:

> . . . the great fear I entertained of my brethren, was occasioned by the many stories I had heard of their cruelty towards the whites—how they were in the habit of killing and scalping men, women and children. But the whites did not tell me that they were in a great majority of instances the aggressors—that they had imbrued their hands in the life blood of my brethren, driven them from their once peaceful and happy homes—that they introduced among them the fatal and exterminating diseases of civilized life. If the whites had told me how cruel they had been to the poor Indian, I should have apprehended as much harm from them. (*Son of the Forest* 23; 1831 ed.)

Apes's autobiography was published at the height of the debate over the Indian Removal Bill, which Andrew Jackson had advocated in his campaign for the presidency in 1828.

The *Life, History, and Travels of Kah-ge-ga-gah-bowh* (1847), by George Copway (Ojibwa, 1818–69), reflects the traditions of the spiritual confessions as well as of the missionary narratives. Copway undoubtedly wrote his autobiography in response both to his popularity as a lecturer and to the government's efforts to remove Ojibwas from ceded territory to central Minnesota. It was later published under the title *The Life, Letters and Speeches of Kah-ge-ga-gah-bowh* (1850).

Born near the mouth of the Trent River in Upper Canada, Copway was raised as a traditional Ojibwa until he was converted to Methodism in 1827. Copway's only formal schooling was the nineteen months he spent at Ebenezer Academy in Jackson, Illinois. After his marriage to Elizabeth Howell, a white woman, Copway served as missionary in Wisconsin, Minnesota, and at Rice Lake in Ontario. Accused of embezzlement by the Saugeen and Rice Lake bands of Ojibwa, he was imprisoned briefly in 1846 and left Canada for the United States. Befriended by American Methodists, Copway launched a new career as a lecturer and writer on Indian affairs. His autobiography went through six editions in a single year. Undoubtedly, part of the book's popularity was due to Copway's characterization of himself as a "noble savage" who recognized that Christianity and education were the salvation of the Indian, a portrayal exemplified in the following passage:

> I loved the woods, and the chase, I had the nature for it, and gloried in nothing else. The mind for letters was in me, but *was asleep*, till the dawn of Christianity arose, and awoke the slumbers of the soul into energy and action. (11; 1850 ed.)

Copway's tender portrayals of Indian family life are designed to counteract the stereotypes of Indian savagery all too common in the popular press. Like Apes, Copway has a strong oratorical style, demonstrated, for example, in his attack on the government's treatment of American Indians and its payments for Indian land in money rather than as an investment in education: "I would now ask, what are millions of money without education? I do not mean that an equivalent should not be given for lands ceded to the government. No; but I do mean that his equivalent should be appropriated in such a way as to produce the greatest benefits and the happiest results" (127; 1850 ed.). His blend of myth, history, and personal experience established a structural pattern followed by later Indian autobiographers.

Few Indians published during the three decades following the publication of Copway's works. From the 1850s to the 1890s, most of the works by Indian authors were histories of woodland tribes from the East and Midwest. White audiences were far more interested in reading the accounts of explorers, settlers, and goldminers who conquered the West than of Indians who suffered the consequences of this conquest. During the last half of the nineteenth century, the public's earlier interest in the "noble but vanquished savage" tribes from the East and Midwest was replaced by its hostility to the fighting tribes of the Far West.

One of the few Indian life histories published in the thirty years after Copway wrote his autobiography was *Life among the Piutes* (1883), by Sarah Winnemucca [Hopkins] (Paiute, c. 1844–91). It is a unique chronicle of Paiute-white relations during the important period from 1844 to 1883. Winnemucca was the only Indian woman writer of personal and tribal history during most of the nineteenth century. Born near the Sink of the Humboldt River in Nevada, Winnemucca was the granddaughter of Truckee, who she claimed was chief of all the Paiutes, and the daughter of Old Winnemucca, who succeeded his father as chief. Because Winnemucca and her family followed Truckee's policy of peaceful coexistence with whites, she spent much of her life serving as a liaison between the Paiutes and whites in her people's native Nevada and in Oregon, where they were later removed. At the end of the Bannock War of 1878, in which many Paiutes participated, Winnemucca accompanied her father and her brother Naches to Washington, D.C., to obtain from Secretary of the Interior Carl Schurz permission for the Paiutes to return to the Malheur Reservation in Washington State. Unfortunately, the government provided neither supplies nor transportation for the tribe's return.

Winnemucca's disillusionment with federal Indian policy and with its agents motivated her to take the Paiute cause to the public. Encouraged by the success of her first lecture in San Francisco, in 1879, she toured the East, delivering more than three hundred lectures. Both her speeches and her book, *Life among the Piutes*, supported the General Allotment Act (1887). *Life among the Piutes* is one of the most imaginative personal and tribal histories of the period. Unlike Apes and Copway, Winnemucca was not influenced by religious autobiographies. With a sharp eye for detail, she re-creates scenes and dialogues that give her book an immediacy missing from many other histories of the period. Particularly interesting are her characterization of her childhood terror of the whites her grandfather so respected, her discussion of the status of women in Paiute society, and her portrayal of her role as a liaison between Indians and whites during the Bannock War. Winnemucca does not hesitate to remind her white readers that Paiute women had more opportunity to influence their councils than did white women. Although Winnemucca admires white achievements, she eloquently attacks the religious hypocrisy of white Christians determined to take all Indian land and exterminate its inhabitants: "your carbines rise upon the bleak shore, and your so-called civilization sweeps inland from the ocean wave; but, oh, my God! leaving its pathway marked by crimson lines of blood, and strewed by the bones of two races, the inheritor and the invader; and I am crying out to you for justice" (207).

By the 1890s and early twentieth century, as noted, many autobiographies of western Indians began to appear. The most influential and widely read Indian autobiographer during this period was Charles Eastman [Ohiyesa] (Sioux, 1858–1939), one of the first Indian doctors. In his lifetime, Eastman moved from the nomadic tribal life of the Santee Sioux to the drawing rooms and lecture halls of America and England, meeting such illustrious people as Matthew Arnold, Henry Wadsworth Longfellow, Ralph Waldo Emerson, Francis Parkman, and Theodore Roosevelt. Though often described as a full-blooded Sioux, Eastman was at least one-quarter white. His mother's grandfather was Seth Eastman, a New Englander, and her mother was at least one-fourth French. Until he was fifteen, Eastman led the life of a traditional Santee Sioux boy, isolated from contacts with whites. The return of his father, Jacob [Many Lightnings], who had been imprisoned for his role in the Minnesota Sioux uprising in 1862, ended this free life. Jacob enrolled his son in school in Flandreau, Dakota Territory. For the next seventeen years, Eastman attended such schools as Dartmouth College (class of 1887) and Boston University Medical School, from which he received his degree in 1890. Eastman became an agency physician at Pine Ridge, just before the Ghost Dance religion swept through the reservation. During this period he met and married Elaine Goodale, a Massachusetts writer and teacher on the Great Sioux Reservation. As a result of policy disputes at Pine Ridge, the Eastmans moved to St. Paul, where Eastman tried unsuccessfully to establish a practice. For the next two decades, Eastman held a variety of positions in Indian affairs and was active in Indian reform movements, including the Society of American Indians. During World War I, the Eastmans purchased a New Hampshire summer camp, for which Eastman served as director. In 1921, the Eastmans separated after the death of a beloved daughter. Eastman moved to Detroit to live near their only son. In 1939, after a tepee in which he had been living caught fire, he suffered smoke inhalation and later contracted both pneumonia and a heart condition, which killed him.

Eastman's collaborator on all his books was Elaine, whose contributions he acknowledged. However, her name as coauthor appears only on *Wigwam Evenings* (1909) and on *Smoky Day's Wigwam Evenings* (1910, a reissue of the earlier work). Describing their collaboration, Elaine later wrote that "Dr. Eastman's books left his hand . . . as a rough draft in pencil, on scratch paper." She then typed copies, "revising, omitting, and re-writing as necessary" (qtd. in Wilson, *Ohiyesa* 131).

Eastman chronicled his life as a Santee Sioux from childhood to age fifteen in *Indian Boyhood* (1902). Written for his children, the book depicts the traditional life of the Sioux before the reservation period. The opening lines express the spirit Eastman hoped to transmit to his readers: "What boy would not be an Indian for a while when he thinks of the freest life in the world? This life was mine. Every day there was a real hunt. There was real game" (20). Eastman's second autobiography, *From the Deep Woods to Civilization* (1916), describes his experiences in the white world; it also reveals a deepening sense of his own Indianness and questions the superiority of white ways. He expresses some of these feelings in his account of his years at Dartmouth (1883–87): "It was here I had most of my savage gentleness and native refinement knocked out of me. I do not complain, for I know that I gained more than their equivalent" (67). The work strongly criticizes government policy, particularly the indifference to the hunger and protest of the Sioux, which Eastman felt led to the spread of the Ghost Dance religion: "Never was more ruthless fraud and graft practiced upon a defenseless people than upon these poor natives by the politicians! Never were there more worthless 'scraps of paper' anywhere in the world than many of the Indian treaties and Government documents!" (99). In all his works, Eastman attempted to serve as a bridge between Indian and white cultures—to reveal to his white audience the worldviews, customs, literature, and history of the Indians so that non-Indian Americans might appreciate and emulate native American virtues.

Eastman's autobiographies inspired other Sioux writers, such as Luther Standing Bear and Zitkala-Ša, to write their personal narratives. Like Eastman, Standing Bear [Ota K'te] (c. 1868–1939) belonged to the generation of Sioux who witnessed the transition from the old nomadic life to that on a reservation. He joined the first class at the Carlisle Indian School, established in 1879 by Richard Henry Pratt, an army officer, to educate young Indians. Standing Bear eventually joined Buffalo Bill's Wild West Show, which toured the United States and England in 1902. By 1912, he had sold his allotted land and settled in California, where he became a movie actor, lecturer, and volunteer for Indian causes. His career as an author began late in life, when he wrote *My People, the Sioux* (1928), assisted by E. A. Brininstool. Especially moving are his descriptions of his journey to and subsequent life at Carlisle. In 1933, he published *Land of the Spotted Eagle*, which focuses far more on Sioux beliefs, customs, and life than did *My People, the Sioux* and is far more critical of white treatment of Indians. Standing Bear also wrote *My Indian Boyhood* (1931), directed to children. Zitkala-Ša [Gertrude Bonnin] (1876–1938) published autobiographical essays in the *Atlantic Monthly* in 1900 and 1901, which were subsequently reprinted in her *American Indian Stories* (1921). Although her literary career ended after her marriage to Raymond T. Bonnin, in 1902, Zitkala-Ša collaborated with William Hanson on the composition of *Sun Dance*, an Indian opera that premiered in 1913 in Vernal, Utah. A zealous advocate of Indian rights, Zitkala-Ša was active in such organizations as the Society of American Indians and the National Council for American Indians, which she founded.

Another Plains Indian who wrote a fine autobiography is Francis La Flesche (Omaha, 1857–1932). Trained as a linguist by the scholar J. Owen

Dorsey, La Flesche became one of the first Indian anthropologists. His major works are "The Omaha Tribe" (1905–06), written with Alice Fletcher, and "The Osage Tribe" (1914–28). *The Middle Five* (1900) describes his life as a student in a Presbyterian mission school in northeastern Nebraska after the Civil War. La Flesche succeeds in his goal of revealing the true nature and character of the Indian boy, by creating lively and amusing portraits of the children, their activities, and their interactions with their parents and school authorities as the boys learn to adjust to a new culture. Another Indian who wrote an autobiography in the first half of the twentieth century is James Paytiamo (Acoma, b. c. 1890). More recently Anna Moore Shaw (Pima, b. 1898) has recorded her autobiography in *A Pima Past* (1974), and Ted Williams (Tuscarora, b. 1930) gives a witty account of his life in *The Reservation* (1976). James McCarthy (Papago, b. 1895), in *A Papago Traveler* (1985), provides an interesting chronicle of his early life on the reservation, his years as a student in Indian schools, and his experiences as a soldier in World War I and laborer who traveled to Europe, China, and Alaska.

Twentieth-century Indian authors have also written literary autobiographies. A splendid example of such a work is *Talking to the Moon* (1945), by John Joseph Mathews (c. 1894–1979), strongly influenced by Osage culture as well as by the writers Thoreau and John Muir. One-eighth Osage, Mathews was raised in Pawhuska, the Osage agency. During World War I, he served in the aviation branch of the Signal Corps in France. He received his BS from the University of Oklahoma in 1920 and his BA in natural science from Oxford University in 1923. While abroad, Mathews attended the School of International Relations in Geneva and traveled widely in Western Europe, Britain, and North Africa. After his marriage, he settled in Los Angeles. When his marriage ended, Mathews returned in 1929 to Pawhuska, where he built his cabin in the blackjack oaks region and lived for the next ten years.

As had Thoreau before him, Mathews withdrew from cities to live alone in order to overcome the separation he felt from nature. In *Talking to the Moon*, Mathews, like Thoreau, uses the seasons as an organizing principle. However, he structures his work according to the Osage names and descriptions of individual months. A spiritual kinship with Thoreau is evident, as well, as Mathews describes his observations of nature and his personal growth in terms of natural cycles; the two also share a strong sense of place. For Mathews, however, the Osages were part of the balance of the blackjacks and the prairie in what is now Oklahoma, and their religion was as much a product of this environment as the Osage people themselves. This balance is revealed in the following passage from "Spring—Planting Moon (April)," which also demonstrates Mathews's polished style:

> All this is woman's work, the female children of the earth planning with Mother Earth and the Moon Woman for the coming of the fruits of the earth; preparing for the nuptials of ageless earth and Grandfather

the Sun and all his male manifestations. Certain ceremonies were performed and songs were sung, and often, as they sang their planting
songs the April rains would slant from the sky with a solitary cloud as
their source, while the sun, still present, made the raindrops sparkle
with life. (47)

Mathews's own beautifully crafted descriptions contrast vividly with his re-
creations of the dialects used by the Osage and white Oklahomans whom
he portrays so accurately. Writing toward the end of World War II, Mathews
celebrates the continuity of Osage traditions and the natural order with
humanity's destructiveness in war.

An equally sophisticated autobiographer is N. Scott Momaday (Kiowa,
b. 1934). Although born at Lawton, Oklahoma, Momaday spent much of
his youth in the Southwest on Navajo, San Carlos Apache, and Jemez
reservations in New Mexico and Arizona, where his Kiowa father and part-
Cherokee mother worked. Momaday returned with his father to Kiowa
country during summers. After receiving a BA from the University of New
Mexico in 1958, Momaday began graduate work in English at Stanford,
where he completed his MA in 1959 and PhD in 1963. He later became a
distinguished professor of the University of Arizona English department.

Momaday's *Way to Rainy Mountain* (1969) chronicles the Kiowas' origin
and migration to Oklahoma, their life both before and after the reservation
period, and his own quest for his tribal roots. The rediscovery of tribal,
ethnic, and family roots was a frequent theme in American Indian and
minority literature during the 1960s and 1970s. In this highly imaginative,
poetic work, Momaday incorporates Kiowa myths, tribal and family history,
and personal reminiscences. An introductory essay, prologue, epilogue,
and two poems frame three chapters that describe the emergence, ascend-
ance, and decline of Kiowa culture. The three chapters are subdivided into
units, each of which contains mythical, historical, and personal narratives
focusing on a particular theme. The book pays tribute to memory—tribal,
family, and personal—and emphasizes the inevitability of change and loss.
Memory and imagination provide the means for transmitting images of
people and events for future generations. The subtle, complex structure
of *The Way to Rainy Mountain* is enhanced by Momaday's simple but highly
poetic style, as illustrated in the excerpt below, which describes Momaday's
reaction to seeing a pronghorn buck in Wyoming:

> But I remembered once having seen a frightened buck on the run, how
> the white rosette of its rump seemed to hang for the smallest fraction
> of time at the top of each frantic bound—like a succession of sunbursts
> against the purple hills. (19)

In *The Names* (1976), a more conventional autobiography, Momaday
makes considerable use of stream-of-consciousness narrative. In the preface, he calls the work "an act of the imagination" (i). The writer gives a

fascinating account of both sides of his family as well as a detailed and poignant description of his boyhood. Like Isak Dinesen in *Out of Africa*, the model for *The Names*, Momaday believed that individuals are molded by the particular location they inhabit. In his emphasis on the importance of early experience and landscape on molding the adult, Momaday combines Wordsworthian literary tradition with American Indian oral traditions. An acclaimed novelist and poet as well as an autobiographer, Momaday has been a major influence on contemporary literature. His fiction and poetry are discussed later in this volume.

One of the most highly acclaimed autobiographies by a contemporary American Indian author is *Blue Highways* (1982) by William Lewis Trogdon, whose book was published under the name William Least Heat Moon (Osage, b. 1939). Born in Kansas City, Missouri, Trogdon, whose father's Osage name is Heat Moon, earned his BA, MA, and PhD from the University of Missouri. (He later earned another BA, in photojournalism.) That same year, Trogdon left his job teaching English at Stephens College, took the name Least Heat Moon, and toured rural America in his van. *Blue Highways*, a best-seller, chronicles the author's physical and spiritual journey across the country. The work is in the tradition of the "road literature" written by de Tocqueville, Steinbeck, and Kerouac. Least Heat Moon is especially successful in his characterizations of rural philosophers and careful descriptions of nature.

Gerald Vizenor's *Interior Landscapes* (1990) is, by turns, poignant, sprightly, and satiric. The book, which incorporates revised sections of "I Know What You Mean, Erdupps MacChurbbs," gives Vizenor's account of his Ojibwa father's ancestry and records important experiences in his evolution as a writer. He vividly re-creates his childhood spent living in poverty with his mother, relatives, or foster parents; his uneasy relationship with his mother; and his eventual love of his stern stepfather, whom his mother abandoned and who died shortly thereafter in an accident at work. In the third grade, Vizenor began to escape into the world of his imaginative trickster friend Erdupps MacChurbbs, where dreams became stories and tricksters raised him in imagination. The motif of the personal and tribal trickster runs through the book as it does Vizenor's other works. Also significant to his emergence as a writer were his army stint in Japan and a course in Japanese Haiku at the University of Minnesota. Vizenor's descriptions of his experiences in the army and on various social-service, journalistic, and academic jobs demonstrate his ability as a satirist and social commentator. The volume also includes Vizenor's encounters with leaders of the American Indian Movement and his investigative reporting of the suicide of Dane Michael White, a thirteen-year-old Indian who hanged himself in jail while court authorities tried to decide his future. Vizenor's autobiography reworks and illuminates a number of incidents described in such earlier works as *Wordarrows* (1978), *Earthdivers* (1981), *The Trickster of*

Liberty (1988), and various essays. These and other works by Vizenor are examined elsewhere.

The genre of narrated autobiographies was introduced in *Black Hawk, an Autobiography* (1833), told by Black Hawk (Sauk, 1767–1838), collected and translated by Antoine Le Claire, and edited in final form by John B. Patterson. A memoir contemporary to Black Hawk's is that of Governor Blacksnake (Seneca). Recorded in Seneca-style English by Benjamin Williams and edited by Thomas Abler under the title *Chainbreaker* (1989), it provides a valuable record of Indian participation in the Revolutionary War.

The narrated autobiographies came of age in the first half of the twentieth century, when anthropologists, who recognized the importance of the life history as a means of understanding tribal ethnography, collected numerous personal narratives. The following narrators collaborated with scholars in preparing excellent ethnographic autobiographies: Sam Blowsnake [Big Winnebago and Crashing Thunder] (Winnebago); Mountain Wolf Woman (Winnebago); Maria Chona (Papago); John Stands in Timber (Cheyenne); James Sewid (Kwakiutl); Left Handed (Navajo); and Albert Yava (Tewa/Hopi). Some subjects told their stories to friends, who recorded them. *Me and Mine* (1969), narrated by Helen Sekaquaptewa (Hopi) and written by Louise Udall, typifies this form.

The most widely read work of this genre is *Black Elk Speaks* (1932), narrated by Black Elk (1863–1950) to John G. Neihardt. Far more literary than other such works, *Black Elk Speaks* records the life and visions of a Sioux holy man in his progress toward becoming a medicine man. It also portrays that tribe's worldviews and customs both before and after the tribe was forced onto the reservation and contains the accounts of the Custer battle told by Black Elk and others. Of particular interest are Black Elk's descriptions of his visions. Raymond J. DeMallie, in *The Sixth Grandfather*, makes clear the crucial role Neihardt played in shaping the final manuscript when he points out that "the book is Black Elk's story as he gave it to Neihardt, but the literary quality and tone of the work are Neihardt's" (51). However, Neihardt did shorten and eliminate some ethnographic details from the description of Black Elk's great vision. In *The Sixth Grandfather*, DeMallie reproduces the original notes taken by Neihardt's daughter, Hilda Neihardt Petri. Less polished stylistically, *Lame Deer: Seeker of Visions*, by John Fire [Lame Deer] (b. 1900) and Richard Erdoes, gives a humorous account of a Sioux who was part holy man and part scamp and who lived after the beginning of the reservation period.

Falling somewhere between narrated and written personal narratives are those recorded in writing by the subjects and later edited by scholars. Among the most interesting of this genre is *The Warrior Who Killed Custer*, recorded in Dakota by Chief Joseph White Bull (Sioux, b. 1850). The long manuscript written by Don Talayesva (Hopi, b. 1890) was revised and restructured extensively by Leo W. Simmons in *Sun Chief.* The manuscript by Refugio Savala (b. 1904) was edited by Kathleen Mullen Sands and published with far less editorial intrusion in *The Autobiography of a Yaqui Poet.* Important for the study of Indian women is Mourning Dove's autobiography and ethnohistory, edited by Jay Miller and published under the title *Mourning Dove: A Salishan Autobiography.* Miller has constructed the volume from the various drafts and fragments prepared by Mourning Dove (Colville), who died before she could complete the manuscript. Using her own life as an example, Mourning Dove devotes several chapters to the role of women. Mourning Dove's other work is discussed elsewhere.

History of Written Literature

EIGHTEENTH AND NINETEENTH CENTURIES

The major genre written by American Indian authors in the late eighteenth and nineteenth centuries was nonfiction prose. In addition to writing autobiographies, Indian authors wrote sermons, protest literature, tribal histories, and travel accounts. They hoped that their prose would make their white audiences recognize Indians' humanity as a people and the significance of their tribal cultures and history. Their efforts paralleled the political developments, such as the Indian Removal Bill of 1830, that threatened the sovereignty of Indian peoples.

The first Indian author to publish in English was Samson Occom (Mohegan, 1723–92), a Presbyterian missionary to the Indians who was renowned for his powerful preaching. Occom was the pupil of the Reverend Eleazar Wheelock, who sent him to England from 1765 to 1768 to raise money for his Indian Charity School in Hanover, New Hampshire, which became Dartmouth College. Occom's *Sermon Preached at the Execution of Moses Paul, an Indian* (1772) so impressed his audience that, after it was published, it became the first Indian best-seller. The sermon combines a deep concern for the effects of alcohol on Indian life with the traditions of the execution sermon then so popular in America and exemplified in the work of Increase Mather and Cotton Mather. Occom, who had been an advocate for his people in their land claims, became an enthusiastic supporter of the plan to remove New England Christian Indians to lands offered by the Oneida in western New York. Before the Revolutionary War, there was considerable white pressure for Indians to remove from New England; the pressure increased after the war, when the Oneidas and other Indians in western New York were persuaded to move to Wisconsin.

One of the most forceful Indian protest writers of the early nineteenth century was William Apes. Appended to the 1833 edition of his *Experience of Five Christian Indians of the Pequod Tribe* is "An Indian's Looking-Glass for the White Man," in which he charges that whites disenfranchised Indians merely because of their skin color. Apes's criticism reflects the enactment of new state laws to abrogate Indian civil rights as well as the passage of the Indian Removal Bill. His *Indian Nullification of the Unconstitutional Laws of Massachusetts, Relative to the Marshpee Tribe* (1835) demonstrates Apes's ability as a writer of protest literature and is a well-documented account of the grievances of the tribe, which he joined and encouraged in its fight for justice. The Mashpee's victory was one of the few that Indians gained during the 1830s, which saw the massive removal of Indians from their lands in the South and Midwest. Apes's final work is the eloquent *Eulogy on King Philip* (1836). First preached at the Odeon at Boston, *Eulogy* illustrates Apes's oratorical power. In the excerpt below, Apes forcefully criticizes the inhuman treatment of the Indians by the Pilgrims. Describing how the Pilgrims paid a poor woman almost one hundred years old a few brass trinkets to atone for kidnapping three sons, Apes asks white women what they would think if someone took their children:

> Should you not think they were beings made more like rocks than men. Yet these same men came to these Indians for support, and acknowledge themselves, that no people could be used better than they were; that their treatment would do honor to any nation; that their provisions were in abundance; that they gave them venison, and sold them many hogheads of corn to fill their stores, besides beans. This was in the year 1622. Had it not been for this humane act of the Indians, every white man would have been swept from the New England colonies. In their sickness too, the Indians were as tender to them as to their own children; and for all this, they were denounced as being savages, by those who received all these acts of kindness. (10)

Following the publication of these works, Apes disappeared from view and nothing is known of his later life.

Many American Indian authors in the nineteenth century wrote histories of their tribes, based on oral traditions. The first Indian to publish such a history was David Cusick (Tuscarora, d. c. 1840). His *Sketches of Ancient History of the Six Nations . . .* may have been published as early as 1825, the date of the preface, but probably was published in 1827. A few paragraphs were added to his twenty-eight-page history in the editions of 1828 and 1848. The histories by Cusick and later writers were responses to the increasing pressures on Indians to remove from lands that whites coveted. By emphasizing the traditions and culture of their tribes, the works reminded their white audiences of the essential humanity of Native Americans.

George Copway published his *Traditional History and Characteristic Sketches of the Ojibway Nation* in 1850; it later appeared under the title *Indian Life and Indian History*. Emphasizing in this work the importance of oral tradition as a basis for Indian history, he chronicles his people's migrations as contained in their legends and discusses their wars with such perpetual enemies as the Iroquois, Huron, and Sioux. In addition, he describes the tribe's religious beliefs, forms of government, language and pictograph writing, hunting, and games. Copway incorporates considerable material from other historians. During this period, too, other Ojibwas were recording the history of their tribe. Peter Jones [Kahkewaquonaby] (1802–56), a Methodist missionary like Copway, wrote *History of the Ojebway Indians* (1861), published posthumously. Covering much of the same material as Copway, Jones also gives an analysis of Ojibwa marriage customs, the structure of the language, and an account of Indian affairs in which he participated. His history is far more authoritative than Copway's. The best and fullest account of the Ojibwas written in the nineteenth century is *History of the Ojibway, Based upon Traditions and Oral Statements* by William Whipple Warren (Ojibwa, 1825–53). Completed in 1852, the book was not published until 1885, over thirty years after Warren's death. Highly respected by Indians and non-Indians, Warren worked as an interpreter and was elected as the only Indian member of the Minnesota state legislature. His *History* provides a general introduction to the Algonkins and to the Ojibwa nation, a detailed history of their origin and migration legends, their movement westward, and their battles with enemy tribes.

These tribal histories encouraged other authors to write accounts of their tribes: Peter Dooyentate Clarke (Wyandot), *Origin and Traditional History of the Wyandotts, and Sketches of Other Indian Tribes of North America* (1870); Chief Elias Johnson (Tuscarora), *Legends, Traditions and Laws, of the Iroquois* (1881); and Chief Andrew J. Blackbird [Mackawdegbenessy] (Ottawa), *History of the Ottawa and Chippewa Indians of Michigan* (1887).

Indians also published accounts of their travels abroad. Maungwudaus, or George Henry (Ojibwa), a lapsed Methodist convert and cousin of Peter Jones, described his adventures with his traveling band of Indian performers in a pamphlet entitled *An Account of the Chippewa Indians* (1848). Copway also described his travels in *Running Sketches of Men and Places, in England, France, Germany, Belgium, and Scotland* (1851), the first full-length travel book by an Indian. Although the volume contains some interesting character sketches of London luminaries, it is primarily a collection of lengthy citations from local guidebooks. Copway briefly published a newspaper, *Copway's American Indian*, between July and the fall 1851.

One of the few Indians to write fiction and poetry in the nineteenth century was John Rollin Ridge (Cherokee, 1827–67), whose *Life and Adventures of Joaquín Murieta* (1854) is the first novel by an Indian author. Ridge was the half-Cherokee grandson of Major Ridge, one of the most influential leaders of the tribe before removal. Ridge himself was only twelve at the time of the forced march to Indian Territory. Both Major Ridge and his son John were assassinated for their role in bringing about the sale of Cherokee lands. Late in his teens, Ridge shot a man—probably in self-defense—and fled in 1850 to the California gold fields, where he worked as a clerk. Writing under the name Yellow Bird, a literal translation of his Cherokee name Cheesquatalawny, Ridge became a regular contributor to such San Francisco periodicals and journals as *Gold Era, Hesperian,* and *Pioneer.* He later became owner and editor of other California newspapers.

In *The Life and Adventures of Joaquín Murieta,* Ridge portrays the mixed-blood Murieta as a Byronic "noble outlaw" who turns to crime after he is victimized by white miners. Ridge echoes the experiences of the Cherokees in his description of how the hard-working, ambitious Murieta is driven off his land by greedy whites. Only after his brother is killed does Murieta devote his life to vengeance against his oppressors. Although Ridge himself developed elaborate plots to avenge the murders of his grandfather and father, he had to be content with the imaginary revenge gained through the exploits of his protagonist. Like the Byronic hero, Murieta is a good man driven to violent deeds by injustice, a gallant gentleman to women, a courageous leader to his men, and an unrelenting enemy to his foes. The romance inspired later Mexican American writers and initiated the flood of subsequent stories about this Robin Hood figure. The novel proceeds at a breathless pace, filled with derring-do and punctuated by gunfire:

> He dashed along that fearful trail as he had been mounted upon a spirit-steed, shouting as he passed:
> "I am Joaquín! kill me if you can!"
> Shot after shot came clanging around his head, and bullet after bullet flattened on the wall of salt at his right. In the midst of the first firing, his hat was knocked from his head, and left his long black hair streaming behind him. (87)

In its emphasis on regionalism in California, the romance also reflects the local-color tradition.

Ridge's collected *Poems* (1868), most of which were written before he was twenty, was published after his death. Although the majority reflect the sentimentality of popular literature of the period, "Arkansas Root Doctor" reveals the author's ability to create a realistic characterization and to use dialect, while "The Humboldt River" vividly describes the toll that the Nevada desert took on the pioneers. An excerpt from this poem portrays the ghastliness of the shores of what he called the "River of Death":

> Weird shores with their alkaline white—
> That loom in the glare of the light;
> Weird bones as they bleach in the sun,
> Where the beast from his labors is done;
> Weird frost-work of poisonous dews
> On shrub and on herb, which effuse
> The death they have drank to the core. (15)

Ridge also wrote a series of essays on the American Indian, which have been recently collected in *A Trumpet of Our Own.*

One of the few novels attributed to an Indian author during this period is *O-gî-mäw-kwe Mit-i-gwä-kî (Queen of the Woods)* (1899), published under the name of Simon Pokagon (Potawatomi, 1830–99). Although this work is often cited as the first novel by a Native American devoted to Indian life, James A. Clifton, who has done extensive studies of the Pokagon band of Potawatomi, states in "Simon Pokagon and the Sand-Bar Case" that Pokagon did not write this posthumously published work (14). The novel combines nostalgic reminiscence for the lost golden age of the Potawatomi with fiery attacks on alcohol, which has destroyed Indian families.

At the turn of the century, Emily Pauline Johnson, a Canadian Mohawk (1861–1913), achieved critical acclaim as a poet and performer of her poetry in her native Canada, the United States, and England. Her work is included here because of its importance to the evolution of American Indian women's literature and because she was one of the most widely read Indian authors in the United States. Many of her short stories appeared in the *Mother's Magazine* and *Boys' World*, journals published in the Chicago suburb of Elgin. In 1910, when Johnson was writing for the *Mother's Magazine*, it had a circulation of over 600,000.

Johnson's father was the Mohawk chief George Henry Martin, and her mother was Emily Susanna Howells, an English-born cousin of the American writer William Dean Howells. The family's home of Chiefswood in Brantford, Ontario, was a gathering spot for Indian and non-Indian visitors. Primarily educated at home by governesses and her mother, Johnson was introduced early to the classics of English and American literature. Her career as a poet and performer began in January 1892 at a Toronto literary evening, when Johnson electrified her audience with a recitation of her poem "A Cry from an Indian Wife," based on the first mixed-blood rebellion (1869–70), led by Louis Riel, against the Canadian government. Subsequently, Johnson crisscrossed Canada and the United States and visited England, performing her works to great praise. Her first two volumes of poetry were *The White Wampum* (1895), almost half of which had Indian themes, and *Canadian Born* (1903). Her poems from these volumes and from various periodicals were collected in *Flint and Feather* (1912). The poetry in this collection tends to be highly romantic and melodramatic. Unfortunately, some of her best poems are not included in the volume. The lyrical "Song My Paddle Sings," describing the west wind on the river as the speaker paddles her canoe, is frequently anthologized, as is the fiery outcry against the whites' mistreatment of the Indian, "As Red Men Die." "The Corn Husker" is an interesting character sketch of an old Indian woman. Several of Johnson's best poems, such as "Morrow Land," "Heidelberg," and "Song," were so personal that she never published them. These lines from "Song" demonstrate her lyricism:

The night-long shadows faded into grey,
Then silvered into glad and golden sunlight
Because you came to me, like a new day
Born of the beauty of an autumn night.
(Qtd. in Keller, *Pauline* 159)

Johnson was, moreover, one of the first Indian women to publish short fiction. Especially interesting is her *Moccasin Maker* (1913), which is primarily a collection of short stories about Indian and non-Indian women in Canada. It also includes a fictional account of the lives of her parents. Her stories reflect the domestic orientation common in popular women's fiction in the nineteenth century; several, focusing on the problems of mixed-blood women in love with white men, introduce a dominant theme of twentieth-century American Indian fiction: the mixed-bloods' search for their place. The most popular of these stories is "A Red Girl's Reasoning," which dramatizes the dilemma of the mixed-blood woman who must choose between her values and her marriage. Reared in the Canadian bush, Christine, the heroine, marries Charlie MacDonald and moves to the city, where she quickly becomes "the rage." The issue that causes Christine to leave her husband is her admission at a party that her parents were never married in the church. When Charlie states that her parents were not legally married, Christine responds, "Why should I recognize the rites of your nation when you do not acknowledge the rites of mine?" (117). Later, when Charlie finally locates her, Christine refuses to take him back. Johnson's stories for boys are collected in *The Shagganappi* (1913). Johnson's work serves as a transition between the nineteenth and twentieth centuries.

1900–67

As the number of Indian authors increased because of education in government-sponsored schools, so did their interest in creative work in a variety of genres.

The first American Indian author to publish satires was Alexander Posey (1873–1907). Through his mother, Mary Phillips, Posey was related to the old and powerful Harjo family. Raised as a Creek, Posey did not learn English until he was twelve. After graduating from Indian University at Bacone, Oklahoma, in 1895, Posey held a number of educational and journalistic posts in Indian Territory. Because of his knowledge of both Creek and English and because of his integrity, he served as a delegate to almost every council or convention in that territory. In 1901 Posey edited the *Indian Journal* at Eufaula, Oklahoma, in which his "Fus Fixico Letters" originally appeared. In these letters, written in Creek-style English, Posey satirized the politics of Indian Territory and the nation. Among the local issues he addressed were allotment, staunchly opposed by many Creeks;

local corruption; white attempts to defraud Indians of their land; and statehood for Indian Territory. The "Letters" were widely reprinted in Oklahoma and in some eastern newspapers as well. Posey's use of dialect and regionalisms was certainly influenced by Robert Burns, whom he greatly admired, and by Finley Peter Dunne, whose satires featuring Mr. Dooley and Mr. Hennessey first appeared in the 1890s. Posey heightened the humor by including well-known Creek elders as characters. Fus Fixico dutifully records the wisdom of his friend Hotgun, who neatly summarizes the Indian problem:

> The missionary he tell the Injin he must lay up treasures in heaven, but he didn't show 'im how to keep body an' soul together on earth an' lay by for the rainy day; an' the school teacher he learn 'im how to read an' shade 'is letters when he write, but didn't teach 'im how to make two blades o' grass grow out o' one; and the philanthropist remind 'im o' the century o' dishonor instead o' the future individual responsibility; an' the government dish out beef an' annuity to 'im instead of a mule an' a plow. Everything like that make the Injin no count, except give jobs to government clerks. (29 June 1906, *Holdenville Times*; qtd. by permission from typescript in the Western History Collections, University of Oklahoma Library)

Posey was also a poet, although he wrote most of his poetry in his youth. After her husband's death, Mrs. Minnie Harris Posey published *The Poems of Alexander Lawrence Posey* (1910), one of the few volumes of poetry by Indian authors in the first half of the twentieth century. Most of the poems are romantic evocations of nature. However, "When Molly Blows the Dinner-Horn" captures the spirit of Burns's "Cotter's Saturday Night." "On the Capture and Imprisonment of Crazy Snake" demonstrates Posey's ability to write protest poetry. Crazy Snake (Chitto Harjo) was imprisoned for his defiance of the government and led a band of Creeks opposed to allotment. The first stanza reveals an anger not present in Posey's other poetry:

> Down with him! chain him! bind him fast!
> Slam to the iron door and turn the key!
> The one true Creek, perhaps the last
> To dare declare, "You have wronged me!"
> Defiant, stoical, silent,
> Suffers imprisonment! (207)

Like Posey, Will Rogers (Cherokee, 1879–1935) was a member of a family prominent in Indian Territory. Rogers's father, Clement Vann Rogers, was a prosperous rancher and banker as well as a member of the tribal senate. Young Rogers left school in 1898 to become a cowboy and entertainer, performing rope tricks. By the beginning of World War i, Rogers had become a regular on the vaudeville circuit, reaching his greatest successes as a stage performer in the Ziegfeld Follies of 1916–18, 1922, and 1924–25. Rogers's famous line "All I know is what I read in the papers" became the preface for his witty commentaries on the national and international scene. His first two books, both published in 1919, consisted of these observations plus other material: *Rogers-isms: The Cowboy Philosopher on the Peace Conference* and *Rogers-isms: The Cowboy Philosopher on Prohibition.* The popularity of Rogers's humor led to a weekly column, which the *New York Times* began syndicating in 1922. Four years later Rogers developed what was to become his most influential written medium—the daily telegram, which eventually ran in 350 newspapers. During the 1920s, he published a series of books based on these columns and on his observations during his many trips abroad: *The Illiterate Digest; Letters of a Self-Made Diplomat to His President, There's Not a Bathing Suit in Russia*, and *Ether and Me.* In his writing and in his stage and movie performances, Rogers adopted the role of the wise innocent—a semiliterate cowboy whose bad grammar and hyperbole gained him instant rapport with average Americans. Rogers represented to them the embodiment of an American hero, unabashed by president or prince, always ready to do verbal battle with the hypocrites of big business or government in order to defend the underdog. Until his death in a plane crash during a tour of Alaska in 1935, Rogers was the most popular humorist of his age.

Another widely read Indian author in the early part of the twentieth century was Charles Eastman. In addition to writing autobiography, Charles Eastman and Elaine Goodale Eastman, his coauthor, wrote nonfiction prose and fiction. In *Red Hunters and the Animal People* (1904), the Eastmans combined traditional legends with adventure and animal stories based on common experiences and observations of Indian hunters. *Old Indian Days* (1907), even more explicitly imaginative than the earlier book, is divided into stories about warriors and those about women. The Eastmans also reinterpreted traditional stories for children in *Wigwam Evenings: Sioux Folktales Retold* (1909), reissued in 1910 under the title *Smoky Day's Wigwam Evenings: Indian Stories Retold.*

Eastman's *Soul of the Indian* (1911) is his fullest statement on ethics. Here he describes the worship of the "Great Mystery" as "silent, solitary, free from all self-seeking" (4). He stresses that Indian faith was not formulated in creeds or forced on those unwilling to receive it. There were no temples and no shrines except those of nature. In *The Indian To-day* (1915), Eastman surveys Indian history, contributions to America, achievements, reservation life, and problems. He also discusses government policies toward the Indian. His *Indian Heroes and Great Chieftains* (1918) is among his most interesting works because of its anecdotes, which the leaders or their contemporaries told to Eastman. Zitkala-Ša included short stories about Sioux life in *American Indian Stories* (1921), as well as essays and the autobiographical pieces.

The first novel by an American Indian woman is *Cogewea, the Half-Blood* (1927), by Mourning Dove [Christine Quintasket] (Colville, 1888–1936). Mourning Dove, who completed only the third grade and a brief stint in business school, spent much of her adult life as a migrant worker in Washington State. Written in collaboration with Lucullus Virgil McWhorter, Mourning Dove's novel focuses on the identity problem of those with mixed-blood and the importance of oral tradition. Although Cogewea, the protagonist, initially rejects a mixed-blood, cowboy suitor for a "crafty Easterner," because accepting him would mean living Indian, she finally realizes the importance of the values he and her Indian grandmother represent. The problems faced by mixed-bloods like Cogewea are vividly portrayed in an incident that occurs during a Fourth of July celebration. Dressed as a white woman, Cogewea enters and wins a "ladies' horse race," only to be denied the prize by a judge who calls her a squaw. When she then enters the race for Indian girls, she is told she has no right to be there because this is a contest for "Indians and not for breeds!" (66). Mourning Dove combines these themes with plot elements from popular westerns. Especially interesting is her use of a strong-willed, independent heroine who is as capable of doing ranch work as any cowboy.

The most controversial writer of the 1920s was Sylvester Clark Long [Long Lance] (Lumbee, 1890–1932). The child of exslaves, Long was a mixed-blood. His mother was white and Lumbee; his father, who never knew his parents, was at least partially African American and claimed white and Indian ancestry. In Winston-Salem, North Carolina, where the family lived, they were categorized as "colored." At age thirteen, Long joined a Wild West show, where he met a Cherokee who taught him some of the language. To get into Carlisle Indian School, Long had his father certify that his son was Cherokee. When Carlisle Cherokee students did not accept him, he took the name Long Lance, suggested by a teacher to help him gain greater credibility as an Indian. An excellent student, Long was later appointed as a Cherokee to West Point, which then excluded blacks. Instead of entering that school, Long enlisted in the Canadian army during World War I. After his service, Long became a journalist in Alberta, where he met members of the Blackfeet tribe. When he published *Long Lance* (1928), he described himself as a Blackfeet chief named Buffalo Child Long Lance. Although the book purported to be Long's autobiography, it is actually a fictional account of growing up on the far western Plains, beginning in the 1890s. Long based much of the book on interviews he conducted in the early 1920s with Canadian Blackfeet and Blood Indians. The book was highly praised by such authorities as Ernest Thompson Seton and Paul Radin. A popular lecturer on Indian themes who addressed his audiences in full tribal regalia, Long also wrote a number of essays published in such journals as *Cosmopolitan* and *McLeans*. The acclaim from his essays and "autobiography" made him a popular figure on Broadway. He costarred in the 1930 Indian film *Silent Enemy*, with Chauncey Yellowrobe (Sioux).

Long's life and career ended quickly and tragically. Contact with his family, whom Long had avoided for over twenty years, was reestablished when his brother came in January 1931 to New York to ask Long for financial help for their father, who was seriously ill. Long thereafter regularly sent money home until shortly before his death. In May, he moved to Los Angeles but became so depressed that he killed himself on 19 March 1932.

The most published American Indian writer of the 1920s was John Milton Oskison (1874–1947). One-eighth Cherokee, Oskison was raised in Oklahoma, graduated from Stanford, and attended Harvard. He later became an editor and feature writer for *Collier's Magazine* and a freelance writer on finance and Indian affairs. Oskison's *Wild Harvest* (1925) and *Black Jack Davy* (1926) are "southwesterns" set in Indian Territory just before statehood and deal with the surge of white settlers into Cherokee land near a town called Big Grove. In *Brothers Three* (1935), Oskison perceptively evaluates these two novels when Henry Odell, the fictional version of the author, describes his first novel as "a mess, misty, sentimental, badly knit, with impossible situations and caricatures of human beings" and the second as "amateurish" but containing "the people and the country I knew" (343–44). Oskison's best novel is *Brothers Three*, which chronicles the efforts of three sons to hold on to the farm established by their father, Francis, and quarter-Cherokee mother, Janet. At the end of the novel, the third son returns from his New York life as a writer and investor to help reestablish the farm. Although the major characters are part Indian, the novel focuses not on Indian life but rather on the importance of honesty, loyalty, hard work, and thrift and on the economic and social history of Oklahoma from the turn of the century through the Depression. A good example of regionalism, *Brothers Three* demonstrates Oskison's ability to create believable characters and realistic dialogue. Although Indianness and issues affecting Indian people are not central to his novels, Oskison did write more explicitly about these subjects in his early essay "Remaining Causes of Indian Discontent" and in his biography, *Tecumseh and His Times* (1938).

During the 1930s, the most accomplished American Indian novelists to emerge were John Joseph Mathews and D'Arcy McNickle (Cree/Salish, 1904–77). Unlike other writers of the 1930s who focused on economic and social issues, Mathews and McNickle emphasized the importance of tribalism and the devastating impact on tribes of the government's assimilationist policies. Mathews's first book was *Wah'Kon-Tah* (1932). Based on the journal of Major Laban J. Miles, the first government agent for the Osage, this fictional account portrays the tribe's determination to retain its traditional ways as Laban attempts to lead them down the white world's road. The last chapter introduces the prototype of the hero of *Sundown* (1934): a young, jazz-age Osage, ashamed of his backward parents but dependent on them for money. Both in this book and in the novel *Sundown*, Mathews vividly portrays how Osage culture was affected by life on the reservation, by allotment, and by the Oklahoma oil boom of the 1920s. (Unlike most tribes, the Osage retained their mineral rights after allotment, which provided income when oil was discovered.)

The parents of the protagonist of *Sundown*, Challenge Windzer, are Osage. The full-blood mother is a traditionalist, while the father, who is one-quarter white, is an assimilationist and a strong advocate of allotment. Windzer is a passive hero who rejects his ancestral past without feeling at home in the white-dominated present. His white education has cut him off from his Indian roots; his cultural separation is completed by a brief stint at the University of Oklahoma and service with the armed forces during World War I. When he returns home after the war, Windzer inherits enough money from the family oil leases to destroy his desire for either education or work. Dreaming of glory, Windzer lives in an alcoholic haze, unable to cope with either the Osage or the white world. Mathews's next book was a biography entitled *Life and Death of an Oilman: The Career of E. W. Marland* (1951). He also published *The Osages: Children of the Middle Waters* (1961), a lengthy and personalized history of his tribe.

The best-written and most polished novel by an Indian writer in the 1930s is McNickle's *Surrounded* (1936). By blood, McNickle was Métis of Cree extraction on his mother's side and white on his father's. His mother's family had settled on the Flathead Reservation, and her children were added to the Flathead rolls by tribal vote, making them eligible for land allotments. After his parents separated, McNickle was sent to Indian boarding school in Oregon. He attended the University of Montana but left just short of graduation; he also briefly attended Oxford and Grenoble. One of the strongest influences on McNickle's writing was his experiences with federal Indian policy gained as an employee of the Bureau of Indian Affairs from 1936 to 1952. McNickle began his career in the BIA under the enlightened leadership of John Collier, a staunch advocate of the Wheeler-Howard Indian Reorganization Act of 1934, which supported tribal autonomy. After the government embarked on a policy of terminating the reservations and eliminating Indian influence in the BIA, McNickle resigned. During the next few years, he worked for American Indian Development, conducting community improvement workshops and directing a health education program for the Navajos in New Mexico. In 1965, he became chair of the Division of Social Sciences of the University of Saskatchewan, Regina, a position he retained until 1971. In addition, McNickle cofounded the National Congress of American Indians and served as the first director of the Center for History of the American Indian, Newberry Library.

McNickle's novel *The Surrounded* chronicles a mixed-blood's search for his place and emphasizes the importance of oral traditions to the cultural survival of the tribe. Published two years after the Indian Reorganization Act, the work movingly describes the disintegration of a tribe as a result of the destruction of its religion and values and the loss of Indian lands to whites. The protagonist, Archilde Leon, is the son of a Flathead woman, renowned for her Catholic piety and for her refusal to abandon Indian ways, and a Spanish father, who after forty years of living among Indians has no insight into their worldviews. The couple has been separated for many years. Returning to his home for a last visit to his parents, Archilde is inadvertently caught up in unpremeditated murders that his mother and his girlfriend commit. His strongly traditional mother and a tribal elder lead him back to the Salish culture he had rejected. Through its emphasis on the role of tribal religion and culture in restoring the tribe, *The Surrounded* offers more hope for the survival of American Indian culture than does Mathews's *Sundown*.

McNickle's *Runner in the Sun* (1954), written for middle-school readers, is one of the few novels published by an Indian author between the 1930s and 1968. Set in the precontact Southwest, this taut novel evokes the life, customs, and beliefs of the ancient cliff dwellers of Chaco Canyon in what is now northwestern New Mexico, as they battle the forces of nature and society that threaten to destroy them. Central to the plot are the adventures of Salt, a teenager being trained to lead his people. Salt survives the efforts of his archenemy, Dark Dealer, to control the village and destroy the young boy. After a hazardous journey to Mexico, Salt brings back a hardy strain of corn that his people can grow to save themselves from starvation. McNickle incorporates the hero twins motif, common in pueblo oral literature, through the character Star Child, who is Salt's age but is more passive than his friend.

McNickle's next novel, *Wind from an Enemy Sky*, was published posthumously in 1978. Here McNickle moves from the clash of two cultures within the individual to that between groups. The plot contrasts the values of the non-Indian culture, symbolized by a dam that cuts off the Indians' water and violates a holy place, with the values of the Indian culture, symbolized by the tribe's sacred Feather-Boy medicine bundle. The plot also contrasts the responses by two brothers, one a traditionalist and the other an assimilationist, to government efforts to alter Indian life-style. The murder of a dam engineer by a young Indian sets off the chain of events that ends in tragedy. As in *The Surrounded*, the clash of cultures ends in the death of the participants. McNickle's forty years of experience in Indian affairs since the publication of his first novel strengthened his belief in the continuing inability of the representatives of the two cultures to communicate their vastly different worldviews to one another. Although McNickle wrote and published some short stories in his youth, he published no other novels. Most of his other books have been histories: *They Came Here First* (1949); *The Indian Tribes of the United States* (1962); *Indians and Other Americans* (1970), with Harold E. Fey; and *Native American Tribalism* (1973). McNickle also wrote a biography of Oliver La Farge entitled *Indian Man* (1971).

Few Indian authors published poetry during the first half of the twentieth century. One of these was Bertrand N. O. Walker [Hen-toh] (Wyandot,

1870–1927), whose *Yon-Doo-Shah-We-Ah* (1924), a volume of dialect poetry, contains some interesting character sketches and narratives, as well as some lyrics that evoke traditional Indian themes. The most accomplished Indian poet in the early twentieth century was [Rolla] Lynn Riggs (Cherokee, 1899-1954). Reared on a farm near Claremore, Oklahoma—then Indian Territory—Riggs entered the University of Oklahoma in 1920. His major published volume of poetry is *The Iron Dish* (1930), which contains delicate lyrics, perceptive descriptions of nature, and some realistic observations. However, it includes only one poem on a specifically Indian theme: "Santo Domingo Corn Dance." Among the loveliest of his poems is the following, in which Riggs effectively blends imagery of touch, sight, and sound. His use of "silver prayer" particularly recalls Keats's use of synaesthesia.

Moon

What I had waited for in the silken wind
Came over me at last. Radiant I stood
In silver. Silver the pavement's end.
Chaste every poplar, every cottonwood.

A light in the *portales* of the hill
Opened the earth. A cricket shook the air.
On Monte Sol guitars of gold, too still
For music, said a silver prayer. (38)

The descriptions of the insects, animals, and plants are in the bucolic tradition of Vergil, Thomson, and Wordsworth. In his "Shadow on Snow," Riggs combines a playful sense of humor with striking imagery. After explaining how he, as a shadow, feels the "need of a mimicry" to say in music "how the moon is one / With the snow, and the snow warmer" than he shall ever be, the speaker concludes with this haunting reflection:

There shall be no more shadows after mine shall go
Hissing over ice cracking the black river glass.
There shall be still a moon, but never a sun,
Never an earth again with its triumphing grass—
Only the moon and the snow. (49)

Riggs is best known as a dramatist, the only Indian author to publish dramas in the first half of the twentieth century. His first play to be produced on Broadway was *Big Lake* (1927), which was not a success. Two of his best plays were folk dramas set in Oklahoma and written during a 1928 Guggenheim fellowship year in Paris: *Borned in Texas*, produced as *Roadside* (1930), and *Green Grow the Lilacs* (1931), which was adapted to become the hit musical *Oklahoma!* (1943). A critical success, *Borned in Texas* deals with the attempts of a high-spirited cowboy on the run from the law for his brawling to win the love of a sharp-tongued but warm-hearted Oklahoma woman. Both *Roadside* and *Green Grow the Lilacs* demonstrate Riggs's ability to capture Oklahoma dialect and folk culture. Also notable is his lyricism and skill in re-creating period and atmosphere.

Riggs's only drama with an Indian theme is *The Cherokee Night* (1936), which deals poignantly with the sense of loss faced by Oklahoma mixed-bloods growing up around Claremore as they became alienated from their Cherokee heritage during the period 1895-1931. Riggs's first attempt to write a play with a contemporary setting was the satirical comedy *Russet Mantle* (1936), produced in New York. Praised as a human comedy, *Russet Mantle* examines the dilemma faced by modern couples who must choose between financial security and romantic love. Critics called the play "wise," "fresh," and "incorrigibly ridiculous" and considered it best thing Riggs had written. Although he continued to write plays, Riggs was unable to equal the success of his earlier work. He did, however, serve as a freelance screenwriter on such films as *Garden of Allah* and *The Plainsman*. In 1942, Riggs enlisted as a private in the United States Army. Although he resided primarily in California and New Mexico before the war, he spent the last years of his life on Shelter Island, New York. In addition to working as a writer, Riggs served as guest author and director of drama at Northwestern University and the University of Iowa.

One of the few Indian authors of mystery and detective fiction is [George] Todd Downing (Choctaw, 1902–74). Raised in Atoka, Oklahoma, Downing received his BA and MA from the University of Oklahoma. He also studied at the National University of Mexico City and conducted tours of Mexico. Downing taught Spanish at the University of Oklahoma and worked in the bilingual program at Southwestern College (now University) in Durant, Oklahoma. His novels, most of which were set in Mexico, include *Murder on Tour* (1933), *The Cat Screams* (1934), *Vultures in the Sky* (1935), *Murder on the Tropic* (1935), *The Case of the Unconquered Sisters* (1936), *The Last Trumpet* (1937), *Night over Mexico* (1937), *Death under the Moonflower* (1938), *The Mexican Earth* (1940), and *The Lazy Lawrence Murders* (1941).

During the 1940s and 1950s, the few Indians who published books returned primarily to the genres of cultural history and autobiography used by earlier authors. Among the writers of this period were Ruth Musk-rat Bronson (Cherokee), *Indians Are People Too* (1944) and Lois Marie Hunter (Shinnecock), *The Shinnecock Indians* (1950). Ella C. Deloria (Sioux) wrote two books during this period. Her *Speaking of Indians* (1944) is a detailed account of how the Sioux retained traditional values after settlement on reservations. *Waterlily*, her only novel, was completed in draft form by 1944 but was not published until 1988. An invaluable portrayal of nineteenth-century Sioux life, *Waterlily* is told from a woman's perspective and traces the life of Waterlily from birth and childhood through marriage, widow-hood, childbirth, and remarriage. In the course of the novel, Deloria authoritatively introduces the reader to Dakota camp life, rituals, kinship systems, and customs.

1968 TO THE PRESENT

The revitalization of Indian pride in the 1960s ushered in an era of creative writing whose quality and quantity were unequaled in the history of Indian literature written in English. The writer whose work began what is called the renaissance of American Indian literature was N. Scott Momaday. After the publication of his highly praised *The House Made of Dawn* (1968) and *Way to Rainy Mountain* (1969), Momaday became the most influential American Indian writer in the late 1960s and early 1970s. *The House Made of Dawn* won the Pulitzer Prize and received more critical acclaim than any previous Indian novel. Through his emphasis on the problems of Indians in contemporary society, on the importance of oral tradition and ritual, and on the use of memory to structure plot, Momaday provided an example that several later Indian novelists followed. Like Mathews and McNickle, he portrays a mixed-blood's quest for a sense of place, tribe, and self. Following the death of his brother and mother, Abel, the protagonist, becomes alienated from his traditional grandfather, the rituals of his pueblo, and the land. In the course of his circular odyssey that takes him from his native Jemez Pueblo, near Albuquerque, to Europe as a soldier during World War II and later to Los Angeles, Abel must conquer a variety of enemies in order to emerge into harmony. Two of these are an albino, whom Abel kills because he believes the man is a witch, and a cruel Chicano policeman, who beats the Indian after he moves to Los Angeles. Abel is aided in rediscovering the importance of Indian rituals and the power of oral tradition by his Jemez grandfather, a Navajo friend, and a Kiowa trickster and minister, as well as by the self-sacrificing love and the example of endurance through suffering demonstrated by his white girlfriend, Millie. Momaday suggests that Abel may become reintegrated into tribal life in the final scene, in which he runs alongside the Jemez dawn runners, participating in a tribal ritual and conscious of his place in the landscape.

Momaday's second novel, *The Ancient Child* (1989), also focuses on a protagonist's ritual journey toward healing and incorporates some of the Kiowa, Pueblo, and Navajo themes and myths that inform *The House Made of Dawn*. The central plot concerns the journey of Lock Setman, called Set, through stages of ritual healing that culminate in his transformation into a bear. Orphaned as a child, Set is adopted by a white man and raised far from his reservation origins. Although he becomes a successful artist, Set feels dissatisfied as he enters middle age. Returning to Kiowa territory after the death of his grandmother, Set meets Grey, a Kiowa-Navajo visionary. Grey, who has absorbed the ritual knowledge and shamanistic powers of her Kiowa great-grandmother, moves back and forth in time through her visions and imagination. She is one of a series of women, undoubtedly emanations of the Navajo goddess Changing Woman, who enable Set to progress toward healing and transformation. Others are his mother, whom he recalls in dim memories; Sister Stella Francesca of the Peter and Paul

Orphanage; and Set's lovers, Lola Bourne and Alais Sancerre. After recovering from a mental breakdown, Set is reunited with Grey in Oklahoma.

The two travel to Navajo country, where they marry. Grey becomes pregnant with his child as Set prepares his mind and body for the final stage of his transformation. In the shadow of Devil's Tower (Tsoai) in Wyoming, Set becomes the bear of the Kiowa legend in which a young boy takes on bear form as he chases his sisters, who climb up a tree stump (Tsoai) and are carried skyward to become the stars of the Big Dipper. Transformation is also the theme of the Piegan story from which the title is derived: an Ancient Boy Child entered camp, spoke a strange language, and disappeared as mysteriously as he came. The Piegans concluded the child must have been a dog or bear. *The Ancient Child* celebrates the power of the myths of the West, Indian and non-Indian. Momaday intertwines stories of mythic and real Indian heroes with those of the outlaw hero, Billy the Kid. Both the writer of stories about Billy and a participant in his life through dream and vision, Grey links the mythology of the Wild West with that of ancient tribal traditions.

In addition to being an autobiographer and novelist, N. Scott Momaday is a fine poet. His *Gourd Dancer* (1976), includes his earlier *Angle of Geese* (1974) and contains many of the themes present in *The Way to Rainy Mountain* and *The House Made of Dawn*, particularly in such poems as "Rainy Mountain Cemetery," "Angle of Geese," and "Bear." A student of Ivor Winters and a scholar of American literature, Momaday uses sharply etched images and a clear style in his lyric poetry. His ability to create a vivid landscape is exemplified in these lines from "Rainy Mountain Cemetery":

> The early sun, red as a hunter's moon,
> Runs in the plain. The mountain burns and shines;
> And silence is the long approach of noon
> Upon the shadow that your name defines—
> and death this cold, black density of stone. (30)

"Bear" reflects the influences of Blake's "Tyger" and Faulkner's treatment of the bear in his fiction. In this poem Momaday effectively captures the power of this animal so sacred to many Indian cultures:

> Seen, he does not come,
> move, but seems forever there,
> dimensionless, dumb,
> in the windless noon's hot glare.
>
> More scarred than others
> these years since the trap maimed him,
> pain slants his withers,
> drawing up his crooked limb. (11)

Especially interesting is the four-poem sequence "The Gourd Dancer," dedicated to his grandfather, Mammedaty, which stresses the importance of place, family, and tribe. The series of poems entitled "Plainview" demonstrates Momaday's skill in writing descriptive-reflective verse. Both "Plainview: 2" and "Delight Song of Tsoai-talee" evoke the spirit of Indian song in their use of repetition.

Like Momaday, Leslie Marmon Silko (Laguna, b. 1948) is a gifted and highly sophisticated storyteller. Silko, who is of mixed Laguna-Mexican-white ancestry, was raised in Laguna Pueblo, New Mexico. It was from her Grandmother Lillie and Aunt Susie Marmon that she heard many of the Laguna stories that inform her work. Silko received her BA from the University of New Mexico in 1969 and briefly enrolled in that university's American Indian law program; more recently she taught at the University of Arizona.

Silko's *Ceremony* (1977) is a response to Momaday's ambivalence about his protagonist's future. Like Momaday, she uses a Pueblo World War ii veteran as the hero and the ritual quest as the central motif for her splendid novel. Silko demonstrates the healing power of tribal ritual and storytelling by reuniting her mixed-blood hero with his tribe at the end of the novel. More overtly than Momaday, she evokes myth and ritual; she not only uses the motif of the ritual journey of the war twins but also structures the novel around the Laguna emergence myth and embeds parts of other myths into the narrative. The protagonist, Tayo, an illegitimate mixed-blood, is raised by an aunt who is embarrassed by his presence. He cherishes the Laguna culture rejected by his progressive cousin, Rocky. Although his decision to join Rocky in enlisting in the army during World War ii leads Tayo to the geographic and psychological hell of a Philippine jungle, the seeds for Tayo's eventual regeneration have been planted in his mind through the lessons from Laguna oral tradition taught him since childhood—stories demonstrating the interdependence of humans and animals on which the harmonious existence of humanity depends. Tayo has survived his descent into the lowest world—that of war—to return to his pueblo, where he must reenact symbolically his tribe's migration from a series of lower worlds to emergence in the present world. Part of this process requires that he overcome hatred of himself and of his white and Indian tormentors, particularly Emo, a modern equivalent of the witches of Laguna mythology. To prepare himself to reenter the ceremonial and communal life of his pueblo, Tayo must participate in rituals, remember ancient stories, and learn lessons taught by Night Swan and T'seh, emanations of the Laguna creator (Thought-Woman). Silko has finished a new novel, *Almanac of the Dead*, which was not available for analysis.

Indian themes are also the focus of Silko's short stories, collected with her poetry and autobiographical commentary in *Storyteller* (1981). Most of these finely crafted stories were published before *Ceremony*. One of the most powerful is "Tony's Story," which, like *Ceremony*, contains the war twins, or hero twins, motif. The story describes how Leon kills a sadistic Chicano state trooper who harasses him because the young Indian has become convinced the policeman is a witch. Also using a traditional motif is "Yellow Woman," a modern version of the Pueblo myths about women who go down to the river to fill their water jars. Seduced by handsome strangers, the women go off with the men but eventually return home. Especially moving is "Lullaby," in which Silko depicts the heartbreak of a Navajo woman whose children are sent away to school and return as strangers. A companion to her alcoholic husband on his periodic drinking trips, the wife sings her sleeping husband an ancient lullaby as he freezes to death in a storm. Considerable humor is revealed in "The Man to Send Rain-clouds," which describes the successful efforts of traditionalists to get a naive local priest to sprinkle plenty of holy water on a dead relative. The priest does not realize they are actually carrying out the ancient ritual of watering a corpse liberally to ensure that it will become a raincloud. Also very funny is "Coyote Holds a Full House in His Hand," which recounts how a Laguna trickster persuades Hopi women that he must feel their thighs as part of a ritual to heal one of their women friends.

Silko includes coyote stories as well in her poetry, much of which was originally published in *Laguna Woman* (1974). "Toe'Osh" combines ancient and modern coyote stories, and "Coyotes and the Stro'ro'ka Dancers" describes the ever-hungry coyotes' unsuccessful attempts to steal food. Many of her poems echo themes in her fiction. For example, the yellow-woman myths are retold in "Cottonwood" and given a modern twist in "Storyteller." "Skeleton Fixer" is a re-creation of a Laguna and Acoma story that emphasizes renewal. Here Silko suggests that Indians, like the Old Badger Man, the skeleton fixer and an animal associated with healing among the Pueblos, can restore the many scattered pieces of Indian culture:

> "Oh poor dear one who left your bones here
> I wonder who you are?"
> Old Skeleton Fixer spoke to the bones
> Because things don't die
> they fall to pieces maybe,
> get scattered or separate,
> but Old Badger Man can tell
> how they once fit together.   (*Storyteller* 243)

Other poems incorporate Silko's sense of place and tribal ancestry, which she combines with contemporary experience, as these lines from "Deer Dance / For Your Return" demonstrate:

> If this
> will hasten your return
> then I will hold myself above you all night
> blowing softly

down-feathered clouds
that drift above the spruce
and hide your eyes
as you are born back
to the mountain.

Years ago
through the yellow oak leaves
antlers polished like stones
in the canyon stream-crossing
     Morning turned in the sky
     when I saw you
     and I wanted the gift
     you carry on moon-color shoulders
     so big
     the size of you
     holds the long winter

You have come home with me before
a long way down the mountain.
The people welcome you. (188)

The eternal interrelationship between animals and humans is the theme of "Deer Song." In the following lines, Silko creates a memorable picture of the ritual death of the deer, which it foresees and is willing to endure in order that its Indian brothers and sisters may survive:

Do not think that I do not love you
if I scream
    while I die.
Antler and thin black hoof
smashed against dark rock—
      the struggle is the ritual
shining teeth tangled in
    sinew and flesh. (201)

Another American Indian writer to gain national recognition in the 1970s is James Welch (Blackfeet/Gros Ventre, b. 1940). After receiving his BA from the University of Montana, Welch began work on an MFA. He has taught at the University of Washington and Cornell University. Like Momaday and Silko, Welch uses the quest motif in his powerful *Winter in the Blood* (1974), which focuses on the search by a nameless hero in his early thirties to learn or remember the truth about his fierce Blackfeet grand-mother's early life, the identity of his grandfather, his parents' relationship, and the deaths of his brother and father. Also like both Momaday and Silko, Welch employs the twin motif: one of the issues the protagonist must resolve is his guilt over being unable to prevent the accidental death of an older brother. At the beginning of the novel, the hero, caught in a cycle of alcoholic violence, feels distant from himself, his family, and nature. Through memory and through insights provided by his mother and Old Yellow Calf, an intermediator, the narrator accepts the truth about his family. These insights enable him to close the distance he feels at the beginning of the novel and offer the possibility that he may stop the cycle of self-destruction engulfing him. In *Winter in the Blood*, Welch realistically depicts reservation life and creates vivid characterizations, especially of women. Using a spare style, he combines tragedy with scenes of Faulknerian humor. The novel also reflects the influence of Emilio Vittorini's *In Sicily* in its use of a nameless hero who returns home to learn about his family and its characterization of a strong mother who has little patience with her husband, whom she considers irresponsible.

Some aspects of the plot of Welch's second novel, *The Death of Jim Loney* (1979), parallel those of *Winter in the Blood*: A protagonist in his thirties cannot integrate the different aspects of his life or the people who enter and leave it. In *Jim Loney*, the protagonist, unable to organize his life because he cannot forget the past, seeks knowledge about his Indian mother and white father, who abandoned their children. The answers are provided by his sister, Kate, who, with her tough-love approach to her brother and ability to cast off the past, bears a strong resemblance to the mother in *Winter in the Blood*. While the nameless narrator of that novel feels separated from his Blackfeet grandmother's tribal heritage, Jim Loney, an urban half-blood, is unable to experience a sense of his Indianness. For him Indians are full-bloods or those who live traditionally. By the end of the novel, Loney, who kills a boyhood friend in a hunting accident, finds release from his psychic dilemma in an act that brings about his own death. Though less sophisticated in structure than *Winter in the Blood*, *The Death of Jim Loney* is a compelling narrative that demonstrates Welch's continuing ability to combine tragedy and humor and create strong characters, particularly Loney's sister, Kate; his father, Ike; and his lover, Rhea. In both novels, Welch captures the dialogue of the people who frequent small-town bars.

Far different is Welch's *Fools Crow* (1986), a historical novel. Here Welch vividly describes the impact of white settlement on a Montana band of Blackfeet in 1870 and gives a colorful and moving account of tribal life of that period. The reactions of two Blackfeet warriors, friends since childhood, to this encroachment is contrasted—Fast Horse, who joins Owl Child's band of renegades in their attacks on whites, and Fools Crow, who lives the life of a traditional Blackfeet and avoids whites as much as possible. Through the portrayal of the maturation of White Man's Dog, later renamed Fools Crow, Welch depicts the life of a warrior who becomes a shaman. Into his detailed account of traditional Blackfeet life, Welch weaves oral narratives, such as the Scarface myth, and ceremonies. Especially delightful are the sections pertaining to the raven, who serves as a messenger from the spirit world and as a liaison between the protagonist and his totem, the wolverine. Welch creates carefully delineated portraits of the individual Blackfeet and the whites they encounter, both real and imaginary. By individualizing the members of the Lone Eaters band and by incorporating Blackfeet ethnohistory, Welch creates a memorable picture of their lives during a crucial period of history.

Before the appearance of his first novel, Welch published his collected poems in *Riding the Earthboy 40* (1971), which contains some powerful protest poetry and reflects the author's reading of Latin American and surrealist poets. His protest poems, such as "Christmas Comes to Moccasin Flat," "Plea to Those Who Matter," and "Blackfeet, Blood and Piegan Hunters," describe the price Indians have paid for white encroachment on their land and culture. Welch summarizes their plight in these lines from "Blackfeet, Blood and Piegan Hunters":

> Comfortable we drink and string together stories
> of white buffalo, medicine men who promised
> and delivered horrible cures for hunger,
> lovely tales of war and white men massacres.
> Meaning gone, we dance for pennies now,
> our feet jangling dust that hides the bones
> of sainted Indians. Look away and we are gone.
> Look back, Tracks are there, a little faint,
> Our song strong enough for headstrong hunters
> Who look ahead to one more kill. (36)

Other poems, such as "Riding the Earthboy 40," pay tribute to the power of the Blackfeet to endure on their land.

Gerald Vizenor (Ojibwa, b. 1934) is one of the most widely published and versatile of the contemporary American Indian authors. Vizenor received his BA from the University of Minnesota, where he also did postgraduate work in Asian studies. From 1953 to 1956, he served in the army in Japan. After holding several positions in social service and employment programs, Vizenor became a journalist for the *Minneapolis Tribune* and contributing editor to the *Twin Citian*. Currently, Vizenor is professor of English and ethnic studies, at the University of California, Santa Cruz.

Vizenor is a masterful writer of nonfiction prose. Many of his articles on his people and on Indian issues in general are collected in *The Everlasting Sky* (1972) and in *The People Named the Chippewa* (1984), which incorporates several pieces from the earlier volume. Particularly impressive are his portraits of actual Indians overcome by the dominant society, such as those of John Ka Ka Geesick, a traditional Ojibwa trapper turned into a turkey-feathered chief by white society (*The People Named the Chippewa*); Dane Michael White, a thirteen-year-old Sioux runaway who hanged himself in a Minnesota jail (*Earthdivers*); and Thomas White Hawk, a young Sioux premedical student convicted of murder and rape (*Wordarrows*).

Wordarrows (1978), *Earthdivers* (1981), and *The People Named the Chip-*

pewa demonstrate Vizenor's skill in combining nonfiction and short fiction. In these works, Vizenor's incisively portrays the wounds suffered by Indians as a result of the cultural conflicts between the white and tribal worlds. In "Laurel Hole in the Day," (*Wordarrows*), Vizenor depicts the destructive efforts of a well-meaning tribal advocate to help an Indian family who had moved to Minneapolis. Many of the wounds Indians suffer are self-inflicted. In "The Sociodowser" (*Earthdivers*), an Indian center board, rallying to the cry "Give us back our land and our vans," hires a shaman to locate its missing vans. Purchased with federal funds to transport Indians to industrial education classes, the vans are used by the center staff for traveling bingo games and other businesses. Such self-destructiveness also affects tribal studies programs. One of Vizenor's best stories in *Earthdivers* is "The Chair of Tears," in which Captain Shammer auctions the Department of Tribal Studies to the highest bidder.

In his fiction, as well as in his mixed-genre works, Vizenor uses many aspects of American Indian oral tradition. *Darkness in Saint Louis Bearheart* (1978), which deals with the quest for ritual knowledge by the culture hero–shaman, Proude Cedarfair. The author's descriptions of the four worlds of Indian people combine the emergence and migration myths of Southwestern tribes with the flood myths of the Algonkian-speaking peoples.

Griever: An American Monkey King in China (1987) won the 1986 Fiction Collective–Illinois State University Award and the 1987 American Book Award for fiction. The novel deals with a mixed-blood Indian who goes to China to teach English, where he transforms himself into a Monkey King, the Chinese trickster, and triumphs over Chinese bureaucracy. Griever gains knowledge of and identifies with the Monkey King through dreams, which free him, like the Monkey King, from time and space. He then becomes a liberator in China, as did the Monkey King. In characterizing Griever as a compassionate trickster and acute observer of society, Vizenor satirizes Chinese as well as white society.

The mixed-blood trickster as liberator, observer, or entrepreneur is a dominant theme in Vizenor's work. *The Trickster of Liberty: Tribal Heirs to a Wild Baronage at Petronia* (1988) contains a whole family of such tricksters, who rebel against conventional systems, establish their ingenious enterprises, and tell trickster stories at such places as White Earth, Berkeley, and China. Vizenor's unpublished screenplay, *Harold of Orange*, completed in 1983, focuses on the trickster as entrepreneur. Harold Sinseer, an eloquent con artist, persuades a gullible foundation board to finance miniature coffee and orange groves (a potted coffee tree and an orange tree) in northern Minnesota. The screenplay won the Minnesota Film-in-the-Cities award and has been made into a thirty-minute film starring the Oneida comedian Charlie Hill.

In addition to being a prolific prose writer, Vizenor is a poet; his haiku is especially imaginative. Early volumes of poetry include *Raising the Moon*

Vines (1964), *Seventeen Chirps* (1965), *Slight Abrasions* (1966; with Jerome Downes), and *Empty Swings* (1967). *Matsushima* (1984) is divided into poems on the four seasons. These lines from the summer section of *Matsushima* exemplify Vizenor's haiku: "bold nasturtiums / dress the barbed wire fences / down to the wild sea" (unpaged). Several of his poems portray the victims of modern society. In "Unhappy Diary Days" he captures the despair and loneliness of a woman preparing to commit suicide:

> Unhooking the hooks
> untying the ties
> she undressed for the garden
> in the moist September light
> she lifted her breasts
> hand over hand in flight
> with young birds
> turning on the wrong trees at dusk
> she crashed through the glass.   (Rosen, *Voices* 33)

Other poems depict the cultural suicide of contemporary urban Indians like his father, Clement, who was murdered when Vizenor was a small child. In "Family Photograph" the poet describes his father as "a spruce / corded for tribal pulp" who left White Earth for Minneapolis, where he shared stories and dreams from a mason jar (Rosen, *Voices* 37). The tragedy of Clement Vizenor's life contrasts with his image in the photograph, in which he smiles as he holds his young son. In "Tribal Stumps" the poet links his father's life in Minneapolis to that of other mixed-bloods: "tribal stumps / from the blood-soaked beams of the city" (32). More optimistic is "Anishinable Grandmothers," which celebrates the importance of forebears as transmitters of Indian culture. They sing "tribal dream songs" and touch the earth with gnarled fingers. Their grandchildren follow, "clumsy and clover stained / tasting the rain / singing / the world will change" (44–45).

Vizenor's commitment to his Ojibwa heritage is reflected not only in such works as *The People Named the Chippewa* and *The Everlasting Sky* but also in *Summer in the Spring: Ojibwa Lyric Poems and Tribal Stories* (1981). This is a reprint of the book with the same title, originally published in 1965 and republished under the title *Anishinabe Adisokan* (1970) and *Anishinabe Nagamon* (1965; rev. 1970). *Summer in the Spring* or *Anishinabe Nagamon* is a collection of traditional Ojibwa songs that Vizenor has reinterpreted, using Frances Densmore's literal translations from her *Chippewa Music* (1910, 1913). *Anishinabe Adisokan* consists of commentary and stories of Ojibwa life, customs, religion, and myths about the culture hero–trickster Naanabozho (also known as Manabozho and Wenebojo). This material was originally published in the White Earth Reservation newspaper *The Progress* (1886–88), edited by Vizenor's mixed-blood ancestor Theodore H. Beaulieu.

Another prolific Ojibwa writer is Louise Erdrich (b. 1954), the author of three acclaimed novels: *Love Medicine* (1984), which won the Critics Circle Award; *Beet Queen* (1986); and *Tracks* (1988). Erdrich and her husband, Michael A. Dorris, collaborate in their fiction, a process she described in an interview:

> We're collaborators, but we're also individual writers. One person sits down and writes the drafts. I sit down and write it by myself or he does, but there's so much more that bears on the crucial moment of writing. You know it, you've talked the plot over, you've discussed the characters. You've really come to some kind of an understanding that you wouldn't have done alone. I really think neither of us would write what we do unless we were together. (Bruchac, *Survival This Way* 85)

Born in North Dakota, Erdrich is German on her father's side and Ojibwa on her mother's; both parents worked for a BIA school in Wahpeton. She received a bachelor's degree from Dartmouth College and a master's from Johns Hopkins. Erdrich's maternal grandfather, Pat Gourneau, was for many years tribal chairman of the Turtle Mountain Chippewa Reservation, located near Belcourt, North Dakota. Formerly editor of the the *Circle*, Boston Indian Council, Erdrich is now a full-time writer.

Erdrich's three published novels, of a planned series of four set in North Dakota, weave an intricate web of relationships among members of individual families and family groups of Indians, mixed-bloods, and whites. Each novel incorporates an image: water in *Love Medicine*, air in *Beet Queen*, earth in *Tracks*. The novels, published in reverse order of their internal chronology, all use multiple narrators who tell parts of the story, which is structured in episodes set in particular years or months.

Tracks, the earliest in terms of plot and the last published, deals with the years between 1912 and 1919, when the North Dakota Chippewas were coping with the effects of allotment. There are three central characters: Nanapush, Pauline Puyat, and Fleur Pillager. Nanapush, named after the Chippewa culture hero, is a witty storyteller and keen observer. Filled with a zest for life, Nanapush is last of his family alive and the last of his tribe to participate in buffalo and bear hunts. Pauline is a jealous, venal mixed-blood who denies her Indian heritage and, after bearing a child, becomes a fanatic nun devoted to punishing her body. Fleur, like Nanapush, is the last survivor of her family, which died in an epidemic. Rescued by Nanapush, Fleur later endures two near-drownings and a gang rape. She retreats to the bush, where she takes Eli Kashpaw as her lover and bears a child of unknown paternity. Fleur's hold over Eli is opposed by his conniving mother, Margaret Kashpaw. Because Fleur miraculously survived near-drowning and seems to possess shamanistic powers, the Chippewa believe that Misshephesu, the mythic horned serpent who dwells in lakes, wants her for his bride and has given her his power.

Beet Queen, set in the off-reservation town of Argus, covers the years from 1932 to 1972, when the area around Argus changed from wheat to sugar-beet farming. In this novel, whose major theme is abandonment and obsessive love, most of the major figures are non-Indian. Abandoned by their mother, Mary and Karl Adare hitch a train to Argus to live with their aunt. There they are separated physically and never reunite emotionally. Stolid, domineering, and hard-working, Mary is loathed by her delicate and pretentious cousin, Sita Kozka. The cousins' relationship deteriorates after Mary wins away Sita's best friend, a mixed-blood named Celestine James. Karl's brief sexual encounter with Wally Pfef, president of the Argus Chamber of Commerce, and his later marriage to Celestine bind together his lovers and Mary through their mutual and obsessive love for Dot, Karl and Celestine's daughter. Unfortunately, this love turns Dot, the Argus Beet Queen, into a selfish, violent brat who denies them affection.

Love Medicine, the first in the series to be published, is a collection of interconnected stories that humorously portrays through several generations the families of the hapless Nector Kashpaw and the two women he loves: his wife, Marie Lazarre Kashpaw, and his mistress, Lulu Nanapush Lamartine. In memory and action, the novel covers the period 1934 to 1983. Nector, son of Margaret Kashpaw, is the center of a love triangle. Despite his physical desire for Lulu, Nector allows himself to be trapped into marriage by Marie Lazarre, to whom he is also attracted. The strong-willed Marie is the illegitimate child of Pauline, who took the name Sister Leopolda after becoming a nun. When Marie goes to the convent school as a young girl, she and Sister Leopolda, whom she does not realize is her mother, are locked in intense physical and psychological battles, as the nun abuses Marie to drive out the devil. Although the ambitious Marie helps Nector to rise to the position of tribal chairman, he lusts after Lulu. Fecund and passionate, Lulu revitalizes the reservation population by bearing numerous children by her husband, his brother, and a variety of lovers. At the end of the novel, when the trio are in an old people's home, the jealous Marie inadvertently is responsible for her husband's death when he chokes on a turkey heart she encouraged him to eat because she thinks it is love medicine. The mutual grief that Marie and Lulu share brings them together.

In addition to being an imaginative novelist, Erdrich is a fine poet whose *Jacklight* (1984) has been highly acclaimed. In the section devoted to narrative poems on Chippewa myths, Erdrich's storytelling powers are particularly evident in the series called "Old Man Potchiko," another name for the Chippewa trickster and culture hero, and "Windigo," the cannibalistic winter demon. Several other poems in the section called "Runaways" deal with growing up Indian or mixed-blood. Among the most powerful of these are "Family Reunion" and "Indian Boarding School: The Runaways." In the latter, Erdrich poignantly portrays the desperate homesickness of these children: "Home's the place we head for in our sleep. / Boxcars stumbling north in dreams / don't wait for us. We catch them on the run" (11).

The volume also contains a moving series of dramatic monologues called "The Butcher's Wife." In one of these, "I Was Sleeping Where the Black Oaks Move," Erdrich's delicate lyricism evokes a sense of longing for a lost past:

> Sometimes now, we dream our way back to the heron dance.
> Their long wings are bending the air
> into circles through which they fall.
> They rise again in shifting wheels.
> How long must we live in the broken figures
> their necks make, narrowing the sky. (67)

Baptism of Desire (1989) focuses on the many forms of that emotion. One group of poems deals with visionary and religious ecstasy and humankind's relations with the divine. The surreal "Hydra," whose fragmented and haunting images recall the Book of Revelation and Blake's prophetic poetry, explores the impact of the snake on the imagination of the speaker: "Blessed one, beating your tail across heaven, / uncoiling through the length of my life, / each bone of the spine a measure, a day, each diamond, each trillum star" (41). Equally powerful is "The Sacraments," which depicts the stages of initiation into religious and visionary life, marked by forms of baptism, communion, confirmation, matrimony, holy orders, and extreme unction. In the segment on communion, the speaker observes the tiny frogs pulling their strange new bodies out of the suckholes and floating upward to break the water's surface, "to one clear unceasing note of need":

> Sometimes, when I hear them,
> I leave our bed and stumble
> among the white shafts of weeds
> to the edge of the pond.
> I sink to the throat,
> and witness the ravenous trilling,
> the low whimper, the acetylene whine
> of the body transformed at last and then consumed
> in a rush of music. (19)

The sensuous imagery of the opening lines of the section on extreme unction evokes Keats's "Ode to Autumn": "the blue steam stalls over the land / and the resinous apples / turn to mash, then to a cider whose thin / twang shrivels the tongue" (23).

Poems in another section, such as "Mary Kroger," "Poor Clare," and "Owls," dramatically portray lust, disillusionment, and longing. Another series of poems examines Erdrich's reactions to pregnancy, childbirth, motherhood, and relations between family members. In "The Fence," the narrator tends a bed of asparagus, whose growth she uses as a metaphor for the development of the baby within her:

> Now it will continue to climb, dragging rude blossoms
> to the other side
> until in summer fruit like green scimitars,
> the frieze of vines, the small body
> spread before me in need
> drinking light from the shifting wall of my body
> and the fingers, tiny stems wavering to mine,
> flex for the ascent. (61)

Michael A. Dorris (b. 1945) is the author of *A Yellow Raft on Blue Water* (1987). Dorris, who is Modoc on his father's side, was reared in Louisville, Kentucky, and in Washington State, Idaho, and Montana. He received a BA from Georgetown University and an MPhil from Yale. From 1972 to 1988, he taught Native American studies and anthropology at Dartmouth College, where he was a full professor. Now an adjunct professor there, he has become a full-time writer.

A Yellow Raft on Blue Water takes the family as its theme. The novel is the first by an Indian author to deal with a mixed-blood character who is part Indian and part African American. In this poignant novel set on a Montana Indian reservation, Dorris tells the stories of three generations of women torn apart by secrets but bound by kinship. Each of the three parts is narrated by one of the protagonists. The first narrator is fifteen-year-old Rayona, whose mother is Indian and whose absent father is African American. Rayona deeply resents her mother Christine, who drags her back to the reservation only to leave her by the side of the road to go off in a friend's pickup. The second is Christine, a devout Catholic who lost her faith when the end of the world she expected failed to occur. Christine no longer has the ability to love since her brother Lee, whom she urged to enlist, was killed in the Vietnam war. Feeling unloved by Ida, her mother, Christine is unable to give Rayona the affection her daughter craves. The third is Ida, a stern, sarcastic woman who asks for three reasons why she should be glad to see her daughter, when Christine announces she has come back home to live. In the course of her story, Ida reveals that she agreed to rear and acknowledge Christine as her own daughter despite the fact that the baby is her half sister—the illegitimate child born of the union between her father and her maternal aunt. Particularly memorable are Dorris's moving characterizations of these women and his skill in creating twists of plot that explain the negative aspects of Christine's and Ida's characters. The novel also contains some wonderfully farcical scenes.

Dorris has also written *The Broken Cord: A Family's On-Going Struggle with Fetal Alcohol Syndrome* (1989). This work of nonfiction portrays Dorris's life with Adam, whom he adopted at age three and whose irreversible mental retardation and physical disabilities are the effects of the syndrome. Dorris combines dramatic personal narrative with information on FAS among American Indians and other populations. The book also contains a moving foreword by Erdrich, describing her experiences with Adam, whom she adopted after she married Dorris. Adam's short autobiography, which concludes the book, illustrates the effects of FAS on intellectual development.

Martin Cruz Smith (Senecu del Sur/Yaqui, b. 1942) has achieved national acclaim for several mystery novels: *Nightwing* (1977), *Gorky Park* (1981), *Stallion Gate* (1986), and *Polar Star* (1989). Born in Reading, Pennsylvania, Smith—whose mother, Louise, was an Indian-rights leader—received his BA from the University of Pennsylvania. He subsequently worked for the *Philadelphia Daily News* before becoming a full-time writer. In 1977 Smith changed his middle name from William to Cruz, the first name of his maternal grandmother. Other novels were written under the name Martin William Smith and under the pseudonyms Nick Carter, Jake Logan, Martin Quinn, and Simon Quinn.

Both the successful *Nightwing* and the highly praised *Stallion Gate* have Indian protagonists who leave their pueblos, serve in the armed forces overseas during wartime, and return to their homelands, where they feel separated from their people and their traditions. The heroes confront forces capable of destroying the human species. In *Nightwing*, the force is an invasion of Mexican bats; in *Stallion Gate*, it is the atomic bomb, created and tested in New Mexico during World War II. The two novels also contrast modern science with ancient Pueblo religion; *Nightwing* in particular uses Hopi mythology, while elements of the trickster are incorporated into the protagonist of *Stallion Gate*.

Gorky Park departs from Indian themes. Set in Moscow, this tightly plotted novel chronicles the efforts of investigator Arkady Renko to find out who was responsible for the bizarre murders of three victims in Gorky Park, whose faces were mutilated to prevent identification; the attempts of an American businessman, John Osborne, to spirit minks out of the country to undercut the Soviet monopoly; and Renko's love for Irina Asanova, Osborne's mistress, whom the detective helps to escape from the Soviet Union. Assisting Renko in solving the mystery is William Kirwill, a tough New York detective who came to Moscow to locate his brother, one of the victims. Smith's sharply focused characterizations, authoritative accounts of Renko's painstaking detective work, and vivid descriptions of Moscow make *Gorky Park* a superb suspense novel. The book was made into a major film.

The sequel, *Polar Star*, is an equally absorbing novel that contains echoes of E. E. Hale's "Man without a Country," Mary Shelley's *Frankenstein*, and Conrad's "Secret Sharer." Renko, who has been thrown out of the Communist Party, interrogated in a psychiatric hospital, and banished to Siberia for helping Irina escape, becomes a worker in the lower depths of the *Polar Star*, a fish-factory ship in the Bering Sea. Considered politically unreliable, Renko has been restricted to the ship for over a year. When the body of one of the women working on the ship surfaces in a fishnet hauled out of the ocean, Renko is assigned to solve the mystery of her death. His assistant is Natasha Chaikovskaya, a former hydroelectric worker who joined the ship's crew to find a husband. Renko is stalked by the grotesquely tatooed Karp Korobetz, whom the former investigator had earlier sent to prison. Still mourning the loss of Irina, Renko finds a respite from his grim life in an affair with Susan Hightower, an American crew member. In his characterizations of the crew of *Polar Star*, Smith creates a microcosm of the social and ethnic diversity of the Soviet Union, a mixture he enriches with the addition of Americans and an Aleut.

Janet Campbell Hale (Coeur d'Alene/Kootenai, b. 1947) is the author of two novels: *The Jailing of Cecelia Capture* (1985) and and *Owl's Song* (1974). Raised on the Coeur d'Alene Reservation in northern Idaho, Hale received her BA from the University of California, where she also began the study of law, and her MA in English from the University of California, Davis. Hale has taught at the University of Washington and Washington State University, Bellingham.

The Jailing of Cecelia Capture portrays an alcoholic urban Indian woman who is separated from her husband and children and is trying to rebuild her life. Hale accurately describes the dilemmas faced by a twentieth-century mixed-blood and by a woman attempting to find her place in the world. As a child, Cecelia was torn between her mother, a mixed-blood who regretted marrying an Indian, and her father, who taught her traditional values but insisted she attend white schools. After the death of her lover and a series of affairs, Cecelia marries a doctoral candidate in literature, hoping to experience his upper-middle class WASP culture and share his memories of a peaceful childhood. Unhappy in her marriage, Cecelia begins drinking; her growing sense of independence and returning sense of Indian identity cause her to leave her family in search of self-awareness. By the end of the novel, she renounces her planned suicide and vows to finish law school and to get enough money to keep her children with her.

Owl's Song, Hale's first novel, focuses on the experiences of Billy, an adolescent who tries to cope with reservation alcoholism and teenage suicide. Sent to live in the city, Billy attempts unsuccessfully to adjust to an urban school unprepared to deal with Indians. The novel is one of the few works about an adolescent urban Indian. Hale has also written a chapbook of poetry, *Custer Lives in Humboldt County* (1978).

Two other important novelists are Anna Walters (Otoe/Pawnee, b. 1946) and Thomas King (Cherokee, b. 1943). Born in Oklahoma and educated at the Institute of American Indian Arts, Santa Fe, New Mexico, Walters has worked for the Navajo Community College Press in Tsaile, Arizona. Her first novel, *Ghost Singer* (1988), is an intriguing blend of mystery and history, which focuses on the history of Navajo-white relations and on whites' inhumane practice of storing Indian skeletons, body parts, and sacred possessions in museums. Walters shows the long-term impact on one Navajo family of the kidnapping and enslavement of tribal members in the nineteenth century. A common practice in the Southwest, the kidnapping of Navajos has been little known outside that area and continued for some time after the abolition of slavery elsewhere in the United States. Willie Begay, a member of this family, becomes a focal point for Walters's treatment of the second theme. While studying his people's history in a Washington, D.C., museum, Begay is stricken by an illness that white doctors seem unable to cure. Like the numerous white employees of the museum who subsequently commit suicide, Willie has seen Indian ghosts, who emerge in the museum to rage against the storage and display of artifacts that prevent their souls from resting. Two medicine men, Wilbur Snake from Oklahoma and Jonnie Navajo, who tries to learn the history of his family members stolen by slave traders, come to Washington to determine what is wrong. Wilbur Snake forcefully states why the ghosts are so angry about the storage of skeletons:

> "A man's body is wondrous too. Old peoples like to think that it's holy too. Any part stands for the whole . . . , a hand, fingers, a breast, the hair. And the body itself—the blood, flesh, and bones—stands for the unseen part of the man . . . , his memory, his mind, and his spirit. A man ain't fully a man without them." (176)

Thomas King's *Medicine River* (1990) is also a first novel. King received degrees from California State University, Chico, and the University of Utah. *Medicine River* is set in the fictional town from which it takes its title, located near the Blood Reserve in Alberta. Like the protagonists of many twentieth-century American Indian novels, King's hero, Will, is a passive mixed-blood who tries to learn more about himself, his family, and the Indians and mixed-bloods of his hometown. A classic distancer at the beginning of the novel, Will, the son of an Indian mother, becomes increasingly involved with the people of Medicine River. The catalyst in his decision to return home and for most of the novel's action is Will's friend Harlen Bigbear. As eager, energetic, and witless as a young Labrador, Harlen is full of enterprises that never quite come off, misguided advice for Will, and rambling stories. King creates accurate portraits of life in an off-reservation town and on the reserve, as well as a memorable character in the farcical but lovable Harlen. King has edited *An Anthology of Canadian Native Fiction*, a special issue of *Canadian Fiction Magazine* (1987), and *The Native in Literature: Canadian and Comparative Perspectives*, papers from the 1984 conference at the University of Lethbridge.

The most controversial contemporary Indian novel is *Seven Arrows* (1972), by Hyemeyohsts Storm (Cheyenne, b. 1935), who was born in Montana and educated at Eastern Montana College. The publication of this novel aroused considerable protest among traditional Cheyenne. It re-counts the decline in the nineteenth century of the Sun Dance ceremony and the Brotherhood of the Shields, a society of healers and diviners who kept the sacred shields that were part of the annual Sun Dance. It consists of stories that cover the period from the Sand Creek Massacre in 1864 to the Custer Battle in 1876. Native religion is also the theme of Storm's *Song of the Heyoehkah* (1981), which deals with the heroine's quest for the ritual knowledge to become a shaman. Other Indian novelists include Dallas Chief Eagle (Sioux), Denton R. Bedford (Munsee), Joseph Bruchac (Abenaki). The only novel by an Eskimo writer is Markoosie's *Harpoon of the Hunter*, the story of Kamik, who survives extreme hardships while on a hunt.

Increasing numbers of Indian authors have written poetry since the 1960s; much of their work has been published by such small firms as Strawberry Press and Contact II Press, both directed by Maurice Kenny (Mohawk poet); Greenfield Review Press, directed by Bruchac; and *Blue Cloud Quarterly*. The American Indian Studies Center of the University of California, Los Angeles, has also published several volumes. The poetry of contemporary Indian authors evidences considerable variety in form and theme: the use of traditional chants; re-creations of myths, especially coyote or trickster stories; nostalgia for a lost past and closeness to nature; at-tachment to place; autobiographical accounts of experience; realistic por-trayals of contemporary Indian life and problems; and feminist approaches to these themes.

Two Southwestern authors who have written fiction but are primarily poets are Paula Gunn Allen and Simon Ortiz. Raised in Cubero, New Mexico, Allen (b. 1939) is Laguna/Sioux on her mother's side and Lebanese on her father's. She received her BA and MFA from the University of Oregon and PhD in American Studies at the University of New Mexico. She has been a professor of Native American studies at the University of California, Berkeley.

In *The Woman Who Owned the Shadows* (1983) Allen brings a feminist perspective to her treatment of the ritual quest present in the works of Momaday, Silko, Vizenor, and Welch. Like all these authors except Welch, she uses a southwestern setting. *The Woman Who Owned the Shadows* focuses on the journey toward spiritual rebirth of the central character, Epiphanie Atencio, a half-blood who feels at home neither in the Southwest nor in San Francisco. In the course of her psychological and spiritual journey toward emergence as a shaman, Epiphanie searches her memory to recall both childhood experiences that reveal the sources of her adult fears and the Keres myths that are the base of her Indian heritage. Her journey is symbolized by her circular migrations between Albuquerque and San Fran-cisco. In her progress toward a visionary state, she is aided by her brother Stephen and the psychic Teresa, who serve as shamans, and by a shamanlike therapist. The novel contains skillful portraits of feminine relationships.

Until the publication of her novel, Allen was best known as a perceptive critic and fine poet. The editor of *Studies in American Indian Literature* (1983) and *Spider Woman's Granddaughters* (1989), she is also the author of *The Sacred Hoop* (1986), a study of the feminine in American Indian culture and literature.

One of the most sophisticated contemporary American Indian poets, Allen writes about traditional and modern Indian culture, personal experience, and feminist issues in language of translucent power. Most of her poetry has been collected in *Shadow Country* (1982). She has published two subsequent volumes: *Wyrds* (1987), a collection of metaphysical poems dedicated to society's outsiders, and *Skins and Bones* (1988), which is divided into "C'Koy'u, Old Woman: Songs of Tradition," "Heyoka, Trickster: Songs of Colonization," and "Naku, Woman: Songs of Generation." Both volumes demonstrate Allen's continuing mastery of simple language and emotional intensity.

Allen's treatment of Indian themes is exemplified in such poems from *Shadow Country* as "Creation," which deals with the Keres creation myth, and "Sandia Crest," which expresses a sense of tribal place. Several poems convey a recognition of Indianness through portrayals of family members. In *Wyrds*, the most moving poem on an Indian theme is "Never Cry Uncle," a tribute to her Uncle Ook. Especially touching in *Skins and Bones* is "Grandma's Dying Poem," in which Allen reflects on her relationship to her dead grandmother:

> She's somehow what your life has been
> all along,
> you realize—your life has been
> a mirror of her ways, the reflection
> slightly different by small changes
> time and fashion make. (62)

Allen concludes the poem with a tribute to the grandmother's care of her as a child and to her fierce defiance of death. "Dear World," in the same volume, portrays her mother's suffering from lupus and the complexities of being both Indian and white: "I know you can't make peace / being Indian and white. / They cancel each other out. / Leaving no one in the place" (56).

Several of Allen's poems express her reactions to personal experience or her sense of the fragility of life. "On the Street: Monument" from *Shadow Country* describes Allen's anguish over the death of a twin son and illustrates the delicate purity of her language:

> I remember wondering how I could
> not break; whether the butterfly in the shade
> of the carefully concealed grave hole was a sign—and if
> anything was ever sacralized. No matter what
> ideologies occurred before that time, my

son was dead.
The good do not deserve anything more
than their virtue. The evil
inherit the earth, regardless of what Marx
has said. (69)

She uses, in *Skins and Bones*, the metaphor of the fallen sparrow in "Something Fragile, Broken" to suggest the frailty of life: "and i am not stone but shell, / blue and fragile. dropped / i splatter" (54).

In "Off Reservation Blues" Allen characterizes the difficulties of self-definition:

If my language is oblique
misunderstandable—
if I confine myself
within demands of imaged time—
I saw true one night:
the keeper and the kept,
saw myself,
how I must
be—not in the forest of *should*—
but actually.   (*Shadow Country* 26)

In other poems, such as "This Is the Watchbird Watching You," Allen depicts how she copes with the anxieties and shadows that haunt her days:

My hands do all the crying. In the dying afternoon
my eyes shun vision. Memories of other times,
of singular uncertainties arise, like clouds
upon the sky, obscure the sinking light.   (*Wyrds* 21)

Many of Allen's poems, particularly in *Skins and Bones*, pay tribute to Indian women. In the section of that volume entitled "C'koy'u, Old Woman: Songs of Tradition," Allen portrays mythical and real Indian women, such as Malinalli (Cortés's mistress), Pocahontas, and Molly Brant. In "Naku, Woman: Songs of Generation" she celebrates the female principle in life and the endurance of women.

Simon Ortiz (Acoma, b. 1941) was raised and has lived in Acoma. A graduate of the University of New Mexico, he received his MFA from the University of Iowa. Ortiz, who served in the United States Army, has taught creative writing and American Indian literature at such institutions as the University of New Mexico and Sinte Gleska College in South Dakota. He has been employed by his tribe.

The editor of a collection of short fiction entitled *Earth Power Coming* (1983), Ortiz has also published two collections of his own short fiction: *The Howbah Indians* (1978) and *Fightin'* (1983), which includes new and collected stories. One of the best of these is "Kaiser and the War," which describes the escalating tragedy of a traditional Indian who is hunted down by the local sheriff and Indian villagers for avoiding the draft. Eventually captured, he kills a man in prison. After his release, Kaiser continually wears a suit given to him by the prison, which grows very shabby and which he wants sent back to the government after his death. (The story is contained in both books.)

Ortiz has published three major volumes of poetry: *Going for the Rain* (1976), *A Good Journey* (1977), and *From Sand Creek* (1981). *Going for the Rain* chronicles Ortiz's circular spiritual and physical journey from Acoma through the United States; the work is grounded in a sense of place and heritage derived from Acoma, memories of which restore Ortiz when he is separated from it. He includes a wry version of the Acoma creation story in "Creation: According to Coyote." The section entitled "Preparation" evokes the memories of the sensory experiences he had as a child in the land around Acoma. "Forming Child" describes the sights and sounds he would show his unborn child, and "My Father's Song" recalls how, when Ortiz and his own father planted corn, the plow unearthed a nest of mice: "I remember the very softness / of cool and warm sand and tiny alive mice / and my father saying things" (20). Subsequent sections focus on the experiences and sensations of his journey, during which he learns that, however alien the land, Indians are everywhere. His disorientation is sharply expressed in "Relocation," in which he describes how the lights, cars, and "deadened glares" of the city "tear his heart" and close his mind (37). In "Hunger in New York," the poet says he feeds himself with song and with the soul of mother earth, whose blessing he asks. The volume contains some incisive portraits of those Ortiz meets. *A Good Journey* continues the motif of travel to and from home and narrates Ortiz's experiences on the road. It also contains a number of poems about his children, as he observes their movements and reactions. In "Canyon de Chelly" he contrasts his own philosophical reflections on the eternal beauty of the canyon with his son's absorption in climbing and putting rocks in his mouth. Ortiz captures the beauty of both the scene and the moment:

> We find gray root, old wood,
> so old, with curious twists
> in it, curving back into curves,
> juniper, pinon, or something
> with hard, red berries in spring.
> You taste them, and they are sweet
> and bitter, the berries a delicacy
> for bluejays. The plant rooted
> fragilely into a sandy place
> by a canyon wall, the sun bathing
> shiny, pointed leaves. (67–68)

The importance of the root is made clear in the final stanza, when the poet perceives it as "wood, an old root, / and around it, the earth, ourselves" (68).

From Sand Creek is an affecting collection of poems that commemorates the massacre of the peaceful Cheyenne and Arapaho at Sand Creek, Colorado, in 1864. Balancing brief commentary with examples, Ortiz describes how the land and its native peoples have been destroyed or demoralized by the dominant society. He particularly memorializes the Indian veterans who suffer from physical and psychological wounds inflicted during America's wars: Toby is so afraid of the glass wall of the hospital that he tends his shadow; Billy has a secret plan to "head east for Kansas, make arrows. / Send word to the IRA" (45). Ortiz vividly expresses the power of honest and healthy anger. After portraying the veteran who cried for his mother and whose ferocious anger "cracked / through the hospital / walls," Ortiz is unable to follow the veteran's example:

> I could have flown
> through the wall
> his anger had opened.
> And strangled him
> to soothed finality.
> But my own dread,
> his own mother,
> my own muscles refused
> the wings needed.
> I could only cry,
>   mangled
> like his anger,
> amazed
> and dismayed. (85)

Ortiz has also written *Fight Back* (1980), a tribute to the Pueblo Indian Revolt of 1680 and the subsequent struggles of Indian people and workers. The volume includes poems and personal essays. In some of the poems, Ortiz combines the traditional song techniques of repetition and incremental development with political protest, as in these lines from "It Will Come":

> Where from is it thundering.
> Thundering, the People working.
> Thundering, the People's voices.
> Thundering, the movement of the struggle.
> Thundering, the power of the Land.
> Thundering, the coming Rain.
> It will come, it will come. (45)

Linda Hogan (Chickasaw, b. 1947) is a poet of considerable thematic range who has also written short stories and a novel. The daughter of a Chickasaw father and a mother descended from a white immigrant Nebraska family, Hogan earned her BA and MA from the University of Colorado. Formerly associate professor of Native American and American studies at the University of Minnesota, Hogan now writes full time.

Hogan is an accomplished fiction writer as well as a fine poet. Her first novel, *Mean Spirit* (1990), describes an Oklahoma Indian community during the oil boom of the 1920s. In her summary of the novel, Hogan emphasizes that the work is based on historical events surrounding the murders of Native Americans, especially women, in Osage County, and that it focuses on the devastation of the land and the Indians by greedy non-Indians. As Hogan points out, the thievery continues on Indian reservations currently under siege by oil, gas, and coal interests. Several of her short stories are collected in *That Horse* (1985).

Hogan's books of poetry include *Calling Myself Home* (1978), *Daughters, I Love You* (1981), *Eclipse* (1983), *Seeing through the Sun* (1985), and *Savings* (1988). *Calling Myself Home* focuses on the author's recollections of her family and growing sense of Indian identity, while *Daughters, I Love You*, reprinted in *Eclipse*, is a forceful protest against nuclear war. In *Seeing through the Sun*, Hogan reveals a wry sense of humor. "The Pond" describes how night changes the pond and old creatures are exposed to "hard air": Asking "What kind / of motel is this anyway?" she concludes that it may be Oklahoma, where the frogs, "evicted for weeping," fall out of room 103, "their toes spread like stars" (20). In "Death, Etc." which recalls Dickinson's "Because I Could Not Stop for Death" (no. 712), Hogan rejects her visitor's arguments: " 'I've seen the beds you visited,' I said. / 'You don't make good corners / and you leave them a mess' " (31). Many of Hogan's poems are personal, like "The Truth Is," which describes the difficulty of balancing her white and Chickasaw sides. Others, such as those in the section called "Daughters Sleeping," deal poignantly with the relationship between mothers and daughters. An excerpt from the title poem of this section reveals Hogan's sensitive insights expressed in simple language:

> Beauties, I want to curve into your skin
> while you sleep,
> to suspend myself in you
> and tell you it is a warm world.
> Would I lie?
> I'll say you are strong
> like a people who lived so long
> on fish, the glass scales
> and white lace of bones piled up
> and blew about their home
> a warm snow. (45)

Savings, which is divided into the sections "Savings" and "Truth of Matter," combines the penetrating observation present in her earlier volumes with a maturity of vision. In the volume's title poem, Hogan acknowledges the futility of saving one's good clothes for life in an attempt to avoid the inevitability of change and decay:

>Night unravels
>the calcium from bones.
>Moths in the closet are growing
>into dark holes they've eaten away
>from fine shirts,
>shirts empty of heartbeats,
>all we should have lived for,
>empty of arms that reach back
>like a sleepless night, for what is saved,
>are the way back
>behind plaster
>to the old world in canyons
>with blood women dancing on walls
>to the earth's drum
>and the mother of deer and corn
>so light the insects appear. (4–5)

"Missing" depicts Hogan's realization of the years of her life that she has forgotten, as she has been caught up in day-to-day concerns. In "The Other Voices," the poet contrasts the physical decay of her body with the "beauties" of her "joyous life" that flows through her veins (45). The duality of life reflected in this poem is expressed also in such poems as "Young Boys," which describes young boys riding their bikes in springtime, unconscious of their "other lives / in swamps" and the "goddesses of inner earth / bent over the cauldron" (21).

Many of her poems focus on the power and beauty of nature, which Hogan often uses as a metaphor for life. Among the most striking of these in *Savings* is "Geraniums"; the flowers remain as a symbol of the life that burns in everything, even in "red flowers / abandoned in an empty house" (17). Several poems in that volume, such as "Rain," "Two Winds," and "Avalanche," emphasize forces in nature. Her sensitive evocations of nature are exemplified in "Landscape of Animals" and "Landing" in *Eclipse* and "Grasshoppers and Old Men," "November," and "Linden Tree" in *Seeing through the Sun*.

Hogan often incorporates a feminist perspective in her verse through descriptions of women's lives and feelings. In "Friday Night," in *Seeing through the Sun*, Hogan expresses her sympathy for an abused Mexican woman who lies crying on the door stoop. More political is "The Women Are Grieving," in which mothers lament the disappearance of their children—"the luminous women / who have lost their bright children" (*Eclipse* 26).

Among the most highly polished poets is Jim Barnes (b. 1933), who is of Welsh and Choctaw ancestry and grew up in Choctaw country—LeFlore County, Oklahoma. After graduating with a BA from Southeastern Oklahoma State University, Barnes received an MA and a PhD from the University of Arkansas. Barnes, who worked as a lumberjack from 1954 to 1959 and taught English at Northeastern Oklahoma State University, has been a full professor of comparative literature at Northeast Missouri State University, Kirksville. In addition, he is the founding editor of *Chariton Review*.

Barnes's three major works of poetry are *The American Book of the Dead* (1982), *A Season of Loss* (1985), and *La Plata Cantata* (1989). His poetry is characterized by penetrating personal observation and strong sense of place expressed in language of crystalline purity. Many of his poems are descriptive-reflective, celebrating what Wordsworth calls "spots of time" associated with specific places. Barnes comments in *Contemporary Authors* that he often chooses places "that have all the signs of having once been full of life but that are neither full of life nor lifeless. This in-betweenness is important in my work" (108: 43–44). In *The American Book of the Dead*, the poet combines images of death, exile, and the wanderer with perceptive descriptions of and incisive commentary on America. "On the Bridge at Fourche Malline River" is particularly Wordsworthian in its blending of past and present observations of nature:

> It has
> been years since you swam this muddy stream
> and, bearing a rock for ballast, walked the bottom
> straight across, bank to bank, in the longest breath
> you ever held. Time and time again, as now,
> you dream that walk. This time it's real. You leave
> your clothes flapping on the rail and jump, wide,
> into the warm water and feel the river
> bottom wrap a gentle skin about your feet.
> As you break upward for breath, you taste
> the sweet meat of earth the river is made of,
> and you remember the earth and that you are home.   (78)

Barnes's identification with his Indian heritage is particularly evident in *A Season of Loss*. "Four Things Choctaw" and "Choctaw Cemetery" evoke his cultural and family roots. In "Halcyon Days" he reminisces about his childhood hunting exploits against pretended adversaries and memorializes his Indian friend Charlie Wolf, who whittled skinning knives and swords from empty apple crates. The volume's title poem conveys Barnes's own sense of loss and his attempt to gain the unity with nature that his ancestors had known: "Our blood was now too thin to know / the half-moon brother, our skin too pale; / yet we, hands out, tried again to sow / our spirit in these stars." It was a "frail effort: our fathers' blood pulsed slow" (27). Barnes blends the traditions of the past with the tragic present in "Right Place, Wrong Time," in which he narrates how an old drunken Sioux summoned up his "grandfathers' ghosts" while Lame Johnny is hanged (15). The poet's vivid imagery in "Boneyard" enables the reader to visualize the parched land where a hundred buffalo died knee-deep in sludge:

> Only the ghosts of hoofs
> that still tramp along
> play on a hot wind
> which has no past.
>
> Only in dead of winter
> do the hoofs grow still,
> when humped clouds
> crowd low against the ground.   (3)

La Plata Cantata continues the emphasis on event, memory, and place that characterizes Barnes's other volumes. In "Touching the Rattlesnake," Barnes poignantly suggests the fragility of life as he recounts his reactions to a neighbor's leg, filled with poison from a rattlesnake bite, and the death of another friend as a result of a snake bite. Several poems, such as "First Cavalry: Holson Valley Road, 1942" and "The War over Holson Valley," deal with the impact of World War II on the poet. Especially moving is "Bombardier," which recaptures his memories of his brother, who was killed over the Netherlands:

> . . . Forty-odd years and still I
> feel him in the air, hear the sputter of
> dying props that do not die, but whir on
> into the dreams I have of this my life
> that is also his life. (28)

Place is one of the dominant themes in the volume. In some cases it is an animal's territory. "Domain" portrays a hawk who has fixed its eyes on a fearful Barnes when he dares to enter its territory. The poem echoes Blake's "Tyger," Hopkins's "Windhover," and Yeats's "Leda and the Swan." Many of the poems describe specific places Barnes has visited. The longest section of the volume is devoted to the series of poems bearing the book's title. "The Palace Cafe" pays tribute to the stoicism and endurance of small-town America. Here, the poet tells us, the people drank to "all the things they should have done before / Armageddon" in the form of catastrophic wind "fell upon" the town (47). Despite their loss, they do not want to leave. "Bandstand" recalls Barnes's boyhood experiences of crawling underneath the structure, a hideout for mischievous boys, budding musicians. He laments its replacement by a concrete-block building: "we need the darkling wind / beneath to lift the music from the fear / of remaining horns" (48). Especially beautiful is "From the Swinging Bridge," which conveys the sensation of being suspended between water and sky:

> Breathless in the rocking air,
> you see your time flow
> in the dark water
> that will not stay
> for shadows on the swinging bridge
> nor ripples on the plane of sky
> twenty feet below.
>
> This parallel time behind
> the deep water you look into
> makes you want to step down
> from the middle
> and sink softly into
> a dim semblance of self
> that lives quite other. (61)

Whereas Barnes's Indian heritage is not the central theme in his poetry, it is in that of Ray A. Young Bear (Mesquakie, b. 1950), a writer of striking imaginative power. Young Bear was raised and still lives in the Mesquakie settlement of Tama, Iowa, and attended the University of Northern Iowa. In addition to being a poet, Young Bear is the lead singer for the Woodland Singers, who perform traditional Mesquakie songs; he is also employed by the Mesquakie Tribe.

Young Bear has published two volumes of poetry: *Winter of the Salamander* (1980) and *The Invisible Musician* (1990). In *Winter of the Salamander*, the poet uses the tribal and contemporary influences on his life to examine the nature of humans and their relation to the landscape. His evocations of experiences and places are often combined with vision and dream so that the real and the unreal merge. An example of this surrealism is the poem entitled "in dream: the privacy of sequence":

> always expecting the winter
> to be a sad one
> i slept after heavy eating of food
> and waited until the portions
> grew alive.
> they sprouted antlers and formed
> into circles,
> fitted themselves perfectly
> into my hollow teeth

> and communicated to each other
> about the comfort and quiet welcome
> they were to receive. . . . (60)

At the same time, Young Bear's ability to create an affectionate portrait grounded in reality is exemplified in "grandmother," in which he says he would recognize the shape of his grandmother a mile away because of her "purple scarf / and the plastic / shopping bag" and her touch because her hands were "warm and damp / with the smell / of roots" (3). That Young Bear is also a keen observer of nature is evident in "the way the birds sat," depicting a bird as "dividing the weather through songs / cleaning the snow and rain / from the underside of its wings" (53). Young Bear searches for understanding in traditional and contemporary Indian life as well as in the distinction between reality and dream, as this excerpt from the poem "Winter of the Salamander" indicates:

> we'd like to understand why we breathe
> the same air, why the dead grow
> in number, the role i play in speaking
> to mouths that darken blue with swollen
> gunpowder burns, chapped lips, and alcohol.
> we keep wondering whether or not we'll ever
> leave in the form of eight sticks.
> we have waited until morning to turn off
> the lights, hoping to catch a glimpse
> of light chasing light. (90)

A theme that pervades *Winter of the Salamander* is that the individual and the tribe can survive the destructive forces present in the mythic and real world. Survival must come through an attempt to heed the lessons taught by nature, tribal elders, and one's own instincts.

Invisible Musician, whose title alludes to the frog as a night singer, continues the emphasis on interrelationship between reality and dream that informs *Winter of the Salamander*. This focus is especially evident in "The Black Antelope Tine," as the lines below illustrate:

> Cree tried to keep our attention on Philippine
> coins, old wax seals and war photographs,
> but I was soon conscious of another strength—
> cool and invisible—emanating from a cast iron
> toy kettle. Her narrations about the deformed
> pearl hunter became inaudible as autumn rain
> exploded on the roof, sending slivers of light
> out into the yard. Sleet. *There was this kind*
> *of power once: tribal celebration dancers*
> *flashed their sequins under the nightlights*
> *and the ground bloated beneath their feet*

until we all stood on what seemed a little
earth. We attempted to balance on its
curvature. Yet the dancers danced when
regalias alone could have disabled anyone.
Sharp triangles of bone in the heel and instep.
Roots to combat sorcery. (75)

Other poems that deal with the mixture of dream and reality are "All Star's Thanksgiving" and "King Cobra."

Many focus on Indian traditions and the interdependence of the people and the land. "The Significance of a Water Animal" deals with the Mesquakie version of the earth-diver myth, the creation of gods, and the origin of the Mesquakie. In "Language of Weather" Young Bear creates a vivid word picture of the landscape just before a summer rain, when the sound of thunder causes his parents to comment that members of the household should release parts of themselves to the clouds, their grandfathers. Both this poem and "Last Time They Were Here" exemplify Young Bear's ability to write fine descriptive-reflective verse. That the poet is a keen observer of the land and its inhabitants is evident as well in these lines from "The First Dimension of Skunk," which evokes a mid-October scene:

On the ground yellow-jacket
bees burrow themselves
into the windfall apples.
On the house the empty body shells
of locusts begin to rattle with
the plastic window covering
torn loose the night previous
in the first sudden gusts of wind.   (36)

The poet includes several traditional Mesquakie songs. In one section, tribal celebration songs are followed by "*Wa ta se Na ka mo ni*, Viet Nam Memorial, *1982*." After questioning why he had to immerse himself in "country, controversy, and guilt," Young Bear concludes that the Mesquakie tradition of honoring veterans in song should be respected: "Surely, the song they presently listened to along with my grandfathers / was the eternal kind which did not stop" (41).

Duane Niatum (Klallam, b. 1938) is a fine poet who has devoted considerable effort to publishing other Indian poets. Niatum spent his early life in Washington, Oregon, California, and Alaska. After enlisting in the navy in 1955, he spent two years in Japan. He received his BA from the University of Washington and his MA from Johns Hopkins. Some of his work was published under the name Duane McGinnis. In 1971, his great-aunt, Mrs. Annie Patsy Duncan, gave him his great-grandfather's name of Niatum, which he subsequently took as his legal name.

Niatum's books include *Ascending Red Cedar Moon* (1969), *After the Death of the Elder Klallam* (1970), *Taos Pueblo* (1973), *Digging out the Roots* (1977), and *Songs for the Harvester of Dreams* (1981). He also edited *Carriers of the Dream Wheel* (1975) and *Harper's Anthology of 20th Century Native American Poetry* (1988), compilations of contemporary American Indian poetry. Many of his works, such as *Digging out the Roots*, trace Niatum's quest for knowledge about his Klallam heritage. Others—such as "Legends of the Moon," a series of descriptive-reflective poems, and "Taos Pueblo," a long place poem, both in *Ascending Red Cedar Moon*—focus on the cultures of other tribes. The pictorial quality of Niatum's imagery and the gentleness of his language are illustrated in lines from "Poem for the People Who Came from the Moon" in *Ascending Red Cedar Moon*:

> Deer meadows end where wind settles
> In the city's heart of mushrooms; the river
> Willows echo Snoqualmie chants to children
> Chasing quail into the arms of afternoon.
> Within their houses rising from the sea,
> Carriers of the dream wheel often sing
> Their rain songs to the stranger. (20)

This volume also contains several beautifully crafted poems on personal themes. Among these is "At a Friend's Houseboat," which describes how Niatum and a companion merge with the beauty of the night:

> The ocher moon flow out
> Our arms: the long, the short,
> The undulating shadows.
>
> After dancing on the lake
> Like moths, we sit
> On the evening's blue montage.   (25)

The section of *Ascending Red Cedar Moon* devoted to the 1960s and *Songs for the Harvester of Dreams* blend the Indian past with the present and future. The later volume contains a series of imaginative nature lyrics, including this excerpt from "Loon":

> Easing effortlessly into evening's darkness,
> It dives for the lower reaches of your eyes.
>
> At its place for dreaming, it builds a nest
> With twigs made from escaping stars. (16)

Niatum's most recent work is *Drawings of the Song Animals* (1990).

A prolific poet who has written extensively on Indian themes and who has also been a mentor to other Indian poets is Maurice Kenny (Mohawk, b. 1929). Kenny was raised in northern New York, near St. Lawrence, and in the foothills of the Adirondacks. Kenny attended Butler, St. Lawrence, and New York universities. After years of traveling across country to work or attend school, he settled in Brooklyn. He is the coeditor of *Contact II*, a poetry journal that also publishes chapbooks, and has been on the faculty of North Country Community College, Saranac Lake, New York.

Kenny's selected poems from 1956 to 1984 are collected in *Between Two Rivers* (1987). Many of the poems are incantatory, such as "I Am the Sun" and "They Tell Me I Am Lost," while others, such as "Mulleins Are My Arms," are Whitmanesque in their appeal to the senses through the vigorous piling up of visual images. The following lines from "Cold Creek" illustrate this aspect of his lyricism:

> trout speckled in April dawn
> silvered with silver of early spring . . .
> song poured to the willows of daylight
> over the sandy banks of the creek
> cold to the toe, cold to the boy
> caught like rainbow trout
> by the hook in the jaw;
> song poured to the grass, minnows
> burnished in the leaping of noon
> over and over down the hills. . . . (28)

In many of his poems, Kenny expresses his nostalgia for the lost tribal past and attacks the injustices inflicted on Indians by whites.

Blackrobe: Isaac Jogues (1982) is a sharply etched collection of re-created letters, journal entries, and dramatic monologues that portray the attitudes of the French; Father Isaac Jogues, a Jesuit priest; and the Mohawks in the mid-seventeenth century, when Jogues tried to convert the Mohawks. Convinced that Jogues brought them back luck, the Mohawks murdered him.

Some of Kenny's most moving poetry is contained in *The Mama Poems* (1984), which won the American Book Award for poetry. Like *Blackrobe*, it is included in *Between Two Rivers*. Especially poignant is "Wake," a tribute to his dead mother. In the following lines, Kenny bids her farewell:

> Women climbed the stairs
> with sleeping children in their arms,
> others carried bowls of succotash
> to tables crowded with hunger
> as men sang songs;
> I touched her stiffness with my lips;
> there was music in her hands
> and I would hear their stories (143)

Also touching are "May 14, 1982," which deals with Kenny's grief, over his mother's death and "The Last Word," a tribute to his father. His most recent collection is *Humors and/or Not So Humorous* (1988), divided into "Greyhounding to Billings, Montana," and "Listening to Leslie Silko Telling Stories." Some of the poems in the first section, such as "After the Reading" and the title poem, recall Kenny's encounters with prejudice on the road. Several in the second part capture the interrelationship between the past and present, animal and human. In "Canyon de Chelly, Navajo," the poet, while looking at the landscape, imagines the lives of Navajos in the distant past and remembers hearing Simon Ortiz tell his son not to forget the massacre of the Navajos by Kit Carson in 1864. In others the focus is the poet's personal response to events. In the "Leslie Silko" title poem, the narrator, riding home on the subway, watches the faces of the passengers and knows that "children will always listen / as the train shuttles from magic / to Brooklyn" (43).

Another poet who combines explorations of Indian roots with graphic portrayals of urban Indian life is Barney Bush (Shawnee/Cayuga, b. 1945). His books include *My Horse and a Jukebox* (1979), *Petroglyphs* (1982), and *Inherit the Blood* (1985), which also contains some fiction. Born in southern Illinois, Bush left home at sixteen to travel across the United States. After attending the Institute of American Indian Arts in Santa Fe, New Mexico, Bush received his bachelor's degree from Fort Lewis College, Durango, Colorado, and his master's from the University of Idaho. Bush's poetry is characterized by realistic portrayals of contemporary Indian life, imaginative evocation of memory, and conversational tone. His poems, which concentrate on Indians across the country rather than on a specific tribe from one particular place, often contrast the grim reality of life away from home with memories of the Indian past or of the reservation. Several of the poems deal with the problems faced by urban Indians. In "City— Sunday" he comments that just as white people do not belong in Indians' country, Indians cannot feel at home on whites' streets: "Life does not begin / here—only ends" (*My Horse and a Jukebox* 15). In "Sidewalk Horses" an urban Indian sees reflected in the "eyes of shadowed doorways" images of late-night singing, dancing, storytelling, and drinking back home that make him long to take one of the "glaring" wooden horses he sees on the sidewalk and "hear / their iron feet dance old time bronco trails on concrete" (*Petroglyphs* 18). Bush is conscious of the self-destructiveness of Indian life, particularly in the cities. He portrays this aspect in "Requiem at the Bar" (*Petroglyphs*) and the untitled poem in *My Horse and a Jukebox* beginning "I think of the lights / and dark nights."

Another theme in Bush's poetry is memory. "Unbridling" recaptures an image from a winter in the past, when, brushing snow from his companion's hair, he "spoke no words / except in song / watched white whirlwinds dancing at / our feet" and felt a sense of loneliness after his friend left (*Petroglyphs* 80). In "It Is Finished," he emphasizes the strength of dreams that are "old before / you say them" and remembers another time:

What crying night wind do
your soulful eyes release
like an invisible lariat to
hold me at a monitos edge   (*Inherit the Blood* 32)

Many of the memories recall home or special moments in time. The sense of home and of lost opportunity is the subject of "Summer of Melons," in which the poet uses the withering of the corn patches one summer as a metaphor for the death of Indian relatives, who had passed on ancient rituals to him. Unknowing and undeserving, he "warred and lost" against the white world as if he had "planned it" (*Petroglyphs* 31). In "This Time above Flagstaff," Bush describes a moment in time when he walked with friends through the clouds above San Francisco peaks:

                                            we
        gaze at sky   each other the
        knowing way   heads
        swaying in time   wanting to
        stay in time with drumming that
        hits us in hard flashes   between
        going and staying   for we know
        we are shadows that   sink deep
        into the lake   after the
        sun is gone. (*Petroglyphs* 23)

Among the many talented women poets who have emerged recently is Joy Harjo (Creek, b. 1951). Harjo received her BA from the University of New Mexico and her MFA in creative writing from the University of Iowa. She is an associate professor at the University of Arizona.

What Moon Drove Me to This? (1979) chronicles the experiences and observations of Noni Daylight, her alter ego. Many of the poems in this volume focus on women. "Answer to Your Letter" describes a marriage gone bad, while "Early Morning Woman" and "To a Black Haired Daughter" stress mother love. In "White Sands" Harjo captures the complexity of mother-daughter relationships as she compares her mother's enthusiasm for her sister's conventional marriage with opposition to Harjo's own.

Most of the poems in *What Moon Drove Me to This*? emphasize Indian life in the past and present, such as "Round Dance Somewhere around Oklahoma City/November Night," "For a Girl I Once Knew," "He Told Me His Name Was Sitting Bull." In "Chicago or Albuquerque," Harjo poignantly describes urban Indians who drink away their sorrow and speak with "an unbearable ache" of their longing to have been hunters and warriors like their ancestors. Like Bush, Harjo is aware of the destructiveness in contemporary Indian life:

it is almost closing time
beginning again
and a warrior
drinks back the distance
before the long night
of the hunt. (6)

In *She Had Some Horses* (1983) Harjo pays tribute to the survival of contemporary Indians, while acknowledging and casting off fear within herself. The opening poem, "Call It Fear," depicts anxiety as an "edge / where shadows and bones of some of us walk / backwards" (13). In "Heartbeat," she ascribes this fear to being curled inside her mother's belly too long: her "mother's heartbeat is a ghostly track / that follows her" (37). Only fierce anger, she concludes, will free her. She lets go of this dark fear in the final poem, "I Give You My Book."

The section entitled "Survivors" honors those who have not succumbed to whites' devastation of native culture. As Harjo comments in the concluding lines of "Anchorage," ". . . who would believe / the fantastic and terrible story of all of our survival / those who were never meant / to survive?" Among the poems that chronicle what Indians have endured are "Woman Hanging from the Thirteenth Floor," "Rain," and "Night Out." In the title section of the volume, which uses traditional song structure, the metaphor of horses suggests the variety of personal responses of Indians to their environments:

She had some horses.
She had horses who whispered in the dark, who were afraid to speak.
She had horses who screamed out of fear of the silence, who
carried knives to protect themselves from ghosts.
She had horses who waited for destruction.
She had horses who waited for resurrection.
She had some horses. (64)

Harjo's most recent volume is *In Mad Love and War* (1990), in which she primarily writes prose poems rather than utilizing the traditional song structure that frames some of the selections in *She Had Some Horses*. In her new book, Harjo includes many eulogies to the victims of racial injustice, such as "For Anna Mae Aquash," "Strange Fruit" (Jacqueline Peters). Some of these portraits are anonymous, including the powerful "Deer Dance," in which the "Indian ruins" drink late at night in a "bar of broken survivors" while watching a drunken Indian woman dance naked on a table: "She was the myth slipped down through dreamtime. The promise of feast we / all knew was coming. / The deer who crossed through knots of a curse to find us" (6). The eulogies to a number of black musicians reveal the poet's love of music. Among these works are "Bird," which describes Harjo's reactions to the movie biography of Charlie Parker, and "Rainy Night," which perceptively imagines how Billie Holiday must have felt as she was dying; in "We Encounter Nat King Cole as We Invent the Future," the narrator recalls listening to the singer's music. A number of the poems are personal. "Autobiography" brings to life Harjo's memories of her father, her child-hood feelings that Indians were different, and her adult encounter with a Jemez man sleeping on the sidewalk in the snow. "Fury of Rain" reveals how her feelings of furious longings explode and celebrates after "guarding the wreck" of her life for thirty-five years. Harjo's fatalism is expressed in her comment that "we are all in the belly of a laughing god / swimming the heavens, in this whirling circle" (16). We do not imagine that one day this god will spit us out. Survival and regeneration are the themes of "Nine Lives," which contains some of the most lyrical poetry in the volume. Noting that she is "downwind of the beer foam and laughter" and that death "with its coat of tender wings" is close to her shoulder while the neighbor's cat fights for all its nine lives, the poet concludes that "We are all spun / within a crescendo of abalone light, unseen beneath the wild storm. / What spins us now, in this neighborhood chrysalis at exactly midnight? / Don't tell me, unless it will turn me into something as perfect as a perfect monarch butterfly" (50). Other personal poems include "Rainy Dawn," a loving trib-ute to her daughter.

In her work, Wendy Rose (Hopi/Miwok, b. 1948) creates both delicate lyrics and harsh protest poems. Rose received her bachelor's and master's degrees from the University of California, Berkeley, where she also did doctoral work in anthropology. An accomplished painter, Rose has taught Native American studies at California State University, Fresno. Much of her work is collected in *Lost Copper* (1980); many of these poems deal with Hopi traditions or Rose's search for her Hopi roots. These themes are combined in such poems as "Walking on the Prayerstick," "To Some Few Hopi Ancestors," and "Hopi Overlay: Turquoise Words Going Home." An excerpt from the latter poem demonstrates Rose's ability to create images of delicate beauty:

> Falling through the years
> like dandelion dust or turquoise
> chipped from the matrix and flying,
> I am set in troubled silver.
> I know there's a first time
> for everything, even closed words,
> even a finishing. (115)

The final section of the volume, "Builder Kachina: Home-Going" describes Rose's 1977 journey to the land of her Hopi father.

Rose is also a forceful protest writer, as these lines from "To Some Few Hopi Ancestors" indicate:

You have engraved yourself
with holy signs, encased yourself
in pumice, hammered on my bones
till you could no longer hear
the howl of the missions
slipping screams through
your silence, dropping dreams
from your wings. (2)

In "Vanishing Point: Urban Indian" Rose bitterly describes the anguish suffered by Indians living in cities. In the bars and "dustless reaches of cold eyes," they vanish and lean "underbalanced into nothing" (12). In the section of the book entitled "Academic Squaw: Reports to the World from the Ivory Tower," Rose satirizes academics' attitudes toward Indians. She protests in the title poem that she is "being trained, / as the bones and clay bowls left open are drained. Grandmother, / we've been framed" (30).

Rose's *What Happened When the Hopi Hit New York* is a series of place poems, in which the author recounts her impressions and experiences as she crisscrossed the country. In "Tehachapi Shadows" she describes this southern California mountain range, whose shadows "in the cut of sky lengthen, fall, / while velvet pillows are rolling east" (2). Also imaginative is "Winter Morning: Northern Nevada," in which she compares the movement of the morning that "dips and shines" to a celestial snake that slides from place to place "in the fluid security / of falling" (9). In "Subway Graffiti: An Anthropologist's Impressions," Rose analyzes the vivid testimonies of a past civilization. The words on the subway walls were once cries for help, of "arrangements made / and treaties abandoned, death threats turned / into rumbles with name and number recorded." Her California-born senses feel the subway "as an earthquake / strangely regular." Here people "rumbled" into each other, "dueling for power (35–36).

Several other talented American Indian women writers have emerged in the 1980s. Among them is Roberta Whiteman (Oneida, b. 1947), whose *Star Quilt* is a highly imaginative work. These stanzas from the title poem demonstrate a keen attention to detail and descriptive power:

These are notes to lightning in my bedroom.
A star forged from linen thread and patches.
Purple, yellow, red like diamond suckers, children

of the star gleam on sweaty nights. The quilt unfolds
against sheets, moving, warm clouds of Chinook.
It covers my cuts, my red birch clusters under pine.

Under it your mouth begins a legend,
and wide as the plain, I hope Wisconsin marshes
promise your caress. The candle locks

us in forest smells, your cheek tattered
by shadow. Sweetened by wings, my mothlike heart
flies nightly among geraniums. (1)

The poet's ability to evoke the delicate beauty of nature and the observer's
autumnal mood is evident in "Nett Lake, Minnesota":

> The only sunlight left bleaches aspens
> far across the lake where they rise like a shout
> above the grey hoods of pine. Down at my feet,
> ripples unravel every reflection
> into glyphs, all shifting form. Loss,
> loss, lost. The constant resonance brings hope
> that colors grow richer in loneliness,
> yet with this rain, autumn fades to embers,
> folding layer after layer
> of scarlet into auburn, magenta into slate. (20)

Two Navajo women authors who write moving and realistic descriptions of tribal life are Luci Tapahonso and Nia Francisco. Tapahonso (b.
1953) has published three books of poetry: *Seasonal Woman* (1982), *One
More Shiprock Night* (1981), and *A Breeze Swept Through* (1987). In the last
volume, Tapahonso celebrates the strength of family ties. "Hills Coffee"
describes her uncle's fondness for her coffee and portrays their loving
relationship. "Dear Alvin" and "Note to a Younger Brother" focus on
Tapahonso's memories of a dead brother and the endurance of her grief.
In "A Spring Poem," she teaches her children to feel good about themselves
and emphasizes that the spirits of the relations they never knew wait to
protect them. Several poems stress the power of women. In "Yes, It Was
My Grandmother," she pays tribute to this woman who trained wild horses
for "pleasure and pay" and hated to cook (17). "Last Year the Piñons Were
Plentiful" describes a woman who leaves her husband to go off with a
handsome stranger she meets at a trading post; "Yáadí lá" humorously
recounts how a Navajo woman gets rid of her husband's lover and regains
her husband (and his paycheck).

Nia Francisco (b. 1952) also focuses on the place of women and family
in *Blue Horses for Navajo Women* (1988). The delicacy of her verse is suggested in these lines from "Newly Fallen Snow Cools": "A Navajo woman's
moment is eternity / long happiness / newly fallen snow cools her heart"
(50). Poems such as "Nabeho Women with Blue Horses" link Francisco's
own life and dreams with Navajo gods and myths. It is from her people,
revived to their original power, that she draws her strength: "I must see
these I must smell I must touch and hear their songs" (27). Several of her
poems, including "Níltsah," "A Voice Called the Child," and "The Only

Daughter within Me," are devoted to childbirth and children. Others, like "Onion and Fried Potatoes," portray the warmth of Navajo family life.

While these poets pay tribute to the strength of tribalism and family, Adrian C. Louis (Paiute, b. 1946) graphically describes, in such poems as "Without Words," from *Fire Water World* (1988), the devastating impact of alcohol and substance abuse on contemporary Indian life:

> We have nothing to live for, nothing to die for.
> Each day we drink and decompose into a different flavor.
> Continuity is not fashionable
> And clashing form is sediment
> Obscuring the bottom of thirst.
> The parched and cracking mouths
> Of our Nations do not demand
> a reason for drinking
> so across America
> we stagger and stumble with contempt for the future
> and with no words of pride for our past. (2)

By chronicling the violence and substance abuse that destroys their lives, Louis forces his readers to face the brutalization of Indians unable to feel at home either in the city or in Indian country. Poems like "Fire Water World," "Her Wake," "Something about Being Indian," "Urban Indian Suite," and "The First of the Month" depict Indians' self-destructive responses to their sense of alienation. In "The Sacred Circle Blues," Louis describes his inability to feel at home either on or off the reservation. "The Bloodwine Epigrams" suggests that by discarding past myths, Native Americans can "discover invisibility and true Indian-ness / in any nameless city" if they seek their own kind: "With clean slates we can invent the past / be it sterile, sweet sparkling, / or gun deadly" (49).

White Corn Sister (1977; 2nd ed., 1981) by Peter Blue Cloud (Mohawk, b. 1935), which the author dedicates to all peoples, suggests that the solutions to the problems of Indians and of humankind as a whole lie in nature, tribalism, and family. In the section of this chapbook entitled "White Corn Sister," a poetic play for voices, Blue Cloud acknowledges not only the dualities of good and evil in life but also the occasional triumph of evil. When evil prevailed, the "Great Good" was remembered "and the strength of clan mothers / spoke through the chiefs / and brought reason / to the people" (24). The Voice of the Hunter reminds the reader that a people lost and a nation scattered should seek one another to be of one mind and to live "the Great Good." Out of this rededication comes renewal:

> The seed corn in earth,
> the newborn child,
> the sun rising as ever

> to warm the good earth,
>   all these,
> in promise to a scattered nation.   (29; 1981 ed.)

The humorous side of contemporary Indian experience is vividly conveyed in *Elderberry Flute Song* (1982), a collection of short stories and poems. Blue Cloud captures the impudence and the incessant hunger of the trickster in "Relativity." To the question of whether he understands the theory of relativity, Coyote responds: "Yes, yes, I do. It's much easier that way. When I'm hungry I just stop at anyone's place and get a meal. Yes, it's really good to know that all creatures are related" (105). In "Why, Coyote, Why?," Blue Cloud shows the importance of the trickster in helping Indians stay in balance:

> and because I am the shadow
> of your wants which you ignore
> and turn your eyes inward
> in self-pity and constant doubt
> while a feast sits waiting
> so close you have but to reach,
> but reach instead neatly formulated
> conclusions based upon your doubt
> to boost your withered ego
> to the level of mental ankles (78)

Space does not permit extended discussion of many other talented poets who write on Indian themes. These include Joseph Bruchac (Abenakie), Diane Burns (Ojibwa/Chemehuevi), Elizabeth Cook-Lynn (Sioux), Anita Endrezze (Yaqui), Diane Glancy (Cherokee), Lance Henson (Cheyenne), Carter Revard (Osage), and Mary Tall Mountain (Athabascan). Although much of the poetry of Ralph Salisbury (Cherokee) does not focus on Indian themes, his *Going to the Water* does.

Many American Indians have become prolific authors of fiction and poetry. Few, however, have written drama. While Gerald Vizenor and Linda Hogan have written plays and screenplays, they have published most of their work in other genres. One contemporary Indian dramatist is Hanay Geiogamah (Kiowa/Delaware, b. 1945), whose *New Native American Drama* includes his satiric dramas *Foghorn, 49,* and *Body Indian.* (Jeffrey Huntsman's introduction to the volume discusses Native American drama). Geiogamah, who received his BA in theater and drama from Indiana University, is artistic director and cofounder of the American Indian Dance Theatre and has been managing editor of the *American Indian Culture and Research Journal.* He has also taught at such institutions as Colorado College and the University of California, Los Angeles.

Body Indian is a moving portrait of urban Indians, degraded by alcoholism and poverty, destroying themselves. *Foghorn*, a multimedia satire, pokes fun at stereotypes of Indians from the arrival of Columbus to the 1973 confrontations at Wounded Knee; the title refers to the foghorns blasted at the Indians who occupied Alcatraz in 1969. The most polished play of the three is *49*, which combines the Indian past, present, and future. The play takes its title from the sings that Indian young people hold late at night after powwows are over. As Geiogamah indicates, the 49s become an emotional release for many Indians who do not take meaningful parts in tribal ceremonies. In all three plays, Geiogamah stresses that, through their traditional culture, Indians must revitalize themselves as individuals and as a group.

The most prolific Indian writer of nonfiction prose is Vine Deloria, Jr. (Sioux, b. 1933). Born in South Dakota, Deloria received a BS from Iowa State University, MTh from the Lutheran School of Theology, and JD from the University of Colorado. The former executive director of the National Congress of American Indians and chair of the Institute for Development of Indian Law, he is professor of Native American studies and political science at the University of Arizona.

Deloria's keen wit, sharp satire, and political insight into the problems of contemporary Indian life are exemplified by *Custer Died for Your Sins* (1969), which contains an interesting essay on Indian humor, and *We Talk, You Listen* (1970). Deloria has also written numerous books on Indian-white relations and Indian religion, including *Of Utmost Good Faith* (1972), *God Is Red* (1973), *Behind the Trail of Broken Treaties* (1974), and *The Metaphysics of Modern Existence* (1979), as well as many volumes on Indian affairs. Like Deloria, a number of other American Indians gained advanced degrees and subsequently published scholarly studies, particularly in the fields of anthropology and history. Many of these works are discussed in the bibliographic review.

American Indians have always had a tradition of creative and oratorical expression. As they were introduced to the written word, Indians used it as a tool both to help preserve their oral traditions and to share them with others. They also used the written word to extend the boundaries of their own creativity into genres outside Indian oral traditions. From the early works written in English by authors like Samson Occom and William Apes to the work of contemporary authors, American Indians have developed an impressive body of literature. What Indians have endured to become writers is poignantly summarized by Jim Barnes in his poem "Contemporary Native American Poetry," which he describes as a kind of scarecrow: "You've seen it ragged against a field, / but you seldom think, at the time, / to get there it had to walk through hell" (*The American Book of the Dead* 85).

Americans can only understand the true literary history of this nation when they have studied the contributions of American Indians. As this survey illustrates, Native Americans' oral and written literary traditions not only remain strong but also continue to grow. The power of Indian culture to inspire tribal people since time immemorial is beautifully summarized Simon Ortiz's "It Doesn't End, of Course":

> It doesn't end.
>
> In all growing
> from all earths
> to all skies,
>
> in all touching
> all things,
>
> in all soothing
> the aches of all years,
> it doesn't end.   (*Going for the Rain* 112)

Note

¹Washington Matthews. "The Night Chant." MAMNH 6 (1902): 142; Bierhorst, *Four Masterworks of American Indian Literature*. Bierhorst greatly condenses the Night Chant in his version.

The "House Made of Dawn," Tsegihi, is a shrine in the Canyon de Chelly, called the White House. It is a two-story cliff house built of yellow sandstone whose upper portion is painted white and whose lower, unpainted portion is yellow. In Navajo symbolism, white is the color of the east and yellow that of the west. Whereas the upper story is sacred to the Hastshéyalti, or Talking God, who is a god of dawn and the east, the lower is sacred to Hasthéhogan, or House God, who is god of the west and evening twilight (Bierhorst, *Four Masterworks* 341).

Part Two

Bibliographic Review

The review of bibliography is divided into the following sections: Section A examines bibliographies and research guides. Section B discusses anthologies, collections, and reinterpretations. It is subdivided into general anthologies, collections and recreations of oral literatures (songs, narratives, and oratory), and collections of life histories and autobiographies. Section C surveys scholarship and criticism and contains several subdivisions: studies of oral literatures (ritual dramas, songs, and narratives), life histories and autobiographies, American Indian literatures in general, individual authors, and teaching Native American literatures. The final section examines works that provide backgrounds for the study of American Indian literatures, with subdivisions for biography, demography, ethnohistory, languages, philosophy and religion, women's studies, and the image of the Indian.

A. Bibliographies and Research Guides

Jack Marken's unannotated *American Indian: Language and Literature* is more helpful as a guide to oral than written literature. An indispensable guide to oral literatures is *Native American Folklore, 1879–1979*, compiled by William M. Clements and Frances M. Malpezzi. Equally indispensable guides to written literature are *A Biobibliography of Native American Writings, 1772–1924* and *Supplement*, compiled by Daniel F. Littlefield, Jr., and James W. Parins, which has sections on Native American writers (including those known only by pen names) and biographical notes. It includes writers not only of belles lettres but also of political documents, tribal addresses, and letters. A good guide to Indian studies that is inadequate for the study of literature is *Guide to Research on North American Indians*, compiled by Arlene B. Hirschfelder, Mary Gloyne Byler, and Michael A. Dorris.

Especially useful overviews of materials on American Indian literature are Ruoff's "American Indian Literatures" and Andrew O. Wiget's "Native American Literature." Michael A. Dorris, "Native American Literature in an Ethnohistorical Context," and Jarold W. Ramsey, "A Supplement to Michael Dorris's 'Native American Literature,' " include substantial bibliographic information in their articles (See "Teaching American Indian Literatures"). *ASAIL Notes* contains bibliographic information on original works and scholarship published in the United States and abroad. *Studies in American Indian Literatures* publishes short articles and bibliographies.

Numerous specialized bibliographies have also been published. H. David Brumble III has compiled two excellent guides to personal narratives: *An Annotated Bibliography of American Indian and Eskimo Autobiographies* and "A Supplement to *An Annotated Bibliography of American Indian and Eskimo Autobiographies*." His *American Indian Autobiography* includes an expanded version of this supplement. *American Indian Novelists*, compiled by Tom Colonnese and Louis Owens, provides brief plot summaries of novels by American Indian authors and includes primary works and selected secondary materials. Important for women's studies is *Native American Women*, compiled by Rayna Green. In addition, *A Bibliographical Guide to the Study of Western American Literature*, compiled by Richard W. Etulain, lists secondary works about western American Indian writers as well as about the image of Indians in western literature. A useful guide to the image of the Indian in American literature is *The American Indian in Short Fiction*, compiled by Peter G. Beidler and Marion F. Egge. *American Indian and Alaska Native Newspapers and Periodicals, 1826–1924*, compiled by Daniel F. Littlefield, Jr., and James W. Parins, is an extensive guide to newspapers and periodicals edited or published by Native Americans as well as to other periodicals focusing on the contemporary affairs of native groups.

Several bibliographies deal with literature for elementary and high school readers. *Books without Bias: Through Indian Eyes*, compiled by Beverly Slapin and Doris Seale, reviews children's books on American Indian subjects and gives recommended reading levels; it also includes reprinted essays by Byler, Dorris, and Joseph Bruchac as well as a checklist of criteria for evaluating children's books. *Literature by and about the American Indian* (1979), compiled by Anna Stensland, stresses books published since 1973 that are appropriate to high-, middle-, and elementary-school readers; this work supplements Stensland's first edition (1973).

Two recent series have greatly increased the bibliographic information available. An extensive series of comprehensive bibliographies on American tribes and culture is published by Scarecrow Press under the editorship of Jack Marken. Particularly suitable for libraries' general collections is the series edited by Francis Jennings, sponsored by the D'Arcy McNickle Center for the History of the American Indian at Newberry Library and published by Indiana University Press. Each annotated bibliography contains approximately two hundred items and an introductory essay. Copies of volumes of this discontinued series can be purchased from the bookstore of the library.

An outdated but informative reference is Frederick W. Hodge's *Handbook of American Indians North of Mexico*. The standard works are the updated volumes, collectively titled *Handbook of North American Indians* and published under the general editorship of William C. Sturtevant. These invaluable guides to tribal ethnohistory contain extensive bibliographies.

Also indispensable for information on tribal backgrounds is Francis P. Prucha's *Bibliographical Guide to the History of Indian-White Relations in the United States* and *Indian-White Relations in the United States*. They include sections on Indian biography, concepts of images of the Indian, and Indian writings. An important new survey on Indian-white relations is Norman Heard's *Handbook of the American Frontier*, which will consist of five volumes: 1. *The Southeastern Woodlands* (published); 2. Northeast; 3. Plains; 4. Southwest; 5. Index, chronology, and bibliography. The handbook includes articles on individuals, events, and ethnohistory.

B. Anthologies, Collections, and Re-creations

ANTHOLOGIES

There is no anthology of oral and written American Indian literatures comparable to the standard surveys of English and American literature. *The Portable North American Indian Reader*, edited by Frederick W. Turner III, reprints a varied selection of myths and tales, narrated autobiographies, and works by a few contemporary authors. However, the texts of the oral selections are sometimes altered. *The Literature of the American Indian*, edited by Thomas E. Sanders and Walter W. Peek, contains more oral than written literature, which primarily consists of works by contemporary authors. It lacks adequate introductions and notes. *American Indian Literature*, edited by Alan R. Velie, includes some lengthy oral selections but omits the ethnographic notes that accompanied the original texts. The written selections are primarily by Oklahoma males. An excellent regional anthology is *The South Corner of Time*, edited by Larry Evers, which includes traditional and contemporary oral literature (some with bilingual texts) as well as written literature, maps, orthographies, and tribal ethnohistories of the Hopi, Navajo, Papago, and Yaqui. Although Abraham Chapman's *Literature of the American Indians* contains some oral narratives and autobiographies, it is primarily an anthology of critical essays, which include the work of several contemporary Indian authors. *The Elders Wrote* by Bernd Peyer is a good anthology of prose written by American Indians from 1768 to 1931. Peyer has collected short stories written by American Indians between 1881 and 1936 in *The Singing Spirit*. A representative anthology of contemporary Indian writing is *The Remembered Earth*, edited by Geary Hobson. An excellent anthology of oral and written literature by Alaskan peoples is *Alaska Native Writers, Storytellers and Orators*, edited by Nora Dauenhauer, Richard Dauenhauer, and Gary Holthaus. The only historical collection of speeches and writings by Canadian Indians is *First People, First Voices*, edited by Penny

Petrone. It contains selections by some authors, such as George Copway, who also lived or published in the United States. *An Anthology of Canadian Native Fiction*, edited by Thomas King, was published as a special issue of *Canadian Fiction Magazine* (1987). Among the few collections of Inuit writing are *Northern Voices*, edited by Petrone, and *Paper Stays Put*, edited by Robin Gedalof.

The work of American Indian women appears in several anthologies: *Spider Woman's Granddaughters*, edited by Paula Gunn Allen, which contains both oral and written literature; *That's What She Said*, edited by Rayna Green; *A Gathering of the Spirit*, edited by Beth Brandt; and *Native American Women*, edited by Linda Hogan. Selections by Indian women are included in *The Third Woman*, edited by Dexter Fisher, a collection of works by minority women.

COLLECTIONS AND RE-CREATIONS
OF ORAL LITERATURES

The chief library sources for collections of oral literatures recorded from the late nineteenth century to the present are the Bulletins and Annual Reports of the Bureau of American Ethnology, Anthropological Papers and Memoirs of the American Museum of Natural History, and Publications of the American Ethnological Society, the American Folklore Society, and the Canadian Museum of Man. Additional resources can be found in the anthropological series published by several universities, notably Columbia and California, Berkeley. The Native American Tribal Religions series of the University of Nebraska Press and the Sun Tracks series of the University of Arizona Press publish twentieth-century collections of oral literatures.

Among the few general anthologies of oral literature suitable for class use is *American Indian Prose and Poetry*, formerly entitled *The Winged Serpent*, edited by Margot Astrov, which includes a variety of North and South American narratives and songs, plus a few orations.

Songs

A good general anthology of songs is A. Grove Day's *Sky Clears*, which has a lengthy introduction. Day also includes some comments on the songs' contexts for the collection, which is arranged by culture areas. He does not, however, include the notes from the original texts. This collection provides broader coverage than does *The Indians' Book*, edited by Natalie Burlin Curtis, originally published in 1907. Curtis does give careful ethnographic introductions and notes, bilingual texts, and musical transcriptions as well as relevant myths and tales. Less reliable is *American Indian Poetry*, edited by George W. Cronyn, which includes some fraudulent Eskimo songs. An excellent collection of Inuit songs is *Eskimo Poems from*

Canada and Greenland, translated by Tom Lowenstein, containing a valuable introduction. William Brandon, in *The Magic World*, and Jerome Rothenberg, in *Shaking the Pumpkin*, have provided free interpretations of standard translations; their work should be viewed as the authors' creative efforts rather than as actual translations.

Frances Densmore, one of the first to study Indian music, has published numerous collections of songs from a variety of tribes, which contain extensive analyses of the cultural and musical contexts. Although scholars today recognize the weaknesses in some of her transcriptions and translations, her collections are valuable starting places. Another early collector was Alice C. Fletcher.

Herbert Joseph Spinden provides a good introduction to the lyrics of Indian music in his collection, *Songs of the Tewa*. Especially useful as a teaching text is Ruth Underhill's *Singing for Power*, which gives the English texts of songs connected with the Arizona Papago's fertility rituals and discusses the contexts in detail. The secular songs of the Lakota are presented in a bilingual edition entitled *Songs and Dances of the Lakota*, edited by Ben Black Bear, Sr., and Ron D. Theisz. *Yaqui Deer Songs/Maso Bwikam*, by Larry Evers and Felipe S. Molina, is an exemplary edition that contains bilingual texts and extensive commentary on the social and ceremonial contexts, vocabulary, and background information. Also valuable is *Run toward the Nightland*, edited by Jack Frederick Kilpatrick and Anna Gritts Kilpatrick, which examines Cherokee song magic and provides sample texts.

Narratives

A useful anthology of narratives for the general reader is John Bierhorst's *Red Swan*, which includes a variety of kinds of stories from forty different tribes and some notes; stories are categorized by theme. *Tales of the North American Indians*, edited by Stith Thompson, is arranged thematically and contains stories from a variety of tribes, although many are excerpts. Thompson's notes give considerable information about where stories using similar motifs can be found. Another general anthology of narratives is *American Indian Mythology*, edited by Alice Marriott and Carol Rachlin.

Narratives have received more scholarly attention than any other genre of American Indian oral literatures. In his landmark studies of the Tsimshian and Kwakiutl tribes, Franz Boas established the principle of analyzing oral literatures as a means of understanding American Indian cultures. Among his works are "Tsimshian Mythology," coauthored with Henry W. Tate; *Kwakiutl Tales; Kwakiutl Culture as Reflected in Mythology*; and *Keresan Texts*. Boas's influence is evident in the work of such scholars as Ruth F. Benedict, Leonard Bloomfield, Ruth L. Bunzel, George A. Dorsey, Pliny E. Goddard, Melville Jacobs, A. L. Kroeber, Robert H. Lowie, Elsie Parsons,

Paul Radin, Edward Sapir, John R. Swanton, and Clark Wissler. The texts edited by these scholars, as well as by such pioneers as James Mooney and Washington Matthews, provide literal translations, careful analyses of the cultural backgrounds of the tribes, and full notes.

Anthropologists and linguists have published new scholarly texts. Excellent examples of bilingual editions suitable for classroom use are *O'othham Hoho'ok A'agitha: Legends and Lore of the Papago and Pima Indians*, edited by Dean Saxton and Lucille Saxton; *Hopitutuwutsi*, by Ekkehart Malotki and Herschel Talashoma; and *Hopi Coyote Tales* and *Stories of Maasaw, a Hopi God*, edited by Malotki and Michael Lomatuway'ma; and *Spirit Mountain*, edited by Leanne Hinton and Lucille J. Watahomigie. Bilingual texts enable students to compare English translations with the native-language versions. The University of Chicago has been publishing bilingual texts through its Native American Texts series, *International Journal of American Linguistics*.

An innovative edition of narratives presented in translation is Dennis Tedlock's *Finding the Center*, based on tape-recorded performances. Tedlock uses special typography to represent the changes in pitch and length of the original performances. Anthony Mattina and Madeline de Sautel provide a fine example of a carefully recorded and annotated text in their translation of *The Golden Woman*, a tribal version of a European story. Theisz's *Buckskin Tokens* is a valuable anthology of tape-recorded, contemporary versions of Sioux stories. Another important collection of Sioux myths is James R. Walker's *Lakota Myth*, edited by Elaine A. Jahner. Harold Courlander's *Hopi Voices*, a fine collection of that tribe's literature, includes a careful introduction and notes. An excellent example of a regional anthology accompanied by detailed introduction and notes is Jarold W. Ramsey's *Coyote Was Going There*. Although the volume contains primarily stories, it includes some speeches as well. One of the few collections of southeastern narratives in print is *Native American Legends*, compiled and edited by George E. Lankford. Primarily consisting of excerpts of stories from the Biloxi, Caddo, Chickasaw, Creek, Natchez, and other tribes, the volume includes an introduction by W. K. McNeil, some notes, and information about printed sources of the narratives.

Other important collections of narratives are the re-creations by such skilled storytellers as George Bird Grinnell, Theodora Kroeber, Walter McClintock, and James Willard Schultz. All but Kroeber were early gatherers of American Indian literatures. A scholarly re-creation is Paul Zolbrod's *Diné bahane': The Navajo Creation Story*, a collation of many versions of this story with careful annotation.

Indians, as individuals and as tribes, have increasingly published accounts of their oral traditions. Boasian-trained scholars Ella C. Deloria (Sioux), William Jones (Fox), and Archie Phinney (Nez Perce), and other scholars, such as John N. B. Hewitt (Tuscarora), Francis La Flesche (Omaha), William Morgan (Navajo), and Arthur C. Parker (Seneca), collected and translated the oral literatures of Native America, adding an important

Indian perspective missing from earlier scholarship. Richard Erdoes and Alfonso Ortiz (San Juan) have compiled *American Indian Myths and Legends*, a thematically organized anthology containing previously published and new versions collected by the authors. As Dell Hymes points out in "Anthologies and Narrators," Ortiz and Erdoes have not documented carefully their treatment of previously published versions (see Swann and Krupat, eds., *Recovering the Word*). Jack F. Kilpatrick and Anna Gritts Kilpatrick (Cherokee) have edited several volumes of Cherokee oral literature, including *Friends of Thunder*.

Less scholarly but valuable nonetheless are the following collections by Native Americans: George Clutesi (Tlingit), *Son of Raven, Son of Deer*; Jesse Cornplanter (Seneca), *Legends of the Longhouse*; Vi Hilbert (Lushootseed), *Haboo: Native American Stories from Puget Sound*; Mourning Dove (Colville), *Tales of the Okanogans*, edited by Donald M. Hines (see an earlier version of these tales in *Coyote Stories*, edited by Heister Dean Guie). *Truth of a Hopi* contains numerous stories told by Edmund Nequatewa (Hopi). Emily Pauline Johnson (Mohawk) re-creates Indian stories, primarily Squamish, in her *Legends of Vancouver*. Bertrand Walker (Wyandot) uses dialect in *Tales of the Bark Lodges*, re-creations of traditional and nontraditional tales; many reflect the influence of the Uncle Remus stories. In *Summer in the Spring*, Gerald Vizenor (Ojibwa) retells Ojibwa myths and reinterprets their songs as translated by Frances Densmore.

Several Sioux have collected their people's stories. Charles Eastman (Sioux) and Elaine Eastman retell stories for young readers in *Smoky Day's Wigwam Evenings* (also issued under the title *Wigwam Evenings*). Other Sioux who have published versions of their tribes' stories are Luther Standing Bear, *Stories of the Sioux*; Zitkala-Ša, *Old Indian Legends*; and James La Pointe, *Legends of the Lakota*. An especially full retelling of Blackfeet narratives is *The Sun Came Down*, by Percy Bullchild. Narratives published under the aegis of individual tribes include *The Way It Was, Inaku Iwacha: Yakima Legends*, project director Virginia Beavert, and *Nu Mee Poom Tit Wah Tit (Nez Perce Legends)*, compiled by Allen P. Slickpoo, Sr., et al. An example of a tribally sponsored history based on oral tradition is *Navajo History*, edited by Ethelou Yazzie. Bill Vaudrin (Ojibwa) gathered anecdotal narratives of the Tanaina Indians in *Tanaina Tales from Alaska*. The Alaska Native Language Center, Fairbanks, Alaskan Methodist University Press, and the University of Alaska Press publish collections of stories of Alaskan Natives.

However, printed editions of narratives are only a pale representation of the original storytelling performance, in which we can see or hear the storyteller create the tale and interact with his or her audience. The best example of videotapes of oral performance is the series of eight entitled *Words and Place*, produced by Larry Evers and directed by Denny Carr. The series presents contemporary authors, singers, and storytellers performing in their southwest communities. Five of the videotapes are recorded in native Indian languages with English subtitles. Each videotape is accompanied by a printed guide containing cultural and historical information. In addition, audiotapes of Theisz's *Buckskin Tokens* are available through Sinte Gleska Bookstore. Audiotapes of Yaqui Deer songs collected in Evers and Molina's *Yaqui Deer Songs* are available from the University of Arizona.

A popular collection of stories is Radin's *Trickster*, a Winnebago cycle for which Radin provides excellent ethnographic notes and Jungian commentary; the volume also includes an essay by Carl Jung. *Wisconsin Chippewa Myths and Tales*, edited by Victor Barnouw, contains Trickster cycles with detailed annotation. Other fine collections of trickster stories are *Hopi Coyote Tales*, edited by Ekkehart Malotki and Michael Lomatuway'ma from stories told by Herschel Talashoma, and *Navajo Coyote Tales*, compiled by Berard Haile. Another good collection is William Bright's *Coyote Stories*, which represents over eighteen languages from a variety of southwestern, Mexican, and Northwest Coast tribes.

Oratory

Excellent collections of ritual oratory of the Southwest are *Rainhouse and Ocean: Speeches for the Papago Year*, edited by Ruth Murray Underhill et al., and *Pima and Papago Ritual Oratory*, edited by Donald M. Bahr, which contains a bilingual text. Both have valuable introductions and notes. Many of the speeches made by Indians fluent in English were written. General anthologies, which emphasize oral rather than written speeches, are *I Have Spoken*, edited by Virgina Armstrong, and *Indian Oratory*, edited by W. C. Vanderwerth. Peter Nabokov includes numerous examples in *Native American Testimony*.

Collections of Life Histories
and Autobiographies

Among the collections of tribal oral life histories are *Navajo Stories of the Long Walk Period*, edited by Ruth Roessel; *Stories of Traditional Navajo Life and Culture*, edited by Broderick H. Johnson from tape-recorded accounts; and *The Zunis: Self-Portrayals*, edited and translated by Alvina Quam. The American Indian Lives series of the University of Nebraska Press, edited by A. LaVonne Brown Ruoff, publishes and reprints autobiographies, biographies, and letters. One volume in this series, *I Tell You Now*, edited by Brian Swann and Arnold Krupat, contains contemporary American Indian authors' moving and delightful accounts of growing up Indian and descriptions of their families.

C. Scholarship and Criticism

STUDIES OF ORAL LITERATURES

A recent and informative collection is *Smoothing the Ground*, edited by Swann, which contains sections on context, translation and literary criticism, analyses of narratives, and discussions of autobiography. An excellent discussion of the relationship between anthologies of oral literature and ethnopoetics is Hymes's "Anthologies and Narrators," in which Hymes uses *American Indian Myths and Legends*, compiled by Richard Erdoes and Alfonso Ortiz, as his example of the strengths and weaknesses of such anthologies.

A critical issue that involves all genres of oral literature is translation. A fine introduction to the problems involved in accurate translation is Tedlock's "On the Translation of Style in Oral Narrative," which traces the history of translation and focuses on Zuni examples. Another important study that has stimulated considerable discussion is Hymes's "Some North Pacific Coast Poems," included in his *"In Vain I Tried to Tell You."* Hymes, who provides a helpful summary of the theories of translation used by collectors and anthologists, advocates a mixture of ethnographic and literary analysis. On the other end of the spectrum is Jerome Rothenberg, whose interpretations of American Indian song appear in the controversial *Shaking the Pumpkin*. Rothenberg sets forth his theories of translation in "Total Translation." William Bevis expresses an opposing view in "American Indian Verse Translations." He examines both the careful translations done by linguists and anthropologists and the free rewritings by such poets as William Brandon and Rothenberg, urging readers to use the translations done by recognized ethnologists. Jeffrey Huntsman summarizes the problems of translation in a variety of genres in "Traditional Native American Literature: The Translation Dilemma," and Swann describes the difficulties involved in developing a theory of translation in "A Note on Translation, and Remarks on Collaboration."

Ritual Dramas: Ceremonies and Rituals

Some of the most helpful criticism of the rituals is the scholarly annotation of editions of individual rites. A body of critical scholarship distinct from textual editions is emerging as well. One of the best collections of essays on ceremonies is *Southwestern Indian Ritual Drama*, edited by Charlotte J. Frisbie. Among the most interesting cultural studies of Navajo ceremonies is Katharine Spencer's *Mythology and Values*, which analyzes the Holyway, Evilway, and Lifeway chants. Andrew O. Wiget takes a literary approach in "Sayatasha's Night Chant." Huntsman considers ceremonies and chants as ritual drama in "Native American Theatre." Carter Revard's "Traditional Osage Naming Ceremonies" summarizes the ceremony as edited by Francis

La Flesche and emphasizes the creativity of the Osage who put together the parts of the ceremony.

Songs

A useful general introduction to American Indian songs is Marcia Herndon's *Native American Music*, which examines the subject from the point of view of the cultures that produced it, contrasts Indian and Western European concepts of music, and summarizes ethnomusicological scholarship on American Indian music. Helpful introductions to the field are David P. McAllester's *Readings in Ethnomusicology* and Bruno Nettl's *North American Indian Musical Styles*. A more recent collection of essays on American Indian song is *Traditional Music of North American Indians*, edited by Charlotte Heth.

An excellent regional guide is Frisbie's *Music and Dance Research of Southwestern United States Indians*, which also contains a substantial bibliography. Scholarly editions of song texts also contain useful commentaries. A good example of the modern techniques in collecting Indian music is Alan Merriam's *Ethnomusicology of the Flathead Indians*. Merriam does not include the lyrics of songs, but he does give a thorough analysis of Salish concepts of music and musicianship, types of songs, instruments, and uses of music.

Nettl's *Blackfoot Musical Thought* analyzes the background, fundamentals, history, place of music in human and supernatural societies, and musicianship of that tribe; few songs are included. In *Songprints*, Judith Vander examines the musical experience of five Shoshone women, providing biographies of each woman, information about the history and contexts of the performance of the songs, bilingual lyrics, and musical transcriptions.

Although much of the research on the songs of native peoples of North America has focused on the music, Densmore emphasizes the importance of the content of Indian songs in her "Words of Indian Songs as Unwritten Literature." Subsequent scholars increasingly have paid greater attention to the lyrics of the songs. However, to focus exclusively on the words, as many recent literary critics have tended to do, divorces the lyrics from their musical and cultural contexts. Excellent discussions are Ruth L. Bunzel's "Introduction to Zuni Ceremonialism" and Gladys A. Reichard's *Prayer: The Compulsive Word*. Among the recent, excellent studies examining the relationship of songs to cultural context are *Yaqui Deer Songs*, by Evers and Molina, and *Havasupai Songs*, by Leanne Hinton. The kind of ethnographic and literary analysis Hymes urges is provided by Kathleen Mullen Sands and Emory Sekaquaptewa in "Four Hopi Lullabies" and Donald M. Bahr's "Pima Heaven Songs." The latter examines the interrelation between Pima Papago and Yuman song myths and the Christian influences in these songs; it contains sixteen songs. William K. Powers includes chapters on Lakota song terminology and song texts in his *Sacred Language*.

Narratives

For a historical perspective on the development of critical approaches to American Indian oral literatures, the work of Boas is an excellent starting point. The introductions and commentaries to Boas and Tate's "Tsimshian Mythology" exemplify their belief that oral literatures mirror the cultures of Indian tribes. Boas's emphasis is on the geographic distribution of narratives and delineation of motif types. Many of his essays are collected in *Race, Language and Culture*. His influence on the criticism of American Indian oral narratives is clearly revealed in the works of his disciples that trace the dissemination of narratives and myth motifs, themes, and elements.

Margaret W. Fisher's "Mythology of the Northern and Northeastern Algonkians in Reference to Algonkian Mythology as a Whole" provides a sound introduction to the broad characteristics and distribution of Algonkian oral literature. More specific in focus are Robert H. Lowie's "Test Theme in North American Mythology" and T. T. Waterman's "Explanatory Element in the Folk-Tales of the North-American Indians."

Most of the criticism of oral narratives has been devoted to the examination of themes, elements, or motifs. The analysis of oral literature through the use of motifs is advocated by Stith Thompson in *Narrative Motif-Analysis as a Folklore Method*, and the results of his research appear in his *Motif-Index of Folk-Literature*. A good starting point for the study of motifs is Gladys A. Reichard's "Literary Types and Dissemination of Myths."

Numerous scholars have studied Indian creation myths. Jeremiah Curtin's *Creation Myths of Primitive America* is devoted primarily to those of the California tribes. Anna Birgitta Rooth examines over three hundred such myths in her "Creation Myths of the North American Indians." In "The Emergence Myth in Native North America," Ermine Wheeler-Voegelin and Remedios W. Moore trace the distribution of this myth and its relation to that of migration. Aileen O'Bryan analyzes Navajo origin myths in *The Diné*, and Katharine Spencer discusses the relationship of these narratives to Navajo life in *Reflections of Social Life in the Navaho Origin Myth*. Zolbrod includes a detailed commentary on the Navajo origin myths in his *Diné bahane'*. In *The Spoken Word and the Work of Interpretation*, Dennis Tedlock examines the Zuni origin myth.

The earth-diver motif has also received considerable scholarly attention. Alan Dundes gives a Jungian interpretation of it as an anal-creation story in "Earth Diver." Earl W. Count discusses the connections between the North American and Eurasian versions of the myth in "The Earth-Diver and the Rival Twins." In "The Earth-Diver," Elli Köngäs-Miranda concludes that, though distributed worldwide, the myth always has four traits: earth covered with water, creator, diver, and the creation of the earth. An important study of the ethnographic implications of the Iroquois version of the myth is William N. Fenton's "This Island, the World on Turtle's Back."

In his "Orpheus and Star Husband," Guy E. Swanton discusses the myth's revelation of tribal corporate structure and gives a useful summary of the approaches taken by earlier scholars. Anna H. Gayton's "Orpheus Myth in North America" is an informative guide to the geographic distribution of this narrative. The definitive study of the myth's religious implications is Åke Hultkrantz's *North American Indian Orpheus Tradition*. In his collection of essays on Indian oral literature, *Reading the Fire*, Ramsey includes a perceptive analysis of the meaning and structure of a Nez Perce Orpheus myth.

Thompson's emphasis on a hypothetical archetype and various subarchetypes in "The Star Husband Tale" has stimulated considerable discussion of this narrative. Claude Lévi-Strauss gives a structuralist analysis of Plains Star-Husband tales in *The Origin of Table Manners*, while Dundes takes a morphological approach in *The Morphology of North American Folktales*. George W. Rich suggests in "Rethinking the Star Husbands" that Dundes's approach to the tale's structure is superior to that of Thompson in dealing with variations. In his articles on the narrative, "A Fifth Analysis of the Star Husband Tale" and "Folktales and Social Structure," Frank W. Young provides good summaries and informed criticism of the major theoretical studies, arguing that considerable research is needed to determine links between social organizations and folktales.

Scholars have devoted considerable discussion to the culture hero–trickster-transformer. In *American Hero-Myths*, Daniel G. Brinton surveys the variety of myths in which the culture hero appears. Far more provocative is Boas's classic "Introduction" to "The Traditions of the Thompson Indians of British Columbia," in which he distinguishes three types of culture hero–trickster-transformer: the egocentric, (who may accidentally benefit humankind); a combination of the egocentric and the altruistic; and two separate characters as culture hero (altruistic) and trickster-transformer (egocentric). Radin gives the fullest discussion of the Winnebago trickster-transformer in his commentaries in *The Trickster*. Critics such as Barbara Babcock-Abrahams have increasingly questioned the accuracy of the organization pattern Radin finds in this cycle. Her " 'Tolerated Margin of Mess' " is an invaluable introduction to the trickster as an ambiguous figure whose power derives from his ability to live interstitially, to confuse, and to escape the structures of society. Like Babcock-Abrahams, Mac Linscott Ricketts rejects Radin's Jungian perspective. In "The North American Indian Trickster," Ricketts concludes that the trickster-transformer–culture hero is a complex but unified figure. Useful introductions to the dimensions of the figure in American Indian oral literature are Wiget's "His Life in His Tail" and William Bright's "Natural History of Old Man Coyote," which traces the mythic history of coyote as trickster. Galen Buller also examines the coyote figure in his "Comanche and Coyote, the Culture Maker." Polly Pope discusses the structure of the "Bumbling Host" episodes in trickster stories in her "Toward a Structural Analysis of North American Trickster Tales." In "Encircling Ikto" Julian Rice analyzes the treatment of incest and avoidance in Sioux trickster tales. Examinations of the trickster in specific tribal literatures include Barre Toelken's "Life and Death in the Navajo Coyote Tales," and Howard A. Norman's "Wesucechak Becomes a Deer and Steals Language." Hymes also includes a discussion of a Kalapuya trickster story in "Anthologies and Narrators." (For further scholarship on the trickster, see "General Literary Studies.")

The erotic element in Hopi literature is examined in Ekkehart Malotki's "Story of the 'Tsimonmanant' or Jimson Weed Girls: A Hopi Narrative Featuring the Motif of the Vagina Dentata." This motif, widespread in the Southwest, is frequently part of coyote or trickster stories. Pat Carr and Willard Gingerich also examine this motif in "The Vagina Dentata Motif in Nahuatl and Pueblo Mythic Narratives."

Several studies have discussed motifs and images in Sioux literature. In "Stone Boy," Elaine Jahner demonstrates how the story of this Lakota culture hero provides a starting point for the analysis of the poetics of the folktale. Jahner illustrates in "Cognitive Style in Oral Literature" the symbolic importance of the circle in Lakota narrative. Rice gives a detailed analysis of the importance of the meadowlark in Sioux literature in "How the Bird That Speaks Lakota Earned a Name," in which he argues for an interpretation of Indian oral literature through the restoration of as much of the traditional symbolic context as possible.

Many of the examinations of oral literature in the twentieth century have been influenced by modern psychology. This influence is evident in Benedict's discussion of dreams in her important introduction to *Zuni Mythology*. It is also present in Astrov's introduction to *American Indian Prose and Poetry* and in her "Concept of Motion as the Psychological Leitmotif of Navaho Life and Literature," as well as in the work of Barnouw, Dundes, and Radin.

Other scholars—such as Clyde Kluckhohn, in "Recurrent Themes in Myths and Mythmaking"—have emphasized what Kluckhohn calls "apparently universal elements" in myth. He stresses that the differences in treatment of various themes between cultures and culture areas are as important as the similarities. Lévi-Strauss seeks the meaning of myths by analyzing their Hegelian dialectal structure and developing universal models for this structure; Edmund Leach provides an excellent overview of his theories in *Claude Lévi-Strauss*. In *Morphology of North American Folktales*, Dundes advocates the division of narrative segments into motifeme sequences in order to deal with mythological micro-units.

A good introduction to Melville Jacobs's pioneering work on the expressive content of narrative is his *Pattern in Cultural Anthropology*. Especially important for understanding Jacobs's concepts is *The Content and Style of an Oral Literature*, in which he advocates the examination of oral literature as a total literary event within a tribal setting. He considers oral stories as a form of drama. Hymes, a structuralist who has elaborated on Jacobs's principles, asserts in *"In Vain I Tried to Tell You"* that traditional Chinookan narratives, which he calls "measured verse," possess linguistically marked presentation segments. Hymes applies his principles to the analysis of corrected versions of texts collected by earlier scholars as well as those he has gathered. Basing his own work on that of Hymes, Ramsey has done some interesting analyses of oral narratives in essays published in *Reading the Fire*.

Tedlock's significant work on oral literature differs from that of Jacobs and Hymes in its emphasis on performed, as opposed to dictated or transcribed, texts. In *The Spoken Word and the Work of Interpretation*, he urges that greater attention be paid to spoken performance as a guide to understanding the structure of Indian narratives. Barre Toelken examines the nature of both oral performance and audience response in his essays on Navajo coyote myths, "The 'Pretty Languages' of Yellowman" and "Poetic Retranslation and the 'Pretty Languages' of Yellowman," written with Tacheeni Scott (Navajo). Wiget analyzes Helen Sekaquaptewa's videotaped performance of a Hopi coyote story in "Telling the Tale."

In "North American Indian Mythography," Anthony Mattina takes strong exception to the canonization of the approaches used by Hymes and Tedlock, which excludes other approaches to the presentation of texts. The task of the mythographer, according to Mattina, is to make texts understandable. Mattina also argues for the use of "Red English," which reproduces the language actually used by the Indian narrators. Mattina's edition and translation of *The Golden Woman* is the subject of Karl Kroeber's "Technology and Tribal Narrative." Kroeber suggests that the self-reflexivity of the narrative is thematically functional.

In "Post-Structuralism and Oral Literature," Krupat discusses postmodern theoretical approaches and berates American Indian literature scholars for not using them. Karl Kroeber shows how the critical concepts of Jacques Derrida and J. Hillis Miller are applicable to American Indian trickster-transformer narratives in "Deconstructionist Criticism and American Indian Literature." His *Traditional American Indian Literatures*, contains native texts and critical analyses by Hymes, Ramsey, Tedlock, Toelken, and himself.

The differences between the approaches of the literary critic and the folklorist in analyzing Indian oral narrative are the subject of *Folklore and Literary Criticism: A Dialogue* in the 1981 issue of the *Journal of the Folklore Institute*, which contains an interesting exchange between Kroeber and five folklorists—Sandra Stahl, Elaine Jahner, Barbara Babcock-Abrahams, Dell Hymes, and Barre Toelken. In his "Scarface vs. Scar-face: The Problem of Versions," Kroeber suggests that narrative equivalence be perceived through literary criticism rather than through the examination of formal textual elements. The issue contains the folklorists' response and Kroeber's rebuttal.

Most of the discussions of Indian oratory are included in scholarly texts, described earlier. In "The Plains Indian as Public Speaker," Theodore Balgooyen provides a careful overview of the uses and forms of Plains oratory. In "Chief Seattle's Speech(es): American Origins and European Reception," Rudolf Kaiser gives a thorough examination of the various texts of this famous speech, regarded as a manifesto of ecological feeling and thinking. Kaiser demonstrates that the version popular in Europe bears no resemblance to the two short speeches Chief Seattle gave in 1855.

Studies of Life Histories and Autobiographies

The best general introduction to American Indian life history is *American Indian Autobiography* by H. David Brumble III. Brumble analyzes the attributes and influence of preliterate traditions of American Indian autobiography as well as the role of editors, ghosts, and amanuenses. Among the autobiographers he discusses are Don Talayesva, Gregorio, Sam Blowsnake, Albert Hensley, Charles Eastman, and N. Scott Momaday. Krupat's *For Those Who Come After* examines the literary influences, structure, and role of the editor in several narrated autobiographies, including *Black Elk Speaks*. In *American Indian Women* Gretchen M. Bataille and Sands analyze the development of women's life histories, primarily focusing on narrated autobiographies. They also discuss in detail the role of the editor/transcriber in shaping these life histories. Ruoff traces the influences of the literary traditions of the spiritual confession, missionary reminiscence, and slave narrative on the autobiographies of Apes, Copway, and Winnemucca in "Three Nineteenth-Century American Indian Autobiographers." In *Plains Indian Autobiographies*, Lynne Woods O'Brien briefly surveys the life histories of Indians of those tribes. William F. Smith, Jr., suggests in "American Indian Autobiographies" that most of these works contain a mixture of narrative and cultural essay and provides examples from nine autobiographies. (For a discussion of *Black Elk Speaks*, see "Studies of American Indian Authors.")

Julie Cruikshank's introduction to *Life Lived like a Story*, by Cruikshank, Angela Sidney, Kitty Smith, and Annie Ned, discusses anthropologists' use and interpretation of autobiography.

General Literary Studies

The best overview of American Indian oral and written literatures is Wiget's *Native American Literature*. Two invaluable volumes that contain essays on both oral and written literatures are *Critical Essays on Native American Literature*, edited by Wiget, and *Recovering the Word*, edited by Swann and Krupat. In *Native American Renaissance*, Kenneth Lincoln discusses some oral literatures and gives close readings of the works of such major contemporary authors as N. Scott Momaday (Kiowa), Leslie Silko (Laguna), James Welch (Blackfeet/Gros Ventre), and Louise Erdrich (Ojibwa). *Native American Literature*, edited by Laura Coltelli, contains essays on both oral and written literature. In "Worlds Made of Dawn" Lester Standiford stresses that contemporary imaginative literature is a hybrid based on a blend of traditional native cultures and Anglo-American literature.

The trickster figure in oral and written literature has received some critical attention. Gerald Vizenor uses postmodern theoretical approaches in "Trickster Discourse," an examination of this popular character, whom he calls a "liberator and healer in narrative, a comic sign, communal signification, and a discourse with imagination" (187). In "Trickster," Robert F. Sayre analyzes Indian humor, using as his example the Winnebago cycle in Paul Radin's *The Trickster*.

Several studies address the issue of the canon and of critical approaches to the field. In the chapter "An Approach to Native American Texts," in *For Those Who Come After*, Krupat suggests that poststructuralism offers a way of approaching Native American literature and argues that including native texts in the canon of American literature can "beneficially alter the pedagogical order" of the schools (26). He applies the theories of Frederic Jameson, Jacques Derrida, and others to the analysis of Indian literature.

Ramsey also addresses the issue of the relation of Native American literature to the traditional canon of American literature in "Thoreau's Last Words and America's First Literatures." He points out that although the image of the Indian has influenced many American writers, Native American literature itself has been ignored. According to Ramsey, the current interest in traditional tribal verbal arts has contributed to the development of a new field of literary study, ethnopoetics.

The influence of oral traditions on written literatures has been the subject of several studies. In *The Sacred Hoop*, Allen discusses the influence of ceremony and the medicine wheel on oral and contemporary Indian literature. She also examines the place of Indian women in Native American oral and written literature, giving a personal account of the challenges faced by a mixed-blood writer. Ruoff analyzes the influence of Indian oral narratives on the novels of John Joseph Mathews (Osage), Momaday, Silko, and Vizenor (Ojibwa) in "The Survival of Tradition."

James Ruppert examines the influence of oral traditions on contemporary poets in "The Uses of Oral Tradition in Six Contemporary Nature American Poets." Included in his analysis are Elizabeth Cook-Lynn (Sioux), Maurice Kenny (Mohawk), Peter Blue Cloud (Mohawk), Wendy Rose (Hopi/ Miwok), Liz Sohappy Bahne (Yakima), and Ray A. Young Bear (Mesquakie). In "Mediation and Multiple Narrative in Contemporary Native American Fiction," Ruppert argues that as mediators between oral and written literature and between Indian and non-Indian cultures, American Indian authors create unique artistic structures. His discussion focuses on Momaday, Silko, and Vizenor.

Jeffrey Huntsman surveys American Indian drama in "Native American Theatre," in which he discusses ceremonies and chants as ritual drama and traces the evolution of modern American Indian dramas written to be produced in theaters. Robert F. Sayre provides examples of Indian humor in oral and written literatures in his essay "Trickster."

Many studies focus on the literature written in English. Wiget surveys the history of this literature in *Native American Literature*, as does Ruoff in "Old Traditions and New Forms," which is updated in the present book. Most of these studies have concentrated on twentieth-century literature. Charles R. Larson's *American Indian Fiction* examines novels written since 1899, primarily focusing on plot analysis. Alan R. Velie's *Four American Indian Literary Masters* provides close readings of the works of Momaday, Welch, Silko, and Vizenor. The political dimensions of contemporary native literature are the focus of *Coyote Was Here*, edited by Bo Schöler. Most of the essays are by American Indians.

In "The First Generation of Native American Novelists," Priscilla Oaks surveys the work of Mathews, D'Arcy McNickle (Cree/Salish), and John Oskison (Cherokee) within the context of the literature of the 1930s. William Bevis, in "Native American Novels," discusses the issue of the Indian point of view in the novels of McNickle, Momaday, Silko, and Welch— works, he feels, that emphasize home and humanize nature. Peter G. Beidler traces contemporary Indian authors' use of the animal motif in "Animals and Human Development in the Contemporary American Indian Novel." In "Short Fiction Writers of the Indian Territory," Daniel F. Littlefield, Jr., and James W. Parins carefully analyze short stories written by William Jones (Fox), Alexander Posey (Creek), and Oskison, placing their work in its literary and historical contexts.

Two major volumes of interviews with native writers have been published. *Winged Words*, edited by Laura Coltelli, includes interviews with writers of both fiction and poetry. This volume and *Survival This Way*, edited by Joseph Bruchac, provide additional insights into American Indian writers' lives and opinions. The interviews in *Survival This Way* are with poets and focus on one of the author's poems, which is reprinted.

Studies of American Indian women in literature include Allen's *Sacred Hoop* and Patricia Smith's "Ain't Seen You Since." Smith and Allen examine the use of landscape among Southwestern women writers in "Earthly Relations, Carnal Knowledge." Allen's *Studies in American Indian Literature* contains a section on Indian women's literature.

Indian journalism is the subject of two books: James E. Murphy and Sharon M. Murphy, *Let My People Know*, and Richard Joseph Morris, editor, *Native American Press in Wisconsin and the Nation*.

The career of Carlos Montezuma (Yavapai), an early twentieth-century doctor and national leader of American Indian affairs who founded the newspaper *Wassaja*, is chronicled in Peter Iverson's *Carlos Montezuma*.

STUDIES OF AMERICAN INDIAN AUTHORS

The Boise State University, Idaho, publishes a series of brief but helpful introductions to the lives and works of Indian writers. Among the best are those on McNickle, Momaday, and Ortiz.

Allen, Paula Gunn (Laguna/Sioux). Her work and that of Joy Harjo (Creek) are discussed in James Ruppert's "Paula Gunn Allen and Joy Harjo: Closing the Distance between Personal and Mythic Space." An excellent analysis of Allen's poetry is Elaine Jahner's "Laddered, Rain-Bearing Rug." Kenneth Lincoln gives insights into the themes of her poetry in his introduction to Allen's *Shadow Country.*

Apes, William (Pequot). The best general introduction to Apes is Kim McQuaid's "William Apes, Pequot, an Indian Reformer in the Jackson Era."

Black Elk (Sioux). Essential to understanding *Black Elk Speaks* is Raymond DeMallie's *Sixth Grandfather,* which compares Neihardt's book with the stenographic notes taken by Neihardt's daughter and provides important ethnographic information. Michael Castro also examines Neihardt's role as transmitter in his chapter "Translating Indian Consciousness." In "*Black Elk Speaks* with Forked Tongue," G. Thomas Couser argues that the work speaks out of both sides of its mouth because it conflates two consciousnesses (in this case, cultures and languages), in one undifferentiated voice and deceives because it does not fully acknowledge the extent and tendencies of its editing. Julian Rice's "*Akicita* of the Thunder" discusses the ethnographic significance of horses in Black Elk's vision. *A Sender of Words: Essays in Memory of John G. Neihardt,* edited by Vine Deloria, Jr., contains many essays on *Black Elk Speaks.*

Copway, George (Ojibwa). The only biographical study of Copway is Donald B. Smith's "Life of George Copway or Kah-ge-ga-gah-bowh (1818–1869)—and a Review of His Writings." In this detailed, authoritative account, Smith pinpoints Copway's deviations from fact in his works and discusses the works in the context of Indian-white relations. Ruoff discusses the literary influences on Copway's *Life, Letters and Speeches* in "George Copway: Nineteenth-Century American-Indian Autobiographer." In "Know-Nothings and Indians: Strange Bedfellows?" Dale T. Knobel examines the relationship between Copway and members of this American political movement who supported his work.

Eastman, Charles A. (Sioux). Raymond Wilson surveys Eastman's life and career in his biography *Ohiyesa: Charles Eastman, Santee Sioux.* David R. Miller supplements this work in "Charles Alexander Eastman, the 'Winner.' " One of the few examinations of Eastman as a writer is Anna L. Stensland's informative "Charles Alexander Eastman," which analyzes Eastman's treatment of history in his stories and biographical portraits.

Erdrich, Louise (Ojibwa). Lillian Brewington, Normie Bullard, and Robert W. Reising have compiled "Writing in Love: An Annotated Bibliography of Critical Responses to the Poetry and Novels of Louise Erdrich and Michael Dorris," which includes interviews, articles, and reviews. Erdrich's *Love Medicine* has been the subject of several studies. In " 'Her Laugh an Ace," William Gleason argues that the unifying vision of Erdrich's novel is redemption, accomplished through an expert and caring use of humor. James McKenzie emphasizes in "Lipsha's Good Road Home" that critics and readers have mistakenly read the novel as an anthropological document instead of a tribute to the Chippewa culture's ability to nourish a small band of people who were neither exterminated nor utterly dissolved in a melting pot.

In "Opening the Text" Robert Silberman examines how *Love Medicine* moves away from the narrow focus of earlier works of fiction toward the historical novel and family saga.

Johnson, Emily Pauline (Mohawk). Johnson's life and work have received considerable attention. The standard biography is Betty Keller's *Pauline*, which contains a good bibliography. Ruoff's introduction to *The Moccasin Maker* contains additional information about Johnson's family and examines the relationship between this collection and women's literature of the period; the volume has a substantial bibliography of works by and about Johnson. Additional discussion of Johnson's life and work is contained in Mrs. W. Garland (Anne) Foster, *The Mohawk Princess*, and Walter McRaye, *Pauline Johnson and Her Friends* and *Town Hall To-night*.

La Flesche, Francis (Omaha). In "Francis La Flesche," Margot Liberty gives a brief overview of the writer's life and career. A view of La Flesche's father and other relatives is presented in Norma Kidd Green's *Iron Eye's Family*.

Long, Sylvester (Lumbee). The definitive biography of Long is Donald Smith's *Long Lance, the True Story of an Impostor*; an abbreviated account is in Smith's "From Sylvester Long to Chief Buffalo Child Long Lance."

McNickle, D'Arcy (Cree/Salish). What little work has as yet been published on McNickle is mostly by James Ruppert, whose *D'Arcy McNickle* provides a good overview of the writer's life and work. In "Textual Perspectives and the Reader in *The Surrounded*" Ruppert uses the novel to illustrate Wolfgang Iser's view on the way fiction differs from ordinary discourse. Ruppert argues that criticism of McNickle's work has lacked insight into the dynamic relation between the four textual perspectives (implied author, plot, characters, and implied reader) and the meaning of the text the reader takes away from the novel. In "Politics and Culture in the Fiction of D'Arcy McNickle" Ruppert compares *Wind from an Enemy Sky* to *The Surrounded* and *Runner in the Sun* and discusses the relation between the novels and the author's definition of culture expressed in *They Came Here First*. The writer's novels are the subject of Louis Owen's " 'Map of the Mind.' "

Mathews, John Joseph (Osage). The fullest biography of Mathews is "Osage Oxonian," by Terry P. Wilson. Carol Hunter examines the Osage backgrounds of *Sundown* in "The Historical Context in John Joseph Mathews' *Sundown*" and "The Protagonist as a Mixed-Blood in John Joseph Mathews's Novel *Sundown*." Ruoff's "John Joseph Mathews's *Talking to the Moon*" analyzes how Mathews combines Osage traditions with the literary techniques derived from his reading of Thoreau and John Muir.

Momaday, N. Scott (Kiowa). The best introduction to Momaday's work is Matthias Schubnell's *N. Scott Momaday*, which particularly emphasizes the non-Indian literary influences on Momaday and includes an extensive bibliography of his publications. Momaday's conversations with Charles L. Woodard are collected in *Ancestral Voice*, by Woodard, which is illustrated by Momaday's paintings and drawings. Martha Scott Trimble gives a brief overview of Momaday's life and work in *N. Scott Momaday*.

The only book-length study of *The House Made of Dawn* is Susan Scarberry-Garcia's *Landmarks of Healing*, which examines Momaday's incorporation of pueblo stories and Navajo chantways. Scarberry-Garcia focuses on his use of the twins motif, animal transformers (especially the bear), and Navajo concepts of healing. Excellent interpretations of *House Made of Dawn* are contained in Larry Ever's "Words and Place" and Floyd Watkins, "Culture versus Anonymity in *House Made of Dawn*." Paula Gunn Allen, in "Bringing Home the Fact," discusses the novel as an act of imagination designed to heal, while Linda Hogan traces Momaday's use of Indian oral tradition in this novel in "Who Puts Together." Momaday's novel is also the subject of Bernard Hirsch's "Self-Hatred and Spiritual Corruption in *House Made of Dawn*." Karl Kroeber argues in "Technology and Tribal Literature" that Momaday invents imaginatively to evoke an "Indianness" for his readers through an Anglo-American literary structure that must prohibit any authentically Indian creative form. Instead he relies on a sense of place and defines the recovery of Indian identity as stemming from an identification with physical locale.

Lincoln gives an especially good analysis of *The Way to Rainy Mountain* in *Native American Renaissance*. His "Tai-Me to Rainy Mountain" traces the evolution of the *Journey to Tai-me* to *The Way to Rainy Mountain* through an examination of the correspondence of Momaday, his publisher, and the press's readers. Especially helpful for teachers is *Approaches to Teaching*

Momaday's The Way to Rainy Mountain, edited by Kenneth Roemer, which includes essays on backgrounds, structure, themes, and teaching the text in composition and literature courses.

Mourning Dove [Christine Quintasket] (Colville). The fullest biography and discussion of her writing are Jay Miller's introduction to *Mourning Dove: A Salishan Autobiography* and his "Mourning Dove: The Author as Cultural Mediator." Dexter Fisher's introduction to *Cogewa* provides a brief overview. Alanna Brown, in "Mourning Dove's Voice in *Cogewea*," distinguishes between Mourning Dove's and Lucullus Virgil McWhorter's contributions to the novel. This topic is also the subject of Mary Dearborn's chapter "Pocahontas's Sisters" in her *Pocahontas's Daughters.*

Occom, Samson (Mohegan). The two standard biographies are *Samson Occom and the Christian Indians of New England,* by W. Deloss Love, and the more recent *Samson Occom,* by Harold Blodgett. Love's biography contains some letters and materials not found elsewhere. Leon Burr Richardson describes Occom's journey to England in *An Indian Preacher in England,* which includes Occom's letters and sections of his diaries as well as letters from the Reverend Nathaniel Whitaker and Eleazar Wheelock.

Ortiz, Simon (Acoma). Wiget's *Simon Ortiz* is a fine survey of his work. Also valuable is Patricia Smith's "Coyote Ortiz: *Canis latrans latrans* in the Poetry of Simon Ortiz," which traces his use of the coyote as trickster-transformer. William Gingerich examines the influence of Ortiz's tribal roots on his work in "The Old Voices of Acoma."

Pokagon, Simon (Potawatomi). There is little literary discussion of Pokagon. The romantic biographical accounts of Pokagon in Cecelia Buechner's *Pokagons* and David H. Dickason's "Chief Simon Pokagon: 'The Indian Longfellow' " are contradicted in James A. Clifton's "Simon Pokagon and the Sand-Bar Case."

Posey, Alexander L. (Creek) Leona G. Barnett, in *"Este Cate Emunkv*: Red Man Always," and Doris Callacombe, in "Alexander Lawrence Posey," trace Posey's life and career. The "Journal of Alexander Lawrence Posey with Annotations," by Edward Everett Dale, provides insights into Posey's life and work, as does Poesy's "Journal of Creek Enrollment Field Party, 1905."

Ridge, John Rollin (Cherokee). The fullest discussion of Ridge's life and work is James W. Parins's *John Rollin Ridge* (1991). Earlier accounts can be found in Angie Debo, "John Rollin Ridge"; Carolyn Thomas Foreman, "Edward W. Bushyhead and John Rollin Ridge, Cherokee Editors in California"; and Franklin Walker, *San Francisco's Literary Frontier.* Joseph Henry

Jackson's *Anybody's Gold* and Remi Nadeau's *Real Joaquín Murieta* describe the evolution of the Murieta legend.

Riggs, [Rolla] Lynn (Cherokee). Thomas Erhard's *Lynn Riggs; Southwest Playwright* retraces Riggs's life and career. More recently, Phyllis Cole Braunlich's *Haunted by Home: The Life and Letters of Lynn Riggs* authoritatively examines the author's life and career, quoting copiously from his letters.

Rogers, Will (Cherokee). Rogers's complete works are being edited by Joseph A. Stout, Jr., for Oklahoma State University Press. Important studies on Rogers include William R. Brown, *The Imagemaker*, and Donald Day, *Will Rogers: A Biography*. *Will Rogers: A Centennial Tribute*, edited by Arrell M. Gibson, contains Blue Clark's "The Literary Will Rogers" and a bibliographic essay.

Rose, Wendy (Hopi/Miwok). Kenneth Lincoln analyzes Rose's *Lost Copper* and discusses the relationship of her poetry to contemporary Indian literature in "Finding the Loss."

Silko, Leslie Marmon (Laguna). A brief but good introduction to Silko's work is Per Seyersted's *Leslie Marmon Silko*. Her novel *Ceremony* is the subject of a special 1979 issue of the *American Indian Quarterly* (edited by Kathleen Mullen Sands), which contains a number of useful essays. In "The Psychological Landscape of *Ceremony*," Allen emphasizes that the healing of the protagonist, Tayo, and the land results from the reunification of the person and the land. Allen incorporated this study into her *Sacred Hoop*. Elaine Jahner, in "An Act of Attention," suggests that events in the novel mark the stages of life for the protagonist. In "Circular Design in *Ceremony*," Robert C. Bell traces Silko's use of the Navajo Red Antway ceremony in the novel. Lincoln's *Native American Renaissance* also contain good analyses of *Ceremony*. Robert Nelson argues in "Place and Vision" that the "interior landscape" of the protagonist's consciousness is both attuned to the pattern of the culture he must reenter and congruent with the terrain of the external world. In "Laguna Symbolic Geography and Silko's *Ceremony*" and "Healing via the Sunwise Cycle in Silko's *Ceremony*," Edith Swan gives a detailed analysis of Silko's use of Laguna and other Indian traditions. James Ruppert, in "The Reader's Lessons in *Ceremony*," discusses Silko's blending of poetry and prose, which reflect the epistemological unity of Laguna narrative aesthetic and world view.

Ruoff examines the Keres influences on Silko's short fiction in "Ritual and Renewal." In "The Devil's Domain: Leslie Silko's 'Storyteller,'" Kathryn Shanley Vangen argues that Silko restores the mute ground of the Alaskan native in her short story at the same time she creates a protagonist who can and does find a way to tell her story. James Ruppert discusses

Silko's use of oral tradition in "Story Telling." In "*Storyteller*: Grandmother Spider's Web," Linda Danielson suggests that Silko expresses her unified revision of the world from her vantage point as a Laguna woman, which reinforces her belief in the centrality of the tribe, the significance of the ordinary lives of men and women, and the values arising from the female power of the primary Keresan deities.

Smith, Martin Cruz (Senecu del Sur/Yaqui). Peter Beidler, in his "Indians in Martin Cruz Smith's *Nightwing*," examines Smith's treatment of this subject and reviews the book.

Vizenor, Gerald (Ojibwa). The most comprehensive study of Vizenor's writing is Ruoff's "Woodland Word Warrior," which surveys Vizenor's work in a variety of genres and traces recurrent themes; it also contains a lengthy, selective bibliography. The *American Indian Quarterly* devoted its Winter 1985 issue (ed. Terry Wilson and Robert Black) to essays on Vizenor's work. Two postmodernist discussions of Vizenor's *Darkness in Saint Louis Bearheart* are Alan Velie's "Trickster Novel" and Louis Owens's " 'Ecstatic Strategies.' "

Welch, James (Blackfeet/Gros Ventre). Welch's *Winter in the Blood* was the subject of a 1978 issue of *American Indian Quarterly* (edited by Peter Beidler), which includes Sand's fine essay "Alienation and Broken Narrative." Ron McFarland has edited *James Welch*, a collection of essays on the author's work. The volume includes Ruoff's revised "Alienation and the Female Principle in *Winter in the Blood*," with a note on ethnohistorical backgrounds, and Sand's perceptive "*Death of Jim Loney*: Indian or Not." The volume also contains a bibliography of Welch's works. Peter Wild gives a brief survey of Welch's writing in *James Welch*. William Thackeray's "Crying for Pity in *Winter in the Blood*" analyzes the novel in terms of the Gros Ventre concept of an age-graded society and the "Crying for Pity Ceremony." His "Animal Allies and Transformers of *Winter in the Blood*" examines Welch's use of animals and of mythology.

In "James Welch's Poetry," Alan Velie discusses the author's use of surrealism and the influence of James Wright and Cesar Vallejo, the Peruvian poet, on Welch's work.

Winnemucca, Sarah [Hopkins] (Paiute). The best biography is Gae Whitney Canfield's *Sarah Winnemucca of the Northern Paiutes*, which examines her life and the ethnohistory of her tribe in detail and has an excellent bibliography. Catharine S. Fowler's "Sarah Winnemucca" is a short biography.

Zitkala-Ša [Gertrude Bonnin] (Sioux). A good overview of the life and works of Zitkala-Ša is Fisher's introduction to her *American Indian Stories*.

Teaching American Indian Literatures

Indispensable for teachers is *Studies in American Indian Literature*, edited by Allen, which includes critical essays, course designs, and an extensive bibliography. A brief introduction to issues in teaching American Indian literature is the special issue of the *Association of Departments of English Bulletin* 75 (1983), which includes Ramsey, "American Indian Literature and American Literature"; Evers, "Continuity and Change in American Indian Oral Literature"; and Ruoff, "Teaching American Indian Authors, 1772–1968." The importance of teaching Indian literatures from a multidisciplinary approach and of understanding their ethnohistorical contexts is stressed by Ramsey in "The Teacher of Modern American Indian Writings as Ethnographer and Critic" and Michael A. Dorris in "Native American Literature in an Ethnohistorical Context." Both Dorris's article and Ramsey's "A Supplement to Michael Dorris's 'Native American Literature' " contain substantial bibliographies. The only book published thus far on teaching an individual Indian author is *Approaches to Teaching Momaday's The Way to Rainy Mountain*, edited by Roemer, discussed earlier.

Backgrounds

Biography

At present there is no bibliography of Indian biography, although biographical volumes are to be included in the current revision of *Handbook of North American Indians*, edited by William C. Sturtevant. The standard nineteenth-century source of Indian biographies is Samuel G. Drake's *Indian Biography, Containing the Lives of More than Two Hundred Chiefs* (1832), which was republished in numerous reprints and revisions with variant titles. Much of this information was incorporated by B. B. Thatcher in *Indian Biography* (1832).

Early in the twentieth century, Charles Eastman published *Indian Heroes and Great Chieftains* (1918). One of Eastman's best works, the book is a series of portraits of Indian leaders, primarily Sioux, based on information conveyed to Eastman by the subjects or by those who knew them. *Great North American Indians*, complied by Frederick J. Dockstader, contains short biographies, of varying degrees of accuracy, of three hundred Indians; the bibliography gives many biographical sources. Several Indian authors are included in this volume and in *American Indian Intellectuals*, edited by Margot Liberty. Biographies of Indian chiefs and political leaders are contained in *American Indian Leaders*, edited by R. David Edmunds, which covers the period from the mid-eighteenth century to the present, and in *Indian Lives: Essays on Nineteenth and Twentieth Century Native American Leaders*, edited by L. G. Moses and Raymond Wilson. *Being and Becoming Indian*, edited by

James A. Clifton, focuses on biographical essays about the sense of identity among mixed-bloods and contains Clifton's essay "Alternate Identities and Cultural Frontiers." For discussions of collections of biographies of Indian women, see "Women's Studies" below.

Demography

The best general introduction to the issues involved in Indian demography is Henry Dobyns's *Their Number Become Thinned*, which contains and excellent introductory essay coauthored with William R. Swagerty. In *American Indian Holocaust and Survival* Russell Thornton chronicles the decimation of the native population in the U.S. since contact; it explores the tribes' ability to withstand the slaughter and examines why Indian populations have grown in the twentieth century.

Ethnohistory

The University of Oklahoma's Civilization of the American Indian series has published an extensive number of tribal histories. The following discussion touches on only some of the general ethnohistories and several of those written by American Indians. An excellent reference for additional histories is the bibliographic essay "Part II. History and Historical Sources" by Michael A. Dorris in *Guide to Research on North American Indians*, complied by Hirschfelder, Byler, and Dorris. Also excellent, but unannotated, are Prucha's *A Bibliographical Guide* and *Indian-White Relations*.

Robert Bieder's *Science Encounters the Indian, 1820–1880* is a good starting point for understanding the evolution of ethnological approaches to the study of American Indians. A fine introduction of the Indian tribes of various areas is Edward H. Spicer's *The American Indians*, which also contains chapters on urban Indians and federal policies toward Native Americans. *The Native Americans*, by Robert F. Spencer, Jesse D. Jennings, et al., provides a general background in American Indian ethnology. Also helpful is *Native American Heritage*, by Merwyn S. Garbarino. Underhill's *Red Man's America* analyzes Indian societies from the Stone Age to the present, using materials from archaeology, ethnology, and history.

Among the best general histories of Indian-white relations are Arrell Morgan Gibson's *The American Indian: Prehistory to the Present*, Angie Debo's *History of the Indians of the United States*, and William T. Hagan's *American Indians*. Debo's book is especially strong in its treatment of the southeastern tribes; Hagan's short history is better in its discussion of the period from contact to 1900 than of the twentieth century.

Edward H. Spicer's *Cycles of Conquest* is the best account of Indian-white relations in the Southwest from 1533 to 1960. In *The Invasion of America* Francis Jennings gives a carefully researched description of the devastation inflicted on native populations by the immigrating Europeans.

Jennings's book is particularly valuable for its treatment of the impact on New England Indians. Debo has written a number of excellent histories of Oklahoma and southeastern Indians. *The Indian and the White Man*, edited by Wilcomb E. Washburn, contains a good collection of documents and pictures. A valuable selection of essays designed for both the scholar and the general reader is *Indians in American History*, edited by Frederick E. Hoxie.

Two popular works that contain some bibliographic references are Dee Brown's *Bury My Heart at Wounded Knee*, a historical account told from the Indian viewpoint, and Dale Van Every's *Disinherited*; the latter focuses on Indian-white relations in the East.

Native Americans have written and edited many books on Indian-white relations and histories of their tribes, which are discussed in part 1. Nineteenth-century authors include William Apes (Pequot), George Copway (Ojibwa), Peter Jones (Ojibwa), William Whipple Warren (Ojibwa), Peter Dooyentate Clarke (Wyandot), Chief Elias Johnson (Tuscarora), David Cusick (Tuscarora), John Rollin Ridge (Cherokee), and Chief Andrew J. Blackbird (Ottawa). Among the twentieth-century writers are Charles Eastman (Sioux), John Milton Oskison (Cherokee), and John Joseph Mathews (Osage).

A major figure in the development of Native American history written from an Indian perspective is D'Arcy McNickle (Cree/Salish). Most of McNickle's books are histories: *They Came Here First* (1949); *The Indian Tribes of the United States* (1962); *Indians and Other Americans*, with Harold E. Fey (1970); and *Native American Tribalism* (1973). The latter is a fine history that is especially good on issues affecting Indians since 1900.

Vine Deloria, Jr. (Sioux), has written numerous studies of Indian-white political and legal issues, including *Behind the Trail of Broken Treaties* (1974); *American Indians and American Justice* (1983) and *The Nations Within: The Past and Present Future of Indian Sovereignty* (1984), both written with Clifford M. Lytle; and *American Indian Policy in the Twentieth Century* (1985).

A well-documented account of the cultural and legal practices that resulted in the ambiguities of modern Indian policy is "The Grass Still Grows, the Rivers Still Flow," by Michael Dorris (Modoc).

Languages

Excellent works on Indian languages are *American Indian Linguistics and Literature*, by William Bright; *Native Languages of the Americas*, edited by Thomas Sebeok; "Indian Linguistic Families of America North of Mexico," by John Wesley Powell; and *Handbook of American Indian Languages*, edited by Boas.

Philosophy and Religion

Familiarity with the world views of North American Indians is important in understanding both oral and written literatures. Because sacred oral literature is so closely interwoven into the fabric of traditional Indian religious life, it is difficult to distinguish between literature and religion. The best general introduction is Sam Gill's *Native American Religions*, a comparative study that provides clear descriptions and explanations of the American Indian concepts of the universe. The most comprehensive comparative analysis of American Indian religions is Hultkrantz's *Religions of the American Indians*, based on a Judeo-Christian world view that sometimes distorts Indian traditions. The volume is divided into a section on tribal religions, which delineates general concepts in American Indian religions, and one entitled "Religions of the American High Culture," which focuses on the religion of the Incas, Mayans, and Aztecs. Hultkrantz uses an evolutionary approach in his discussion of the religions of "high" or "nuclear" cultures. The bibliography is a good guide to the field. Underhill provides a sound general survey in *Red Man's Religion*.

In addition to *Native American Religions*, Gill has published two more recent studies of the field. *Native American Religious Action* is a collection of essays that elaborate his belief that, whereas historians of religion focus on texts, American Indians perform their religion; to neglect the performative element, Gill emphasizes, is to overlook the orality of Indian cultures. Less successful is *Mother Earth*, in which Gill argues that the widely held notion that American Indians have always believed in a goddess, Mother Earth, is in error; such a belief, Gill asserts, was not found until Anglo-Americans arrived and taught it to Indians.

Two volumes designed for the general audience and including insightful essays on traditional and current religious movements and world views are *Teachings from the American Earth*, edited by Dennis Tedlock and Barbara Tedlock, and *Seeing with a Native Eye*, edited by Walter Holden Capps.

Most of the tribal histories written by Indians and cited above contain sections on Indian worldviews and religions, as do autobiographies and collections of oral literatures. A fine scholarly study of Tewa oral traditions is *The Tewa World* (1969) by Alfonso Ortiz (San Juan). Ortiz combines anthropological perspectives and Tewa oral traditions to elucidate the dualism present in the beliefs of his tribe. Other Indian authors have used different approaches. One of the first Indians to write a book on Indian religion was Charles Eastman (Sioux), whose *The Soul of the Indian* (1911) is his most fully developed statement of his concept of Indian ethics. Eastman's work is designed to present to a general audience a pan-Indian description of religion, based on a Sioux model. More recently, Vine Deloria, Jr. (Sioux), has written two volumes on Indian religion. In *God Is Red* (1973) Deloria forcefully contrasts American Indian and Judeo-Christian worldviews, which he outlines in broad strokes and presents with satiric wit. More scholarly in tone is *The Metaphysics of Modern Existence* (1979), in which he suggests that the new metaphysics can be based on the kinds of worldviews tribal societies have espoused. This provocative study is stronger in its interpretation of tribal beliefs than in its analysis of modern non-Indian religious and philosophical thought.

Numerous studies of the religions of specific tribes are available. A fine examination of the Sioux is Joseph Epes Brown's *Sacred Pipe*, based on Black Elk's account of the seven rites of this pipe. William K. Powers has written several excellent studies of Sioux religion: *Oglala Religion* gives a detailed survey of the structural and symbolic relationships between such areas as myth, ritual, and social organization of the Oglala; *Yuwipi: Vision and Experience in Oglala Ritual* explains similar relationships among three rituals—the vision quest, sweat lodge, and Yuwipi (a modern curing ritual); *Sacred Language* examines the nature of supernatural discourse in Lakota and includes a chapter on song texts.

Peter Powell has done an extensive study of Cheyenne religion in his two-volume *Sweet Medicine*. Volume 1 treats the history of Cheyenne ceremonialism as it was affected by contact with other Indians and with whites; volume 2 explores rituals and presents myths and songs. Ruth Landes's *Ojibwa Religion and the Midéwiwin*, a major study of that religion, describes the procedures and myths associated with its ceremony.

Though criticized by some Pueblo people, Elsie C. Parsons's *Pueblo Indian Religion* is an important guide to that group's beliefs. Hamilton Tyler has prepared several volumes that popularize Pueblo mythology: *Pueblo Birds and Myths*, *Pueblo Animals and Myths*, and *Pueblo Gods and Myths*. Essential to understanding Navajo religious practices and beliefs are Gladys A. Reichard's *Navaho Religion* and Gill's *Sacred Words*. Karl W. Luckert, who has written many excellent books on Navajo religious beliefs and ceremonies, edits the series American Tribal Religions, University of Nebraska Press.

Women's Studies

In her introductory essay to the bibliography *Native American Women*, Rayna Green reviews popular and scholarly writings about Indian women. *The Sacred Hoop*, by Paula Gunn Allen, is a personal starting point for studying the place of women in Indian society and literature. In the first section of the book, Allen argues that the role of Indian women has been subverted or ignored by non-Indians. A careful anthropological and ethnohistorical approach to the topic is *The Hidden Half*, edited by Patricia Albers and Beatrice Medicine, which contains a fine collection of studies of Indian women. An important discussion of the leadership role played by Indian women is Carolyn Thomas Foreman's *Indian Women Chiefs*. In *Yaqui Women* Jane Holden Kelley explores the lives of four women as a means of understanding the role of women in that culture. Also excellent is Marla N. Powers's *Oglala Women*, which examines women's roles, duties, and pleasures as well as the sacred and secular representations of their life cycle. For collections of writings by and about Indian women, see the discussion of anthologies.

Image of the Indian

Authors and critics in the United States have long been fascinated by the image of the Native American. Indeed, far more study has been devoted by literary scholars to this image in American literature than to Native American literature itself. The most influential study is Roy H. Pearce's *Savagism and Civilization*. Published earlier as *The Savages of America*, this classic work examines the impact of the image of the Indian on American literature from 1609 to 1851. Also good is Albert Keiser's *Indian in American Literature*. William J. Scheick analyzes the treatment of the mixed-blood in popular fiction written by non-Indians in *The Half-Blood: A Cultural Symbol in the 19th Century American Fiction*.

A broad but excellent study by Robert F. Berkhofer, Jr., is *The White Man's Indian*, an examination of the development of whites' perceptions of Indians that determined their behavior toward the natives of the New World. The book contains a section on literature. In *Regeneration through Violence* Richard Slotkin emphasizes the cultural anxieties expressed in accounts of Indian wars of the colonial period and of the mythical hero Daniel Boone of the early Republic. Richard Drinnon, in analyzing the impact of whites' attitudes toward nonwhites in *Facing West*, describes how these attitudes fostered white imperialism in the United States, the Philippines, and Vietnam. *Beyond Geography*, by Frederick W. Turner III, is an imaginative treatment that traces the philosophical origins of Western European worldviews and examines their impact on Native American peoples.

Several books deal with Indian stereotypes. Eugene Jones explores the image of Indians in dramas written by whites in his *Native Americans as Shown on the Stage, 1753–1916*; he concludes that these characterizations masked whites' fear of Indians as obstacles to the fulfillment of their desire to settle in the New World. The study includes a checklist of plays and other theater works featuring American Indian characters, 1658–1982. *The Pretend Indians*, edited by Gretchen Bataille and Charles L. P. Silet, reprints essays on Indian stereotypes in myth and media and on images of the Indian in American films. Vine Deloria, Jr., also treats the subject of Indian stereotypes in *Custer Died for Your Sins* (see "American Indian Authors").

As this introduction to Indian literature and bibliographic review of works about the subject indicates, much research remains to be done on oral literatures and written literature from 1772 to 1967. Anthropologists and linguists have undertaken most of the work on oral literatures, while literary scholars have devoted their energies primarily to the study of contemporary written literature. Additional literary scholarship is needed to provide authoritative texts of oral and written literatures and criticism that are multidisciplinary in their approach, utilizing the techniques and knowledge of ethnohistory, linguistics, and literature.

Part Three

A Selected Bibliography of American Indian Literatures

Abbreviations of Frequently Cited Works

AA	*American Anthropologist*
AICRJ	*American Indian Culture and Research Journal*
AIQ	*American Indian Quarterly*
AL	*American Literature*
APAMNH	Anthropological Papers of the American Museum of Natural History
ARBAE	Annual Report of the Bureau of American Ethnology
BBAE	Bulletin of the Bureau of American Ethnology
CE	*College English*
CO	*Chronicles of Oklahoma*
CUCA	Columbia University Contributions in Anthropology
IJAL	*International Journal of American Linguistics*
JAF	*Journal of American Folklore*
JFI	*Journal of the Folklore Institute*
MAAA	*Memoirs of the American Anthropological Association*
MAFS	*Memoirs of the American Folklore Society*
MAMNH	Memoirs of the American Museum of Natural History
PAES	Publications of the American Ethnological Society
SAIL	*Studies in American Indian Literatures*
SFQ	*Southern Folklore Quarterly*
WAL	*Western American Literature*

A. Bibliographies and Research Guides

Bataille, Gretchen M., and Charles L. P. Silet. *Images of American Indians on Film: An Annotated Bibliography.* New York: Garland, 1985.

Beidler, Peter G., and Marion F. Egge, comps. *The American Indian in Short Fiction: An Annotated Bibliography.* Metuchen: Scarecrow, 1979.

Brumble, H. David, III, comp. *An Annotated Bibliography of American Indian and Eskimo Autobiographies.* Lincoln: U of Nebraska P, 1981.

———. "A Supplement to *An Annotated Bibliography of American Indian and Eskimo Autobiographies.*" *WAL* 17 (1982): 243–60. Expanded in *American Indian Autobiography.* Berkeley: U of California P, 1988. 211–57.

Clements, William M., and Frances M. Malpezzi, comps. *Native American Folklore, 1879–1979: An Annotated Bibliography.* Athens: Swallow, 1984.

Colonnese, Tom, and Louis Owens (Cherokee), comps. *American Indian Novelists: An Annotated Critical Bibliography.* New York: Garland, 1985.

Etulain, Richard W., comp. *A Bibliographical Guide to the Study of Western American Literature.* Lincoln: U of Nebraska P, 1982.

Green, Rayna (Cherokee), comp. *Native American Women: A Contextual Bibliography.* Newberry Library Center for History of the American Indian. Bibliography. Bloomington: Indiana UP, 1983.

Handbook of American Indians North of Mexico. Ed. Frederick W. Hodge. 2 vols. Washington: GPO, 1907–10. New York: Rowan, 1970; St. Clair Shores: Scholarly, 1971; Westport: Greenwood, 1971.

Handbook of North American Indians. Ed. William C. Sturtevant. Rev. ed. Washington: Smithsonian Institution. 20 vols. in progress. *Arctic.* Ed. David Damas. Vol. 5 (1984). *California.* Ed. Robert F. Heizer. Vol. 8 (1978). *Great Basin.* Ed. Warren D'Azevedo. Vol. 11 (1986). *Northeast.* Ed. Bruce G. Trigger. Vol. 15 (1978). *Subarctic.* Ed. June Helm. Vol. 6 (1981). *Southwest.* Ed. Alfonso Ortiz. Vol. 9 (1979): Pueblo; Vol. 10 (1983): Non-Pueblo.

Heard, Norman J. comp. *The Southeastern Woodlands.* Vol. 1 of *Handbook of the American Frontier: Four Centuries of Indian-White Relationships.* Native American Resources 1. Metuchen: Scarecrow, 1987.

Hirschfelder, Arlene B., Mary Gloyne Byler (Cherokee), and Michael A. Dorris (Modoc), comps. *Guide to Research on North American Indians.* Chicago: American Library Assn., 1983.

Kroeber, A. L., comp. *The Handbook of Indians of California.* ARBAE 78 (1925). Berkeley: California Book Co., 1953.

Littlefield, Daniel F., Jr. (Cherokee), and James W. Parins, comps. *American Indian and Alaska Native Newspapers and Periodicals, 1826–1924.* Westport: Greenwood, 1984.

———, comps. *A Biobibliography of Native American Writers, 1772–1924.* Native American Bibliography 2. Metuchen: Scarecrow, 1981.

———, comps. *A Biobibliography of Native American Writers, 1772–1924: A Supplement.* Native American Bibliography 5. Metuchen: Scarecrow, 1985.

Marken, Jack, comp. *The American Indian: Language and Literature.* Goldentree Bibliographies. Arlington Heights: AHM, 1978.

Murdock, George P. *Ethnographic Bibliography of North America.* 4th ed., rev. Timothy J. O'Leary. 5 vols. New Haven: Human Relations Area Files, 1975.

Prucha, Francis P., comp. *A Bibliographical Guide to the History of Indian-White Relations in the United States.* Chicago: U of Chicago P, 1977.

———, comp. *Indian-White Relations in the United States: A Bibliography of Works Published 1975–1980.* Lincoln: U of Nebraska P, 1982.

Ruoff, A. LaVonne Brown. "American Indian Literatures: A Guide to Anthologies, Texts, and Research." Allen, *Studies in American Indian Literature* 281–309.

———. "American Indian Literatures: An Introduction and Bibliography." *American Studies International* 24.2 (1986): 2–52.

Slapin, Beverly, and Doris Seale, comps. *Books without Bias: Through Indian Eyes.* 2nd enl. ed. Berkeley: Oyate, 1988.

Stensland, Anna, comp. *Literature by and about the American Indian: An Annotated Bibliography.* 2nd ed., with Aune M. Fadum. Urbana: NCTE, 1979.

———. *Literature by and about the American Indian: An Annotated Bibliography for Junior and Senior High School Students.* Urbana: NCTE, 1973.

Thompson, Stith. *Motif-Index of Folk-Literature: A Classification of Narrative Elements in Folk-Tales, Ballads, Myths, Fables, Medieval Romances, Exempla, Fabliaux, Jest-Books and Local Legends.* 2nd ed., rev. and enl. 6 vols. Bloomington: Indiana UP, 1955–58.

Wiget, Andrew O. "Native American Literature: A Bibliographic Survey of American Indian Literary Traditions." *Choice* June 1986: 1503–12.

B. Anthologies, Collections, and Re-creations

ANTHOLOGIES

Included here are anthologies containing both oral and written literatures and those containing only written literatures. Collections of oral literatures are listed under that category.

Allen, Paula Gunn (Laguna/Sioux), ed. *Spider Woman's Granddaughters: Traditional Tales and Contemporary Writing by Native American Women.* Boston: Beacon, 1989.

Bartlett, Mary Dougherty, ed. *The New Native American Novel: Works in Progress.* Albuquerque: U of New Mexico P, 1986.

Brandt, Beth (Mohawk), ed. *A Gathering of the Spirit: North American Indian Women's Issue.* Spec. issue of *Sinister Wisdom* 22–23 (1983): 1–223.

Bruchac, Joseph (Abenaki), ed. *Songs from This Earth on Turtle's Back: Contemporary American Indian Poetry.* Greenfield Center: Greenfield Review, 1983.

Chambers, Leland H., ed. *Native American Literature.* Spec. issue of *Denver Quarterly* 14 (1980): 1–112.

Dauenhauer, Nora (Tlingit), Richard Dauenhauer, and Gary Holthaus, eds. *Alaska Native Writers, Storytellers and Orators.* Spec. issue of *Alaska Quarterly Review* 4.3–4 (1986). Also available is Patricia H. Partnow, *Teacher's Guide.* (Anchorage: Alaska Humanities Forum, 1988).

Day, David, and Marilyn Bowering, eds. *Many Voices: An Anthology of Contemporary Canadian Indian Poetry.* Vancouver: Douglas, 1977.

Erdoes, Richard, and Alfonso Ortiz (San Juan), eds. *American Indian Myths and Legends.* New York: Pantheon, 1984.

Evers, Larry, ed. *The South Corner of Time: Hopi, Navajo, Papago, Yaqui Tribal Literature.* Sun Tracks 6. Tucson: U of Arizona P, 1980.

Fisher, Dexter [Alice Poindexter], ed. *The Third Woman: Minority Women Writers of the United States.* Boston: Houghton, 1980.

Gedalof, Robin [McGrath], ed. *Paper Stays Put: A Collection of Inuit Writing.* Edmonton: Hurtig, 1980.

Green, Rayna (Cherokee), ed. *That's What She Said: Contemporary Poetry and Fiction by Native American Women.* Bloomington: Indiana UP, 1984.

Highwater, Jamake, ed. *Words in the Blood: Contemporary Indian Writers of North and South America.* New York: NAL, 1984.

Hill, Roberta (Oneida), and Brian Swann, eds. *Native American Issue.* Spec. issue of *Shantih* 4 (1979): 1–68.

Hobson, Geary (Cherokee), ed. *The Remembered Earth: An Anthology of Contemporary Native American Literature.* 1979. Albuquerque: U of New Mexico P, 1981.

Hogan, Linda (Chickasaw), ed. *Native American Women.* Spec. issue of *Frontiers* 6 (1981): 1–133.

Jahner, Elaine, ed. *American Indians Today: Their Thought, Their Literature, Their Art.* Spec. issue of *Book Forum* 5 (1981): 310–432.

Katz, Jane B. *I Am the Fire of Time: The Voices of Native American Women.* New York: Dutton, 1977.

King, Thomas (Cherokee), ed. *An Anthology of Canadian Native Fiction.* Spec. issue of *Canadian Fiction Magazine* 60 (1987).

Milton, John R., ed. *The American Indian Speaks.* Vermillion: Dakota P, 1969. Pub. simultaneously as spec. issue of *South Dakota Review* 7 (1969).

———, ed. *American Indian II.* Vermillion: Dakota P, 1971. Pub. simultaneously as spec. issue of *South Dakota Review* 9 (1971).

Nabokov, Peter, ed. *Native American Testimony: An Anthology of Indian and White Relations: First Encounter to Dispossession.* Preface Vine Deloria, Jr. (Sioux). New York: Crowell, 1978. Harper, 1979. Primarily oratory.

Niatum, Duane (Klallam), ed. *Carriers of the Dream Wheel: Contemporary Native American Poetry.* Native American Ser. San Francisco: Harper, 1975.

———. *Harper's Anthology of 20th Century Native American Poetry.* New York: Harper, 1988.

Ortiz, Simon J. (Acoma), ed. *Earth Power Coming: Short Fiction in Native American Literature.* Tsaile: Navajo Community College Press, 1983.

Petrone, Penny, ed. *First People, First Voices.* Toronto: U of Toronto P, 1983.

———. *Northern Voices: Inuit Writing in English.* Toronto: U of Toronto P, 1988.

Peyer, Bernd, ed. *The Elders Wrote: An Anthology of Early Prose by North American Indians, 1768–1931.* Berlin: Dietrich Reimer, 1982.

———, ed. *The Singing Spirit: Early Short Stories by North American Indians.* Tucson: U of Arizona P, 1989.

Rosen, Kenneth, ed. *The Man to Send Rain Clouds: Contemporary Stories by American Indians.* New York: Viking, 1974.

———, ed. *Voices of the Rainbow: Contemporary Poetry by American Indians.* New York: Viking, 1975.

Sanders, Thomas E. (Cherokee), and Walter W. Peek (Narragansett/Wampanoag), eds. *The Literature of the American Indian.* New York: Glencoe, 1973.

Turner, Frederick W., iii, ed. *The Portable North American Indian Reader.* New York: Viking, 1974.

Velie, Alan R., ed. *American Indian Literature: An Anthology.* Norman: U of Oklahoma P, 1979.

COLLECTIONS AND RE-CREATIONS
OF ORAL LITERATURE

Armstrong, Virginia, ed. *I Have Spoken: American History through the Voices of the Indians.* Introd. Frederick W. Turner iii. Athens: Swallow-Ohio UP, 1971.

Astrov, Margot, ed. *American Indian Prose and Poetry.* New York: Capricorn, 1962.

Previously pub. as *The Winged Serpent: An Anthology of American Indian Poetry* (1946).

Bahr, Donald M. *Pima and Papago Ritual Oratory: A Study of Three Texts.* San Francisco: Indian Historian, 1975.

Barbeau, Marius, ed. *Huron and Wyandot Mythology.* Canadian Geological Survey Museum Bull. Anthropological Ser. 11 (1915).

————, ed. *Huron-Wyandot Traditional Narratives in Translations and Native Texts.* Anthropological Ser. 50. Bull. National Museum of Canada 165 (1960).

Barnouw, Victor, ed. *Wisconsin Chippewa Myths and Tales and Their Relation to Chippewa Life.* Madison: U of Wisconsin P, 1977.

Beavert, Virginia, project dir. (Yakima). *The Way It Was, Inaku Iwacha: Yakima Legends.* Yakima: Franklin, 1974.

Benedict, Ruth F., ed. *Tales of the Cochiti Indians.* 1931. Introd. Alfonso Ortiz (San Juan). Albuquerque: U of New Mexico P, 1981.

————, ed. *Zuni Mythology.* CUCA 21 (1935). Rpt. 2 vols. New York: AMS, 1969.

Bierhorst, John, ed. *Four Masterworks of American Indian Literature.* 1974. Tucson: U of Arizona P, 1984.

————, ed. *The Red Swan: Myths and Tales of the American Indians.* New York: Farrar, 1976.

————, ed. *The Sacred Path: Spells, Prayers and Power Songs of the American Indians.* New York: Morrow, 1983.

Bingham, Sam, and Janet Bingham, eds. *Between Sacred Mountains: Navajo Stories and Lessons from the Land.* Tucson: U of Arizona P, 1982.

Black Bear, Ben, Sr. (Sioux), and Ron D. Theisz, eds. *Songs and Dances of the Lakota.* Rosebud: Sinte Gleska College Press, 1976.

Bloomfield, Leonard, ed. *Menomini Texts.* PAES 12 (1928). New York: AMS, 1974.

Boas, Franz, ed. *Keresan Texts.* 2 vols. PAES 8 (1928). New York: AMS, 1974.

————, ed. *Kwakiutl Culture as Reflected in Mythology.* MAFS 28 (1935). Millwood: Kraus, 1970.

————, ed. *Kwakiutl Tales.* 2 (1910). New York: AMS, 1969.

————, ed. *Kwakiutl Tales. New Series, Part I. Translations.* CUCA 26.1 (1935).

————, ed. *Kwakiutl Tales. New Series, Part II.* CUCA 26.2 (1943).

————, ed. *Tsimshian Texts.* BBAE 27 (1902). St. Claire Shores: Scholarly, 1977.

Boas, Franz, and George Hunt, eds. "Kwakiutl Texts." MAMNH 5 (1902): 1–270.

————, eds. "Kwakiutl Texts." 2nd ser. MAMNH 14.1 (1906): 1–269.

Boas, Franz, and Henry W. Tate, eds. "Tsimshian Mythology." ARBAE 31 (1909 –10): 29–1037. New York: Johnson, 1970.

Boyd, Maurice, ed. *Kiowa Voices.* Vol. 1. *Ceremonial Dance, Ritual and Song.* Vol. 2. *Myths, Legends and Folktales.* Fort Worth: Texas Christian UP, 1981–83.

Brandon, William, ed. *The Magic World: American Indian Songs and Poems.* New York: Morrow, 1970.

Bright, William, ed. *Coyote Stories.* IJAL Native American Texts 1. Chicago: U of Chicago P, 1978.

Bullchild, Percy (Blackfeet). *The Sun Came Down: The History of the World as My Blackfeet Elders Told It.* Native American Ser. San Francisco: Harper, 1985.

Bunzel, Ruth L., ed. "Zuni Origin Myths." ARBAE 47 (1929–30): 545–609.

————, ed. "Zuni Ritual Poetry." ARBAE 47 (1929–30): 611–835.

————, ed. *Zuni Texts.* PAES 15 (1933). New York: AMS, 1974.

Cameron, Anne, comp. *Daughters of Copper Woman.* Vancouver: Press Gang, 1981.

Clutesi, George (Tlingit). *Son of Raven, Son of Deer: Fables of the Tse Shat People.* Illus. Clutesi. Sidney, BC: Gray's, 1975.

Cornplanter, Jesse (Seneca). *Legends of the Longhouse.* 1938. Iroquois Reprints. Ohswehen: Irografts, 1986.

Courlander, Harold, ed. *Hopi Voices: Recollections, Traditions, and Narratives of the Hopi Indians.* Albuquerque: U of New Mexico P, 1982.

Cronyn, George W., ed. *The Path on the Rainbow: An Anthology of Songs and Chants from the Indians of North America.* Introd. Mary Austin. New York: Liveright, 1918. Repub. enl., as *American Indian Poetry: The Standard Anthology of Songs and Chants.* New York: Liveright, 1934, 1970.

Curtin, Jeremiah, ed. *Creation Myths of Primitive America in Relation to the Religious History and Mental Development of Mankind.* 1898. New York: Bloom, 1969. New York: Arno, 1980.

Curtin, Jeremiah, and J. N. B. Hewitt (Tuscarora), ed. "Seneca Fiction, Legends, and Myths." ARBAE 32 (1911): 37–813.

Curtis, Natalie Burlin, ed. *The Indians' Book: Songs and Legends of the American Indians.* 1907. 2nd ed. 1923. New York: Dover, 1968.

Day, A. Grove, ed. *The Sky Clears: Poetry of the American Indians.* 1951. Lincoln: U of Nebraska P, 1964.

Deloria, Ella C. (Sioux), ed. *Dakota Texts.* PAES 17 (1932). New York: AMS, 1974. Ed. Agnes Picotte (Sioux) and Paul N. Pavich. Vermillion: Dakota P, 1978. The latter omits the Sioux texts.

Densmore, Frances, ed. *Chippewa Music.* BBAE 45 (1910). Millwood: Kraus, n.d.

———, ed. *Chippewa Music, II.* BBAE 53 (1913). Millwood: Kraus, n.d.

———, ed. *Chippewa Music.* Music Reprint Ser. 2 vols. New York: Da Capo, 1972.

———, ed. *Menominee Music.* BBAE 102 (1932).

———, ed. *Papago Music.* BBAE 90 (1929). Music Reprint Ser. New York: Da Capo, 1972.

———, ed. *Pawnee Music.* BBAE 93 (1929). Music Reprint Ser. New York: Da Capo, 1972

———, ed. *Teton Sioux Music.* BBAE 61 (1918). Music Reprint Ser. New York: Da Capo, 1972. Saint Claire Shores: Scholarly, 1977.

———, ed. *Yuman and Yaqui Music.* BBAE 110 (1932). Music Reprint Ser. New York: Da Capo, 1972.

Dixon, Roland. "Shasta Myths." *JAF* 23 (1910): 8–37.

Dorsey, George A., ed. *The Pawnee Mythology.* Pub. of the Carnegie Inst. (1906). New York: AMS, 1974.

Eastman, Charles A. (Sioux), and Elaine Goodale Eastman. *Wigwam Evenings: Sioux Folktales Retold.* Boston: Little, 1909. Repub. as *Smoky Day's Wigwam Evenings: Indian Stories Retold.* Boston: Little, 1910.

Evers, Larry, and Felipe S. Molina (Yaqui). *Yaqui Deer Songs/Maso Bwikam: A Native American Poetry.* Sun Tracks 14. Tucson: U of Arizona P, 1987.

Fletcher, Alice C., ed. "The Hako: A Pawnee Ceremony." ARBAE 22.2 (1900–01): 5–368.

———, ed. See also La Flesche, Francis.

Goddard, Pliney E., ed. "Myths and Tales from the San Carlos Apache." APAMNH 24.1 (1918). New York: AMS, 1980.

Griffis, Joseph (Osage). *Indian Circle Stories.* Burlington: Free Press, 1928.

Grinnell, George Bird. *Blackfoot Lodge Tales*. 1892. Lincoln: U of Nebraska P, 1962.

———. *By Cheyenne Campfires*. 1926. Lincoln: U of Nebraska P, 1971.

———. *Pawnee Hero Stories and Folk Tales: With Notes on the Origin, Customs, and Character of the Pawnee People*. 1889. Introd. Maurice Frink. Lincoln: U of Nebraska P, 1961.

———. *The Punishment of Stingy and Other Indian Stories*. 1901. Introd. Jarold W. Ramsey. Lincoln: U of Nebraska P, 1982.

Haile, Berard, O.F.M., ed. *Navajo Coyote Tales: The Curly Tó Aheedlíinii Version*. American Tribal Religions 8. Ed. with introd. Karl W. Luckert. Lincoln: U of Nebraska P, 1984.

———, ed. *Origin Legend of the Navaho Flintway*. Publications in Anthropology and Linguistics 38. Chicago: U of Chicago P, 1943. New York: AMS, 1978.

———, ed. *The Upward Moving and Emergence Way: The Gishin Biyè Version*. American Tribal Religious 7. Lincoln: U of Nebraska P, 1981.

———. *Waterway*. American Tribal Religions 5. Lincoln: U of Nebraska P, 1979.

———. *Women versus Men: A Conflict of Navajo Emergence: The Curly Tó Aheedlíinii Version*. Ed. Karl W. Luckert. American Tribal Religions 6. Lincoln: U of Nebraska P, 1982.

Hale, Horatio, ed. *The Iroquois Book of Rites*. 1883. Ed. with introd. William N. Fenton. Toronto: U of Toronto P, 1963.

Hewitt, John N. B. (Tuscarora), ed. "Iroquoian Cosmology, First Part." ARBAE 21 (1899–1900): 127–339.

———, ed. "Iroquoian Cosmology, Second Part: With Introduction and Notes." ARBAE 43 (1925–26): 449–819.

———. *Iroquoian Cosmology*. 2 pts. in 1. Rpt. vols. above. New York: AMS, 1974.

Hilbert, Vi (Lushootseed), trans. and ed. *Haboo: Native American Stories from Puget Sound*. Foreword and introd. Thom Hess. Seattle: U of Washington P, 1985.

Hinton, Leanne. *Havasupai Songs: A Linguistic Perspective*. Ars Linguistica 6. Tubingen: Narr, 1984.

Hinton, Leanne, and Lucille J. Watahomigie (Hualapai), eds. *Spirit Mountain: An Anthology of Yuman Story and Song*. Sun Tracks 10. Tucson: U of Arizona P, 1984.

Jacobs, Melville, ed. *Clackamas Chinook Texts*. 2 vols. Indiana U Research Center in Anthropology, Folklore, and Linguistics Pub. 8 and 11. Bloomington: Indiana UP, 1958–59.

———. *The Content and Style of an Oral Literature: Clackamas Chinook Myths and Tales*. Chicago: U of Chicago P, 1959.

———. *The People Are Coming Soon: Analyses of Clackamas Chinook Myths and Tales*. Seattle: U of Washington P, 1960.

Johnson, Elias (Tuscarora). *Legends, Traditions and Laws of the Iroquois or Six Nations, and History of the Tuscarora Indians*. 1881. New York: AMS, 1978.

Johnson, Emily Pauline (Mohawk). *Legends of Vancouver*. 1911. Vancouver: McClelland, 1912, 1961.

Jones, William (Fox), ed. *Fox Texts*. Ed. Franz Boas. PAES 1 (1907). New York: AMS, 1978.

———, ed. *Ojibwa Texts*. Ed. Truman Michelson. PAES 7.1 (1917); 7.2 (1919).

Kilpatrick, Jack Frederick, and Anna Gritts Kilpatrick (Cherokee), eds. *Friends of Thunder: Folktales of the Oklahoma Cherokees*. Dallas: Southern Methodist UP, 1964.

———, eds. *Run toward the Nightland: Magic of the Oklahoma Cherokees*. Dallas: Southern Methodist UP, 1967.

———, eds. *Walk in Your Soul: Love Incantations of the Oklahoma Cherokees*. Dallas: Southern Methodist UP, 1965.

Klah, Hosteen (Navajo), and Mary C. Wheelwright. *Navaho Creation Myth: The Story of Emergence*. 1942. New York: AMS, 1977.

Kroeber, A. L., ed. "Gros Ventre Myths and Tales." APAMNH 1.3 (1907): 55–139.

———, ed. *Yoruk Myths*. Berkeley: U of California P, 1976.

Kroeber, Theodora. *The Inland Whale*. Foreword Oliver La Farge. Bloomington: Indiana UP, 1959.

La Flesche, Francis (Omaha), ed. "The Osage Tribe." ARBAE. "Rites of the Chiefs." 36 (1914–15): 37–597. New York: Johnson, 1970. "Rite of Vigil." 39 (1917–18): 31–630. "Two Versions of the Child-Naming Rite." 43 (1925–26): 23–164. "Rite of Wa-x'be." 45 (1927–28): 523–833.

La Flesche, Francis (Omaha), and Alice C. Fletcher, eds. "The Omaha Tribe." ARBAE 27 (1905–06): 17–642. Rpt. as 2 vols. New York: Johnson, 1970. Lincoln: U of Nebraska P, 1972.

———. "A Study of Omaha Indian Music." *Papers of the Peabody Museum* 1.5 (1893): 1–152.

Lankford, George E., comp. and ed. *Native American Legends. Southeastern Legends: Tales from the Natchez, Caddo, Biloxi, Chickasaw, and Other Nations*. Introd. W. K. McNeil. American Folklore. Little Rock: August House, 1987.

La Pointe, James (Sioux). *Legends of the Lakota*. San Francisco: Indian Historian, 1976.

Lewis, Richard. *I Breathe a New Song: Poems of the Eskimo*. Introd. Edmund Carpenter. New York: Simon, 1971.

Lowenstein, Tom, trans. *Eskimo Poems from Canada and Greenland*. Poetry Ser. Pittsburgh: U of Pittsburgh P, 1973.

Lowie, Robert H., ed. "Myths and Traditions of the Crow Indians." APAMNH 25.1 (1918). New York: AMS, 1974.

Luckert, Karl, ed. *Coyoteway: A Navajo Healing Ceremony*. Tucson: U of Arizona P, 1979.

———, ed. *A Navajo Bringing-Home Ceremony: The Claus Chee Sonny Version of Deerway Ajilee*. American Tribal Religions 3. Lincoln: U of Nebraska P, 1978.

———, ed. *The Navajo Mountain and Rainbow Bridge Religion*. American Tribal Religions 1. Lincoln: U of Nebraska P, 1977.

Malotki, Ekkehart, and Michael Lomatuway'ma (Hopi), eds. *Hopi Coyote Tales/Istutuwutsi*. 1978. American Tribal Religions 9. Lincoln: U of Nebraska P, 1984.

———. *Maasaw: Profile of a Hopi God*. American Tribal Religions 11. Lincoln: U of Nebraska P, 1987.

———. *Stories of Maasaw, a Hopi God*. American Tribal Religions 10. Lincoln: U of Nebraska P, 1987.

Malotki, Ekkehart, and Herschel Talashoma (Hopi). *Hopitutuwutsi: Hopi Tales*. Sun Tracks 9. Tucson: U of Arizona P, 1983.

Marriott, Alice, and Carol K. Rachlin, eds. *American Indian Mythology*. New York: Crowell, 1968.

Matthews, Washington, ed. "The Mountain Chant: A Navajo Ceremony." ARBAE 5 (1883–84): 379–467. Glorieta: Rio Grande, 1971.

————, ed. *Navaho Legends.* MAFS 5 (1897). Millwood: Kraus, 1969.

————, ed. "The Night Chant, a Navajo Ceremony." MAMNH 6 (1902). New York: AMS, 1974.

Mattina, Anthony, and Madeline de Sautel (Colville), trans. *The Golden Woman: The Colville Narrative of Peter J. Seymour.* Tucson: U of Arizona P, 1985.

McAllester, David P., and Susan W. McAllester. *Hogans: Navajo Houses and House Songs.* Middletown: Wesleyan UP, 1980.

McClintock, Walter. *The Old North Trail: or Life, Legends and Religion of the Blackfeet Indians.* 1910. Lincoln: U of Nebraska P, 1965.

Mooney, James, ed. "Myths of the Cherokee." ARBAE 19.1 (1897–98): 3–575. St. Claire Shores: Scholarly, 1970.

Morgan, William (Navajo), Robert W. Young, and Hildegard Thompson. *Coyote Tales.* Washington: Bureau of Indian Affairs, 1949.

Morrisseau, Norval (Ojibwa). *Legends of My People, the Great Ojibway.* Ed. Selwyn H. Dewdney. Toronto: Ryerson, 1965.

Mourning Dove [Christine Quintasket] (Colville). *Coyote Stories.* [Ed. Heister Dean Guie.] Notes by Lucullus Virgil McWhorter. Foreword Chief Standing Bear (Sioux). 1933. New York: AMS, 1977.

————. *Tales of the Okanogans.* Ed. Donald M. Hines. Fairfield: Ye Galleon, 1976.

Nelson, Edward W. *The Eskimo about Bering Strait.* ARBAE 18 (1896–97). New York: Johnson, 1971.

Nequatewa, Edmund (Hopi). *Truth of a Hopi: Stories Relating to the Origin, Myths, and Clan Histories of the Hopi.* 1936. Flagstaff: Northland, 1967.

Norman, Howard A., comp. and trans. *The Wishing Bone Cycle: Narrative Poems from the Swampy Cree Indians.* Preface Jerome Rothenberg. 1972. Rev. and exp. Santa Barbara: Ross-Erickson, 1982.

O'Bryan, Aileen, ed. *The Diné Origin Myths of the Navaho Indians.* BBAE 163 (1956).

Oman, Lela Kiana (Putu/Noorvik). *Eskimo Legends.* 2nd ed. Anchorage: Alaska Methodist UP, 1975.

Parker, Arthur C. (Seneca), ed. *Seneca Myths and Folktales.* Publication Ser. 27. Buffalo Hist. Soc. (1923). New York: AMS, 1978.

Parsons, Elsie C., ed. *Tewa Tales.* MAFS 19 (1926). Millwood: Kraus, 1971.

Phinney, Archie (Nez Perce), ed. *Nez Percé Texts.* CUCA 25 (1934). New York: AMS, 1969.

Radin, Paul, ed. *The Trickster: A Study in American Indian Mythology.* 1956. Commentaries by Karl Kerényi and Carl G. Jung. New introd. Stanley Diamond. New York: Schocken, 1972.

Ramsey, Jarold W., ed. *Coyote Was Going There: Indian Literature of the Oregon Country.* Seattle: U of Washington P, 1977.

Rothenberg, Jerome, ed. *Shaking the Pumpkin: Traditional Poetry of the Indian North Americas.* Garden City: Doubleday, 1972.

Sapir, Edward, and Jeremiah Curtin, eds. *Wishram Texts, Together with Wasco Tales and Myths.* PAES 2 (1909). New York: AMS, 1974.

Saxton, Dean, and Lucille Saxton, eds. *O'othham Hoho'ok A'agitha: Legends and Lore of the Papago and Pima Indians.* Tucson: U of Arizona P, 1973.

Schoolcraft, Henry Rowe. *Algic Researches, Comprising Inquiries Respecting the Mental Characteristics of the North American Indians.* 2 vols. 1839. New York: Garland, 1979.

————. *The Myth of Hiawatha, and Other Oral Legends, Mythologic and Allegoric, of the North American Indians.* 1856. Millwood: Kraus, 1971.

Schultz, James Willard. *Why Gone Those Times? Blackfoot Tales.* Ed. Eugene Lee Silliman. Civilization of the American Indian 127. Norman: U of Oklahoma P, 1973.

Skinner, Alanson, and John V. Satterlee (Menominee), eds. "Folklore of the Menomini Indians." APAMNH 13 (1915): 217–557. New York: AMS, 1977.

Slickpoo, Allen P., Sr. (Nez Perce), et al., comp. *Nu Mee Poom Tit Wah Tit (Nez Perce Legends).* Lawai: Nez Perce Tribe, 1972.

Spinden, Herbert J., ed. and trans. *Songs of the Tewa.* 1933. Santa Fe: Sunstone, 1976.

Standing Bear, Luther [Ota K'te] (Sioux). *Stories of the Sioux.* 1934. Lincoln: U of Nebraska P, 1988.

Stirling, Matthew W., ed. *Origin Myth of Acoma and Other Records.* BBAE 135 (1942). Saint Claire Shores: Scholarly, n.d.

Swanton, John R. "Tlingit Myths and Texts." BBAE 39 (1904–05).

Tedlock, Dennis, trans. *Finding the Center: Narrative Poetry of the Zuni Indians.* Lincoln: U of Nebraska P, 1972.

————, trans. *Popol Vuh: The Mayan Book of the Dawn of Life.* New York: Simon, 1985.

Theisz, Ron D., ed. *Buckskin Tokens: Contemporary Oral Narratives of the Lakota.* Rosebud: Sinte Gleska College Press, 1975.

Thompson, Stith, ed. *Tales of the North American Indians.* 1929. Bloomington: Indiana UP, 1966.

Turner, Frederick W., III, ed. *The Portable North American Indian Reader.* New York: Viking, 1974.

Underhill, Ruth Murray. *Singing for Power: The Song Magic of the Papago Indians of Southern Arizona.* 1938. Berkeley: U of California P, 1976.

Underhill, Ruth Murray, et al., eds. *Rainhouse and Ocean: Speeches for the Papago Year.* 1979. American Tribal Religions 4. Lincoln: U of Nebraska P, 1981.

Vanderwerth, W. C., ed. *Indian Oratory: Famous Speeches by Noted Indian Chieftains.* 1971. Foreword William R. Carmack. Civilization of the American Indian 110. Norman: U of Oklahoma P, 1979.

Vaudrin, Bill (Ojibwa), ed. *Tanaina Tales from Alaska.* Introd. Joan B. Townsend. Civilization of the American Indian 96. Norman: U of Oklahoma P, 1969.

Vizenor, Gerald. *Summer in the Spring: Ojibwa Lyric Poems and Tribal Stories.* Minneapolis: Nodin, 1981. Reprints *Anishinabe Adisokan: Tales of the People* (Minneapolis: Nodin, 1970) and *Anishinabe Nagamon: Songs of the People* (Minneapolis: Nodin, 1965; rev. 1970).

Walker, Bertrand N. O. [Hen-toh] (Wyandot). *Tales of the Bark Lodges.* Oklahoma City: Harlow, 1920.

Walker, James R. *Lakota Myth.* Ed. Elaine A. Jahner. Lincoln: U of Nebraska P, 1983.

Welsch, Roger, ed. *Omaha Indian Myths and Trickster Tales.* Athens: Ohio UP, 1981.

White, Leslie A., ed. "The Acoma Indians." ARBAE 47 (1929–30): 17–192. New preface. New foreword by the author. Glorieta: Rio Grande, 1973.

Wissler, Clark, and D. C. Duvall (Blackfeet), eds. "Mythology of the Blackfoot Indians." APAMNH 2.1 (1908). New York: AMS, 1975.

Wyman, Leland C., ed. *Blessingway.* Tucson: U of Arizona P, 1970.

———. *The Red Antway of the Navaho.* Navajo Religion 5. Santa Fe: Museum of Navajo Ceremonial Art, 1965.

Yazzie, Ethelou (Navajo), ed. *Navajo History.* 1 vol. Many Farms: Navajo Community College Press, 1971.

Zepeda, Ofelia (Papago), ed. *Mat Hekid O Ju: O'odham Ha-Cegitodag/When It Rains: Papago and Pima Poetry.* Sun Tracks 7. Tucson: U of Arizona P, 1982.

Zitkala-Ša [Gertrude Bonnin] (Sioux). *Old Indian Legends, Retold by Zitkala-Ša.* 1901. Glorieta: Rio Grande, 1976. Introd. Agnes Picotte (Sioux). Lincoln: U of Nebraska P, 1985.

Zolbrod, Paul G. *Diné bahane': The Navajo Creation Story.* Albuquerque: U of New Mexico P, 1984.

Collections of Life Histories
and Autobiographies

Cruikshank, Julie, Angela Sidney, Kitty Smith, and Annie Ned. *Life Lived like a Story: Stories of Three Yukon Native Elders.* American Indian Lives. Lincoln: U of Nebraska P, 1991.

Johnson, Broderick H., ed. *Stories of Traditional Navajo Life and Culture.* Tsaile: Navajo Community College Press, 1977.

Kelley, Jane Holden. *Yaqui Women: Contemporary Life Histories.* Lincoln: U of Nebraska P, 1978.

Quam, Alvina, ed. and trans. *The Zunis: Self-Portrayals.* Albuquerque: U of New Mexico P, 1972. New York: NAL, 1974.

Roessel, Ruth H., ed. *Navajo Stories of the Long Walk Period.* Tsaile: Navajo Community College Press, 1973.

Swann, Brian, and Arnold Krupat, eds. *I Tell You Now: Autobiographical Essays by Native American Writers.* American Indian Lives. Lincoln: U of Nebraska P, 1987. Short autobiographies by Paula Gunn Allen (Laguna/Sioux), Jim Barnes (Choctaw), Joseph Bruchac (Abenaki), Barney Bush (Shawnee/Cayuga), Elizabeth Cook-Lynn (Sioux), Jimmy Durham (Cherokee), Jack Forbes (Powhatan/Delaware/Saponi), Diane Glancy (Cherokee), Joy Harjo (Creek), Linda Hogan (Chickasaw), Maurice Kenny (Mohawk), Duane Niatum (Klallam), Simon Ortiz (Acoma), Carter Revard (Osage), Wendy Rose (Hopi/Miwok), Ralph Salisbury (Cherokee), Mary Tall Mountain (Athabascan), Gerald Vizenor (Ojibwa).

C. American Indian Authors

Narrated life histories are designated by *; for these narratives and autobiographies, the name of the author is given first, followed by the name(s) of the collaborator(s). For additional works by Indian authors, see sects. B, E, and F. Chapbooks of poetry that have been incorporated into collected works are not listed separately.

Allen, Paula Gunn (Laguna/Sioux). *Shadow Country.* Foreword Kenneth Lincoln. Native American Ser. Los Angeles: U of California P, 1982. Poetry.

―――. *Skins and Bones: Poems 1979–87*. Albuquerque: West End, 1988. Poetry.

―――. *The Woman Who Owned the Shadows*. San Francisco: Spinster's Ink, 1983. Fiction.

―――. *Wyrds*. San Francisco: Taurean Horn, 1987. Poetry.

*Anauta (Eskimo). Heluiz Chandler Washburne. *Land of the Good Shadows: The Life Story of Anauta, an Eskimo Woman*. New York: Day, 1940. Autobiography.

Apes, William (Pequot). *Eulogy on King Philip, as Pronounced at the Odeon, in Federal Street, Boston, by the Rev. William Apes, an Indian*. Boston: Author, 1836. Non-fiction.

―――. *The Experience of Five Christian Indians of the Pequod Tribe or, An Indian's Looking-Glass for the White Man*. Boston: Dow, 1833. Repub. as *Experience of Five Christian Indians, of the Pequod Tribe*. 2nd ed. Boston: Printed for the Publisher, 1837. Biographies, autobiography, and nonfiction.

―――. *A Son of the Forest: The Experience of William Apes, a Native of the Forest, Comprising a Notice of the Pequod Tribe of Indians*. New York: Author, 1829. Repub. as *A Son of the Forest: The Experience of William Apes, a Native of the Forest*. 2nd ed., rev. and cor. New York: Author, 1831. Autobiography.

Arnett, Carroll (Cherokee). *Tsalagi: Poems*. New Rochelle: Elizabeth, 1976. Poetry.

Aupaumut, Hendrick (Mohegan). *A Narrative of an Embassy to the Western Indians, from the Original Manuscript of Hendrick Aupaumut, with Prefatory Remarks by Dr. B. H. Coates*. Pennsylvania Hist. Soc. Mem. 2.1 (1827): 61–131. Autobiography.

Barnes, Jim (Choctaw). *The American Book of the Dead*. Urbana: U of Illinois P, 1982. Poetry.

―――. *The Fish on Poteau Mountain*. Fort Wayne: Cedar Creek, 1980. Poetry.

―――. *La Plata Cantata: Poems*. West Lafayette: Purdue UP, 1989. Poetry.

―――. *A Season of Loss: Poems*. West Lafayette: Purdue UP, 1985. Poetry.

―――. *This Crazy Land*. Inland Boat Ser. Tempe: Porch, 1980. Poetry.

Bedford, Denton R. (Munsee). *Tsali*. San Francisco: Indian Historian, 1972. Fiction.

Bennett, Kay (Navajo). *Kaibah: Recollections of a Navajo Girlhood*. Los Angeles: Western Lore, 1964. Autobiography.

*Betzinez, Jason (Apache). Wilbur Sturtevant Nye. *I Fought with Geronimo*. 1959. Lincoln: U of Nebraska P, 1987. Autobiography.

*Black Elk (Sioux). John G. Neihardt. *Black Elk Speaks*. 1932. Introd. Vine Deloria, Jr. Lincoln: U of Nebraska P, 1979. New York: Washington Square, 1972. Autobiography.

*Black Hawk (Sauk). Antoine Le Claire and John B. Patterson. *Black Hawk, an Autobiography*. 1833. Ed. with new introd. Donald Jackson. Urbana: U of Illinois P, 1955. Autobiography.

*Blacksnake (Seneca). Benjamin Williams (Seneca). *Chainbreaker*. Ed. Thomas Abler. American Indian Lives. Lincoln: U of Nebraska P, 1989. Autobiography.

*Blowsnake, Sam [Big Winnebago and Crashing Thunder] (Winnebago). Paul Radin. *The Autobiography of a Winnebago Indian*. 1926. Foreword and appendix Arnold Krupat. Lincoln: U of Nebraska P, 1983. Autobiography.

Blue Cloud, Peter (Mohawk). *Elderberry Flute Song: Contemporary Coyote Tales*. Trumansburg: Crossing, 1982. Narrative poetry and short stories.

―――. *Turtle, Bear and Wolf*. Preface Gary Snyder. Mohawk Nation via Rooseveltown: Akwesasne Notes, 1976. Poetry.

―――. *White Corn Sister*. New York: Strawberry: 1977. 2nd ed., 1981. Poetry.

Brown, Emily Ivanoff. [Tecasuk] (Inupiat). *The Roots of Tecasuk: An Eskimo Woman's Family Story*. 1974. Rev. ed. Anchorage: Northwest, 1981.

Bruchac, Joseph (Abenaki). *Ancestry*. Lewiston: Great Raven, 1980. Poetry.

——, ed. *Breaking Silence: An Anthology of Contemporary Asian-American Poets*. Greenfield Center: Greenfield Review, 1983. Poetry.

——. *The Dreams of Jesse Brown*. Austin: Cold Mountain, 1977. Fiction.

——. *Entering Onondaga*. Austin: Cold Mountain, 1978. Poetry.

——, ed. *The Light from Another Country: Poetry from American Prisons*. Greenfield Center: Greenfield Review, 1984. Poetry.

——. *No Telephone to Heaven*. Merrick: Cross-Cultural Communications, 1984. Poetry.

——. *There Are No Trees inside the Prison*. Southharpswell: Blackberry, 1978. Poetry.

——. *This Earth Is a Drum*. Austin: Cold Mountain, 1977. Poetry.

——. *Translator's Son*. Merrick: Cross-Cultural Communications, 1980. Poetry.

Bruchac, Joseph, and William Witherup, eds. *Words from the House of the Dead: Prison Writings from Soledad*. 1971. 2nd ed. Contemporary Anthology Ser. Trumansburg: Crossing, 1974. Poetry.

Burns, Diane (Ojibwa/Chemehuevi). *Riding the One-Eyed Ford*. New York: Contact II, 1981. Poetry.

Bush, Barney (Shawnee/Cayuga). *Inherit the Blood*. New York: Thunder's Mouth, 1985. Poetry and fiction.

——. *My Horse and a Jukebox*. Foreword Kenneth Lincoln. Native American Ser. 4. Los Angeles: U of California P, 1979. Poetry.

——. *Petroglyphs*. Greenfield Center: Greenfield Review, 1982. Poetry.

Carter, Forrest [Asa](Cherokee). *The Education of Little Tree*. 1979. Foreword Rennard Strickland (Cherokee). Albuquerque: U of New Mexico P, 1986. Fictionalized autobiography.

——. *Gone to Texas: The Rebel Outlaw, Josey Wales*. 1973. New York: Buccaneer, 1985. Fiction.

——. *Josey Wales: Two Westerns by Forrest Carter*. Afterword Lawrence Clayton. Albuquerque: U of New Mexico P, 1989. Fiction. Includes *Gone to Texas* (1973) and *Vengence Trail of Josey Wales* (1976).

——. *The Outlaw Josey Wales*. 1973. New York: Dell, 1976. Fiction. Original title of the book above.

——. *The Vengence Trail of Josey Wales*. 1976. New York: Dell, 1977. Fiction.

Chief Eagle, Dallas (Sioux). *Winter Count*. 1967. Denver: Golden Bell, 1968. Fiction.

*Chona, Maria (Papago). Ruth Murray Underhill. *The Autobiography of a Papago Woman*. MAAA 46 (1936). New York: Holt, 1979. Autobiography.

Conley, Robert J. (Cherokee). *The Witch of Goingsnake and Other Stories*. Foreword Wilma P. Mankiller (Cherokee). Norman: U of Oklahoma P, 1988. Short fiction.

Cook-Lynn, Elizabeth (Sioux). *Seek the House of Relatives*. Marvin: Blue Cloud Quarterly, 1983. Poetry.

——. *Then Badger Said This*. New York: Vantage, 1977. Poetry, narratives, history.

Copway, George (Ojibwa). *The Life, History, and Travels of Kah-ge-ga-gah-bowh (George Copway)*. . . . Albany: Weed and Parsons, 1847. Rev. ed. *The Life, Letters and Speeches of Kah-ge-ga-gah-bowh, or G. Copway*. . . . New York: Benedict, 1850. Autobiography.

———. *Running Sketches of Men and Places, in England, France, Germany, Belgium, and Scotland.* New York: Riker, 1851. Nonfiction.

Deloria, Ella C. (Sioux). *Waterlily.* Biography by Agnes Picotte (Sioux). Afterword Raymond J. DeMallie. Lincoln: U of Nebraska P, 1988. Fiction; completed by 1944.

Deloria, Vine, Jr. (Sioux). *Custer Died for Your Sins: An Indian Manifesto.* 1969. Norman: U of Oklahoma P, 1988. Nonfiction.

———. *We Talk, You Listen: New Tribes, New Turf.* New York: Macmillan, 1970. Nonfiction.

Dorris, Michael A. (Modoc). *The Broken Cord: A Family's On-Going Struggle with Fetal Alcohol Syndrome.* Foreword Louise Erdrich (Ojibwa). New York: Harper, 1989. Nonfiction.

———. *A Yellow Raft on Blue Water.* New York: Holt, 1987. New York: Warner, 1988. Fiction.

Downing, [George] Todd (Choctaw). *The Case of the Unconquered Sisters.* Garden City: Doubleday, 1936. Fiction.

———. *The Cat Screams.* Garden City: Doubleday, 1934. Fiction.

———. *Death under the Moonflower.* Garden City: Doubleday, 1938. Fiction.

———. *The Last Trumpet: Murder in a Mexican Bull Ring.* Garden City: Doubleday, 1937. Fiction.

———. *The Lazy Lawrence Murders.* New York: Doubleday, 1941. Fiction.

———. *The Mexican Earth.* New York: Doubleday, 1940. Nonfiction.

———. *Murder on the Tropic.* Garden City: Doubleday, 1935. Fiction.

———. *Murder on Tour.* New York: Putnam's, 1933. Fiction.

———. *Night over Mexico.* Garden City: Doubleday, 1937. Fiction.

———. *Vultures in the Sky.* Garden City: Doubleday, 1935. Fiction.

Eastman, Charles A. [Ohiyesa] (Sioux). *From the Deep Woods to Civilization: Chapters in the Autobiography of an Indian.* 1916. Introd. Raymond Wilson. Lincoln: U of Nebraska P, 1977. Autobiography.

———. *Indian Boyhood.* 1902. New York: Dover, 1971. Autobiography.

———. *Old Indian Days.* 1907. Rapid City: Fenwyn, 1970. Fiction.

———. *Red Hunters and the Animal People.* 1904. New York: AMS, 1976. Fiction.

Endrezze, Anita (Yaqui). *Burning the Fields.* Lewiston: Confluence, 1983. Poetry.

———. *The North People.* Marvin: Blue Cloud Quarterly, 1983. Poetry.

Erdrich, Louise (Ojibwa). *Baptism of Desire: Poems.* New York: Harper, 1989. Poetry.

———. *Beet Queen.* New York: Holt, 1986; Bantam, 1987. Fiction.

———. *Jacklight: Poems.* New York: Holt, 1984. Poetry.

———. *Love Medicine.* New York: Holt, 1984. New York: Bantam, 1987. Fiction.

———. *Tracks.* New York: Holt, 1988. New York: Harper, 1989. Fiction.

Francisco, Nia (Navajo). *Blue Horses for Navajo Women.* Greenfield Center: Greenfield Review, 1988. Poetry.

Geiogamah, Hanay (Kiowa/Delaware). *New Native American Drama: Three Plays.* Introd. Jeffrey Huntsman. Norman: U of Oklahoma P, 1980. Drama.

Glancy, Diane (Cherokee). *Offering: Poetry and Prose.* Duluth: Holy Cow! 1988. Poetry and prose.

———. *One Age in a Dream.* Minneapolis: Milkweed, 1986. Poetry.

Grayson, George W. (Creek). *A Creek Warrior for the Confederacy: The Autobiography of Chief G. W. Grayson.* Ed. with introd. W. David Baird. Civilization of the American Indian 189. Norman: U of Oklahoma P, 1988. Autobiography.

Griffis, Joseph (Osage). *Tahan: Out of Savagery into Civilization.* New York: Doran, 1915. Autobiography.

Hale, Janet Campbell (Coeur d'Alene/Kootenai). *Custer Lives in Humboldt County.* Greenfield Center: Greenfield Review, 1978. Poetry.

———. *The Jailing of Cecelia Capture.* 1985. Albuquerque: U of New Mexico P, 1987. Fiction.

———. *Owl's Song.* 1974. New York: Avon, 1976. Fiction.

Harjo, Joy (Creek). *In Mad Love and War.* Middletown: Wesleyan UP, 1990. Poetry.

———. *She Had Some Horses.* New York: Thunders' Mouth, 1983. Poetry.

———. *What Moon Drove Me to This?* New York: I. Reed, 1979. Poetry.

Harjo, Joy (Creek), and Stephen Strom. *Secrets from the Center of the World.* Tucson: U of Arizona P, 1989. Poetry and photographs.

Henry, George [Maungwudaus] (Ojibwa). *An Account of the Chippewa Indians, Who Have Been Travelling among the Whites, in the United States, England, Ireland, Scotland, France and Belgium. . . .* Boston: Author, 1848. Nonfiction.

Henson, Lance (Cheyenne). *Buffalo Marrow on Black.* Edmond: Full Count, 1981. Poetry.

———. *Naming the Dark.* Norman: Point Riders, 1976. Poetry.

———. *Selected Poems, 1970–1983.* Greenfield Center: Greenfield Review, 1985. Poetry.

Hogan, Linda (Chickasaw). *Calling Myself Home.* Greenfield Center: Greenfield Review, 1978. Poetry.

———. *Daughters, I Love You.* Monograph Ser. Denver: Lorreto Heights, 1981. Poetry.

———. *Eclipse.* Foreword Kenneth Lincoln. Native American Ser. 6. Los Angeles: U of California P, 1983. Poetry.

———. *Mean Spirit.* New York: Atheneum, 1990. Fiction.

———. *Savings.* Minneapolis: Coffee House, 1988. Poetry.

———. *Seeing through the Sun.* Amherst: U of Massachusetts P, 1985. Poetry.

Hogan, Linda (Chickasaw), and Charles C. Henderson. *That Horse.* Acoma: Pueblo of Acoma, 1985. Short fiction.

Johnson, Emily Pauline (Mohawk). *Canadian Born.* Toronto: Morang, 1903. Poetry.

———. *Flint and Feather.* Toronto: Musson, 1912. Markam: PaperJacks, 1973. Poetry.

———. *The Moccasin Maker.* 1913. Ed. with introd. and notes by A. LaVonne Brown Ruoff. Tucson: U of Arizona P, 1987. Fiction and nonfiction.

———. *The Shagganappi.* Introd. Ernest Thompson Seton. Vancouver: Briggs, 1913. Short fiction.

———. *The White Wampum.* London: Bodley Head, 1895. Poetry.

Kenny, Maurice (Mohawk). *Between Two Rivers: Selected Poems, 1956–84.* Fredonia: White Pine, 1987. Poetry.

———. *Humors and/or Not So Humorous.* Buffalo: Swift Kick, 1988. Poetry.

———. *Is Summer This Bear.* Saranac Lake: Chauncey, 1985. Poetry.

King, Thomas (Cherokee). *Medicine River.* Toronto: Penguin, 1990. Fiction.

La Flesche, Francis (Omaha). *The Middle Five: Indian Schoolboys of the Omaha Tribe.*

1900. Foreword David A. Baereis. Madison: U of Wisconsin P, 1963. Lincoln: U of Nebraska P, 1978. Autobiography.

*Lame Deer [John Fire] (Sioux). Richard Erdoes. *Lame Deer: Seeker of Visions.* New York: Simon, 1972. Autobiography.

Least Heat Moon, William [William L. Trogdon] (Osage). *Blue Highways: A Journey into America.* Boston: Little, 1982. Autobiography.

*Lee, Bobbi (Cree). Don Barnett and Rick Sterling. *Bobbi Lee, Indian Rebel: Struggles of a Native Canadian Woman.* Vol. 1. Richmond, BC: Liberation Support Movement Information Center, 1975. Autobiography.

*Left Handed (Navajo). Walter Dyk. *Son of Old Man Hat: A Navaho Autobiography.* Foreword Edward Sapir. 1938. Lincoln: U of Nebraska P, 1967. Autobiography.

Long, Sylvester Clark [Long Lance] (Lumbee). *Long Lance: The Autobiography of a Blackfoot Indian Chief.* New York: Cosmopolitan, 1928. Fiction.

———. *Redman Echoes: Comprising the Writings of Chief Buffalo Child Long Lance and Biographical Sketches by His Friends.* Los Angeles: Frank Wiggins Trade School, Dept. of Printing, 1933. Mixed genre.

Louis, Adrian C. (Paiute). *Fire Water World.* Albuquerque: West End, 1989. Poetry.

———. *Muted War Drums.* New York: Strawberry, 1977. Poetry.

———. *Sweets for the Dancing Bear.* Marvin: Blue Cloud Quarterly, 1979. Poetry.

Markoosie (Eskimo). *Harpoon of the Hunter.* Montreal: McGill–Queen's UP, 1970. Fiction.

Mathews, John Joseph (Osage). *Life and Death of an Oilman: The Career of E. W. Marland.* Norman: U of Oklahoma P, 1951. Biography.

———. *Sundown.* 1934. Introd. Virginia H. Mathews. Norman: U of Oklahoma P, 1988. Fiction.

———. *Talking to the Moon.* 1945. Foreword Elizabeth Mathews. Norman: U of Oklahoma P, 1981. Autobiography.

———. *Wah'Kon-Tah: The Osage and the White Man's Road.* Civilization of the American Indian 3. Norman: U of Oklahoma P, 1932, 1968. Fiction.

McCarthy, James (Papago). *A Papago Traveler: The Memories of James McCarthy.* Ed. John G. Westover. Sun Tracks 13. Tucson: U of Arizona P, 1985. Autobiography.

McNickle, D'Arcy (Cree/Salish). *Indian Man: A Biography of Oliver La Farge.* Bloomington: Indiana UP, 1971. Biography.

———. *Runner in the Sun: A Story of Indian Maize.* 1954. Afterword Alfonso Ortiz (San Juan). Albuquerque: U of New Mexico P, 1987. Fiction.

———. *The Surrounded.* 1936. Introd. William Towner. Albuquerque: U of New Mexico P, 1978. Fiction.

———. *Wind from an Enemy Sky.* 1978. Afterword Louis Owens (Cherokee). Albuquerque: U of New Mexico P, 1988. Fiction.

*Mitchell, Frank (Navajo). Charlotte Johnson Frisbie and David P. McAllester. *Navajo Blessingway Singer: The Autobiography of Frank Mitchell, 1881–1967.* Tucson: U of Arizona P, 1978. Autobiography.

Momaday, N. Scott (Kiowa). *The Ancient Child.* New York: Doubleday, 1989. Fiction.

———. *Angle of Geese and Other Poems.* Boston: Godine, 1974. Poetry.

———. *The Gourd Dancer: Poems.* New York: Harper, 1976. Poetry.

———. *The House Made of Dawn.* New York: Harper, 1968, 1989. Fiction.

————. *The Journey of the Tai-me.* Santa Barbara: Privately printed, 1967. Autobiography, myth, history.

————. "The Man Made of Words." *Indian Voices: The First Convocation of American Indian Scholars.* Ed. Rupert Costo. San Francisco: Indian Historian, 1970. 49 –84. Chapman, ed. *Literature of the American Indians.* 96–110.

————. *The Names: A Memoir.* 1976. Sun Tracks 16. Tucson: U of Arizona P, 1987. Autobiography.

————. *The Way to Rainy Mountain.* Albuquerque: U of New Mexico P, 1969. Autobiography, myth, history.

*Mountain Wolf Woman (Winnebago). Nancy Oestreich Lurie. *Mountain Wolf Woman, Sister of Crashing Thunder: The Autobiography of a Winnebago Indian.* Ann Arbor: U of Michigan P, 1961. Autobiography.

Mourning Dove [Christine Quintasket] (Colville). *Cogewea, the Half-Blood: A Depiction of the Great Montana Cattle Range.* With notes and biographical sketch by Lucullus Virgil McWhorter. 1927. Introd. Dexter Fisher. Lincoln: U of Nebraska P, 1981. Fiction.

————. *Mourning Dove: A Salishan Autobiography.* Ed. Jay Miller. American Indian Lives. Lincoln: U of Nebraska P, 1990. Autobiography.

Niatum, Duane (Klallam). *After the Death of the Elder Klallam.* Santa Fe: Baleen, 1970. Poetry.

————. *Ascending Red Cedar Moon.* Native American Ser. New York: Harper, 1969. Poetry.

————. *Digging out the Roots.* Native American Ser. New York: Harper, 1977. Poetry.

————. *Drawings of the Song Animals: New and Selected Poems.* Duluth: Holy Cow! 1990. Poetry.

————. *Songs for the Harvester of Dreams.* Seattle: U of Washington P, 1981. Poetry.

————. *Taos Pueblo: Poems.* Greenfield Center: Greenfield Review, 1973. Poetry.

Oandasan, William (Yuki). *A Branch of California Redwood.* Foreword Kenneth Lincoln. Native American Ser. 4. Los Angeles: U of California P, 1980. Poetry.

————. *Round Valley Songs.* Minneapolis: West End, 1984. Poetry.

Occom, Samson (Mohegan). *A Choice Collection of Hymns and Spiritual Songs Intented [sic] for the Edification of Sincere Christians of All Denominations.* London: Green, 1774. Songs.

————. *A Sermon Preached at the Execution of Moses Paul, an Indian Who Was Executed at New-Haven, on the 2d of September 1772.* Bennington: William Watson, 1772. Nonfiction.

Ortiz, Simon J. (Acoma). "Always the Stories: A Brief History and Thoughts on My Writing." Schöler, *Coyote Was Here* 57–69.

————. *Fight Back: For the Sake of the People, for the Sake of the Land.* INAD Literary Journal (Inst. for Native American Development, Native American Studies, Univ. of New Mexico) 1.1 (1980). Poetry and nonfiction.

————. *Fightin': New and Collected Stories.* New York: Thunder's Mouth, 1983. Short fiction.

————. *From Sand Creek.* New York: Thunder's Mouth, 1981. Poetry.

————. *Going for the Rain.* New York: Harper, 1976. Poetry.

————. *A Good Journey.* 1977. Sun Tracks 12. Tucson: U of Arizona P, 1986. Poetry.

————. *The Howbah Indians.* Tucson: Blue Moon-U of Arizona P, 1978. Short fiction.

————. "Interview." Coltelli, *Winged Words* 103–19.

Oskison, John Milton (Cherokee). *Black Jack Davy.* New York: Appleton, 1926. Fiction.

——. *Brothers Three.* New York: Macmillan, 1935. Fiction.

——. *Wild Harvest: A Novel of Transition Days in Oklahoma.* New York: Appleton, 1925. Fiction.

Paytiamo, James (Acoma). *Flaming Arrow's People, by an Acoma Indian.* New York: Duffield, 1932. Autobiography.

Pokagon, Simon (Potawatomi). *O-gî-mäw-kwe Mit-i-gwä-kî (Queen of the Woods). Also Brief Sketch of the Algaic Language.* 1899. Berrien Springs: Hardscrabble, 1972. Fiction.

Posey, Alexander (Creek). *The Poems of Alexander Lawrence Posey.* Ed. Mrs. Minnie H. Posey. Memoir by William Elsey Connelly. Topeka: Crane, 1910. Poetry.

Revard, Carter (Osage). *Ponca War Dancers.* Norman: Point Riders, 1980. Poetry.

Ridge, John Rollin [Cheesquatalawny; Yellow Bird] (Cherokee). *The Life and Adventures of Joaquín Murieta, the Celebrated California Bandit.* 1854. Introd. Joseph Henry Jackson. Norman: U of Oklahoma P, 1977. Fiction.

——. *Poems.* San Francisco: Payot, 1868. Poetry.

Riggs, [Rolla] Lynn (Cherokee). *Big Lake.* New York: French, 1925. Drama.

——. *Green Grow the Lilacs.* New York: French, 1931. Drama.

——. *The Iron Dish.* Garden City: Doubleday, 1930. Poetry.

——. *Roadside.* Foreword Arthur Hopkins. New York: French, 1930. Drama.

——. *Russet Mantle* and *The Cherokee Night.* New York: French, 1936. Drama.

——. *This Book, This Hill, These People: Poems by Lynn Riggs.* Tulsa: Lynn Chase, 1982. Poetry.

Rogers, Will (Cherokee). *Complete Works.* Ed. Joseph A. Stout, Jr. The Writings of Will Rogers. Stillwater: Oklahoma State UP. Nonfiction.

——. *Convention Articles.* Ser. 2, vol. 1. 1976.

——. *Ether and Me, or "Just Relax."* 1929. Ser. 1, vol. 1. 1973.

——. *How to Be Funny and Other Writings.* Ser. 5, vol. 3. 1983.

——. *The Illiterate Digest.* 1924. Ser. 1, vol. 3. 1974.

——. *Letters of a Self-Made Diplomat to His President.* 1926. Ser. 1, vol. 6. 1977.

——. *More Letters of a Self-Made Diplomat.* Ed. Steven K. Gragert. Ser. 5, vol. 2. 1982.

——. *Radio Broadcasts of Will Rogers.* Ed. Steven K. Gragert. Ser. 6, vol. 1. 1983.

——. *Rogers-isms: The Cowboy Philosopher on the Peace Conference.* New York: Harper, 1919. Rpt. in *Complete Works.* Ser. 1, vol. 5. 1975.

——. *Rogers-isms: The Cowboy Philosopher on Prohibition.* New York: Harper, 1919. Rpt. in *Complete Works.* Ser. 1, vol. 4. 1975.

——. *There's Not a Bathing Suit in Russia and Other Bare Facts.* 1927. Ed. Joseph A. Stout. Ser. 1, vol. 2. 1973.

——. *Will Rogers's Daily Telegrams.* Ed. James M. Smallwood and Steven K. Gragert. Ser. 3. Vol. 1: *The Coolidge Years, 1926–1929.* 1978. Vol. 2: *The Hoover Years, 1929–1931.* 1978. Vol. 3: *The Roosevelt Years, 1933–1935.* 1979.

——. *Will Rogers's Weekly Articles.* Ed. James M. Smallwood and Steven K. Gragert. Ser. 4. Vol. 1: *The Harding-Coolidge Years, 1922–1925.* 1980. Vol. 2: *The Coolidge Years, 1925–1927.* 1980. Vol. 3: *The Coolidge Years, 1927–1929.* 1981. Vol. 4: *The Hoover Years, 1929–1931.* 1981. Vol. 5: *The Hoover Years, 1931–1933.* 1982. Vol. 6: *The Roosevelt Years, 1933–1935.* 1982.

Rose, Wendy (Hopi/Miwok). *Lost Copper*. Banning: Malki Museum, 1980. Poetry.

———. *What Happened When the Hopi Hit New York*. New York: Contact II, 1982. Poetry.

Salisbury, Ralph (Cherokee). *Going to the Water: Poems of a Cherokee Heritage*. Eugene: Pacific, 1983. Poetry.

———. *Spirit Beast Chant*. Marvin: Blue Cloud, 1982. Poetry.

Sanchez, Carol Lee (Laguna/Sioux). *Conversations from the Nightmare*. San Francisco: La Galleria, 1975. Poetry.

———. *Message Bringer Woman*. San Francisco: Taurean Horn, 1976. Poetry.

*Savala, Refugio (Yaqui). Kathleen Mullen Sands. *The Autobiography of a Yaqui Poet*. Tucson: U of Arizona P, 1980. Autobiography.

*Sekaquaptewa, Helen (Hopi). Louise Udall. *Me and Mine: The Life Story of Helen Sekaquaptewa*. Tucson: U of Arizona P. 1969. Autobiography.

*Sewid, James (Kwakiutl). James P. Spradley. *Guests Never Leave Hungry: The Autobiography of James Sewid, a Kwakiutl Indian*. New Haven: Yale UP, 1969. Autobiography.

Shaw, Anna Moore (Pima). *A Pima Past*. Foreword Edward H. Spicer. Tucson: U of Arizona P, 1974. Autobiography.

Silko, Leslie Marmon (Laguna). *Almanac of the Dead*. Forthcoming.

———. *Ceremony*. New York: Viking, 1977. New York: Penguin, 1986. Fiction.

———. *Laguna Woman*. Greenfield Center: Greenfield Review, 1974. Poetry.

———. *Storyteller*. 1981. New York: Arcade, 1989. Poetry and fiction.

Smith, Martin Cruz (Senecu del Sur/Yaqui). *The Analog Bullet*. New York: Leisure, 1977, 1981. Fiction. Under name of Martin William Smith.

———. *Gorky Park*. New York: Random, 1981. New York: Ballantine, 1982. Fiction.

———. *Gypsy in Amber*. New York: Ballantine, 1982. Fiction.

———. *Gypsy in Amber* and *Canto for a Gypsy*. Garden City: Doubleday, 1971. Fiction.

———. *The Indians Won*. New York: Belmont, 1970. Fiction. Under name of Martin William Smith.

———. *Nightwing*. New York: Norton, 1977. Fiction.

———. *Polar Star*. New York: Random, 1989. Fiction.

———. *Stallion Gate*. New York: Random, 1986. Fiction.

*Standing Bear, Luther [Ota K'te] (Sioux). E. A. Brininstool. *Land of the Spotted Eagle*. 1933. Foreword Richard N. Ellis. Lincoln: U of Nebraska P, 1978. Autobiography.

———. *My Indian Boyhood, by Chief Luther Standing Bear, Who Was the Boy Ota K'te (Plenty Kill)*. 1931. Lincoln: U of Nebraska P, 1988. Autobiography.

*———. E. A. Brininstool. *My People, the Sioux*. 1928. Introd. Richard N. Ellis. Lincoln: U of Nebraska P, 1975. Autobiography.

*Stands in Timber, John (Cheyenne). Margot Liberty. *Cheyenne Memories*. 1967. Lincoln: U of Nebraska P, 1972. Autobiography.

Storm, Hyemeyohsts (Cheyenne). *Seven Arrows*. New York: Harper, 1972. Fiction.

———. *Song of Heyoehkah*. New York: Harper, 1981. Fiction.

Strete, Craig Kee (Cherokee). *Death Chants*. Introd. Salvador Dali. New York: Doubleday, 1988. Short fiction.

———. *Dreams That Burn in the Night*. New York: Doubleday, 1985. Short fiction.

———. *To Make Death Love Us*. New York: Doubleday, 1987. Fiction.

*Talayesva, Don C. (Hopi). Leo W. Simmons. *Sun Chief: The Autobiography of a Hopi Indian*. 1942. New Haven: Yale UP, 1974. Autobiography.

Tall Mountain, Mary (Athabascan). *Nine Poems*. San Francisco: Friars, 1977. Poetry.

———. *There Is No Word for Goodbye*. Marvin: Blue Cloud Quarterly, 1982. Poetry.

Tapahonso, Luci (Navajo). *A Breeze Swept Through*. Albuquerque: West End, 1987. Poetry.

———. *One More Shiprock Night*. San Antonio: Tejas Art, 1981. Poetry.

———. *Seasonal Woman*. Santa Fe: Tooth of Time, 1982. Poetry.

Vizenor, Gerald (Ojibwa). *Darkness in Saint Louis Bearheart*. St. Paul: Truck, 1978. Fiction. *Bearheart*. Minneapolis: U of Minnesota P, 1990. Fiction; retitled reprint.

———. *Earthdivers: Tribal Narratives on Mixed Descent*. Minneapolis: U of Minnesota P, 1981. Fiction and nonfiction.

———. *Empty Swings*. Minneapolis: Nodin, 1967. Poetry.

———. *The Everlasting Sky: New Voices from the People Named the Chippewa*. New York: Macmillan, 1972. Nonfiction.

———. *Griever: An American Monkey King in China*. Bloomington: Fiction Collective-Illinois State UP, 1987. Minneapolis: U of Minnesota P, 1990. Fiction.

———. *Harold of Orange*. 1983. Film and unpublished screenplay.

———. "I Know What You Mean, Erdupps MacChurbbs." *Growing Up in Minnesota: Ten Writers Remember Their Childhoods*. Ed. Chester Anderson. Minneapolis: U of Minnesota P, 1976. 79–111.

———. *Interior Landscapes: Autobiographical Myths and Metaphors*. Minneapolis: U of Minnesota P, 1990. Autobiography.

———. *Matsushima: Pine Islands*. Minneapolis: Nodin, 1984. Poetry.

———. *The People Named the Chippewa: Narrative Histories*. Minneapolis: U of Minnesota P, 1984. Fiction and nonfiction.

———. *Raising the Moon Vines: Original Haiku in English*. Minneapolis: Callimachus, 1964. Minneapolis: Nodin, 1964. Poetry.

———. *Seventeen Chirps: Haiku in English*. Minneapolis: Nodin, 1964, 1968. Poetry.

———. *Slight Abrasions: A Dialogue in Haiku*. With Jerome Downes. Minneapolis: Nodin, 1966. Poetry.

———. *Tribal Scenes and Ceremonies*. 1976. With new essays. Minneapolis: U of Minnesota P, 1990. Nonfiction.

———. "Trickster Discourse: Comic Holotropes and Language Games." Vizenor, *Narrative Chance* 187–211.

———. *The Trickster of Liberty: Tribal Heirs to a Wild Baronage at Petronia*. Emergent Literatures. Minneapolis: U of Minnesota P, 1988. Fiction.

———. *Wordarrows: Indians and Whites in the New Fur Trade*. Minneapolis: U of Minnesota P, 1978. Fiction and nonfiction.

Walker, Bertrand N. O. [Hen-Toh] (Wyandot). *Yon-Doo-Shah-We-Ah (Nubbins)*. Oklahoma City: Harlow, 1924. Poetry.

Walsh, Marnie (Sioux). *A Taste of the Knife*. Boise: Ahsahta, 1976. Poetry.

Walters, Anna Lee (Otoe/Pawnee). *Ghost Singer*. Flagstaff: Northland, 1988. Fiction.

———. *The Sun Is Not Merciful*. Ithaca: Firebrand, 1985. Short fiction.

Welch, James (Blackfeet/Gros Ventre). *The Death of Jim Loney*. 1979. New York: Penguin, 1987. Fiction.

———. *Fools Crow*. New York: Viking, 1986. Fiction.

————. *Riding the Earthboy 40.* Native American Ser. New York: Harper, 1971. Rev. ed. New York: Harper, 1976. Poetry.

————. *Winter in the Blood.* 1974. New York: Penguin, 1986. Fiction.

*White Bull, Chief Joseph (Sioux). James H. Howard. *The Warrior Who Killed Custer: The Personal Narrative of Chief Joseph White Bull.* Lincoln: U of Nebraska P, 1968. Autobiography.

Whiteman, Roberta Hill (Oneida). *Star Quilt.* Foreword Carolyn Forche. Minneapolis: Holy Cow! 1984. Poetry.

Williams, Ted (Tuscarora). *The Reservation.* Syracuse: Syracuse UP, 1976. Autobiography.

Winnemucca, Sarah [Hopkins] (Paiute). *Life among the Piutes: Their Wrongs and Claims.* Ed. Mrs. Horace Mann. 1883. Bishop: Chalfant, 1969. Autobiography and nonfiction.

*Yava, Albert (Tewa/Hopi). Harold Courlander. *Big Falling Snow: A Tewa-Hopi Indian's Life and Times and the History and Traditions of His People.* New York: Crown, 1978. Autobiography.

Young Bear, Ray A. (Mesquakie). *The Invisible Musician.* Duluth: Holy Cow! 1990. Poetry.

————. *Winter of the Salamander: The Keeper of Importance.* Native American Ser. 10 New York: Harper, 1980. Poetry.

Zitkala-Ša [Gertrude Bonnin] (Sioux). *American Indian Stories.* 1921. Introd. Dexter Fisher. Lincoln: U of Nebraska P, 1986. Mixed genre: autobiography, fiction, nonfiction.

D. Scholarship and Criticism

STUDIES OF ORAL LITERATURES

Astrov, Margot. "The Concept of Motion as the Psychological Leitmotif of Navaho Life and Literature." *JAF* 63 (1950): 45–56.

Austin, Mary Hunter. "Aboriginal." *The Cambridge History of American Literature.* 3 vols. in 1. New York: Macmillan, 1946. 610–34.

Babcock-Abrahams, Barbara. "The Story in the Story: Metanarration in Folk Narrative." Bauman, *Verbal Art* 61–79.

————. " 'A Tolerated Margin of Mess': The Trickster and His Tales Reconsidered." *Journal of the Folklore Institute* 11 (1975): 147–86. Wiget, *Critical Essays on Native American Literature* 153–85.

Bahr, Donald M. "A Format and Method for Translating Songs." *JAF* 96 (1983): 170–82.

————. "On the Complexity of Southwest Indian Emergence Myths." *Journal of Anthropological Research* 33 (1977): 317–49.

————. "Pima Heaven Songs." Swann and Krupat, *Recovering the Word* 198–246.

Balgooyen, Theodore J. "The Plains Indian as a Public Speaker." David H. Grover, ed. *Landmarks in Western Oratory.* Laramie: Graduate School and Western Speech Assn., 1968.

Barnes, Nellie. "American Indian Verse: Characteristics of Style." Bull. of the Univ. of Kansas, Humanistic Studies 2 (1921): 1–64.

Bauman, Richard. *Story, Performance, Event: Contextual Studies of Oral Narrative.* Studies in Oral and Literate Culture 10. Cambridge: Cambridge UP, 1986.

————. *Verbal Art as Performance*. 1977. Prospect Heights: Waveland, 1984.

Bauman, Richard, and Joel Sherzer, eds. *Explorations in the Ethnography of Speaking*. New York: Cambridge UP, 1974.

Ben-Amos, Dan, ed. *Folklore Genres*. Austin: U of Texas P, 1976.

Bevis, William. "American Indian Verse Translations." Chapman, *Literature of the American Indians* 308–23.

Boas, Franz. "Introduction to James Teit, 'The Traditions of the Thompson Indians of British Columbia.' " Boas, *Race, Language and Culture* 407–24.

————. *Race, Language and Culture*. 1940. Chicago: U of Chicago P, 1982.

Bright, William. *American Indian Linguistics and Literature*. Berlin: Mouton, 1984.

————. "The Natural History of Old Man Coyote." Krupat and Swann, *Recovering the Word* 339–87.

Brinton, Daniel G. *American Hero-Myths: A Study of the Native Religions of the Western Continent*. 1882. New York: Johnson, 1970.

Buller, Galen. "Comanche and Coyote, the Culture Maker." Swann, *Smoothing the Ground* 245–58.

Bunzel, Ruth L. "An Introduction to Zuni Ceremonialism." ARBAE 47 (1929–30): 467–544.

Carr, Pat, and Willard Gingerich. "The Vagina Dentata Motif in Nahuatl and Pueblo Mythic Narratives: A Comparative Study." *New Scholar* 8.1 (1981). Swann, *Smoothing the Ground* 187–203.

Cohen, Percy. "Theories of Myth." *Man* ns 4 (1969): 337–53.

Count, Earl W. "The Earth-Diver and the Rival Twins: A Clue to Time Correlation in North-Eurasiatic and North American Mythology." *The Civilizations of Ancient Americans. Selected Papers of the Twenty-Ninth International Congress of Americanists*. Ed. Sol Tax. Chicago: U of Chicago P, 1952. 55–62.

Curtin, Jeremiah. See sect. B.

Densmore, Frances. *The American Indians and Their Music*. 1926. New York: Johnson, n.d.

————. "The Belief of the Indian in a Connection between Song and the Supernatural." BBAE 151 (1953).

————. "The Words of Indian Song as Unwritten Literature." *JAF* 63 (1950): 450–58.

Dundes, Alan. "Earth Diver: Creation of the Mythopoeic Male." *AA* 64 (1962): 1032–51.

————. *The Morphology of North American Folktales*. Folklore Fellows Communications 195. Helsinki: Suomalainen Tiedeakatemia, 1964.

————. "Texture, Text, and Context." *SFQ* 28 (1964): 251–65.

————. *The Study of Folklore*. Englewood Cliffs: Prentice, 1965.

Evers, Larry, and Felipe Molina. See sect. B.

Evers, Larry, and Paul Pavich. "Native Oral Traditions." Lyon and Taylor, *A Literary History of the American West* 11–28.

Farrer, Clare R. "Singing for Life: The Mescalero Apache Girls' Puberty Ceremony." Frisbie, *Southwestern Indian Ritual Drama* 125–59.

Fenton, William N. "Horatio Hale." *The Iroquois Book of Rites*. Ed. Horatio Hale. 1883. Ed. Fenton. Toronto: U of Toronto P, 1963. vii–xxvii.

————. "This Island, the World on Turtle's Back." *JAF* 75 (1962): 283–300. Wiget, *Critical Essays on Native American Literature* 133–53.

Fine, Elizabeth C. *The Folklore Text: From Performance to Print.* Bloomington: Indiana UP, 1984.

Finnegan, Ruth. *Oral Poetry: Its Nature, Significance, and Social Context.* Cambridge: Cambridge UP, 1977.

Fisher, Margaret W. "The Mythology of the Northern and Northeastern Algonkians in Reference to Algonkian Mythology as a Whole." *Man in Northeastern North America.* Ed. Frederick Johnson. Papers of the Robert S. Peabody Foundation for Archaeology 3. Andover: Phillips Acad., 1946. 226–62.

Folklore and Literary Criticism: A Dialogue. Spec. issue of *JFI* 18.2–3 (1981): 95–156.

Foster, Michael K. *From the Earth to beyond the Sky: An Ethnographic Approach to Four Longhouse Iroquois Speech Events.* National Museum of Man, Mercury Ser., Canadian Ethnology Service Paper 20. Ottawa: National Museums of Canada, 1974.

Frisbie, Charlotte Johnson. *Kinaaldá: A Study of the Navaho Girl's Puberty Ceremony.* Middletown: Wesleyan UP, 1967.

———. *Music and Dance Research of Southwestern United States Indians: Past Trends, Present Activities, and Suggestions for Future Research.* Detroit Studies in Music Bibliography 36. Detroit: Information Coordinators, 1977.

———, ed. *Southwestern Indian Ritual Drama.* Albuquerque: U of New Mexico P, 1980.

Gayton, Anna H. "The Orpheus Myth in North America." *JAF* 48 (1935): 263–93.

Haile, Berard, O.F.M. "Navaho Chantways and Ceremonials." *AA* 40 (1938): 639–52.

Hallowell, A. Irving. *Culture and Experience.* 1955. Philadelphia: U of Pennsylvania P, 1974.

Herndon, Marcia (Cherokee). *Native American Music.* Norwood: Norwood, 1980.

Heth, Charlotte (Cherokee), ed. and introd. *Traditional Music of North American Indians.* Los Angeles: Dept. of Music, U of California, 1980. Spec. issue of *Selected Reports on Ethnomusicology.*

Hoebel, E. Adamson. "Song Duels among the Eskimo." *Law and Warfare: Studies in the Anthropology of Conflict.* Ed. Paul Bohannan. American Museum Sourcebooks in Anthropology. Garden City: Natural History, 1967.

Hofman, Charles. *Frances Densmore and American Indian Music: A Memorial Volume.* Contributions from the Museum of the American Indian, Heye Foundation 23 (1968).

Hultkrantz, Åke. *The North American Indian Orpheus Tradition: A Contribution to Comparative Religion.* Ethnographical Museum of Sweden 2. Stockholm: Statens Ethnolografiska, 1957.

Huntsman, Jeffrey. "Traditional Native American Literature: The Translation Dilemma." *Native American Literature.* Spec. issue of *Shantih: A Journal of International Writing and Art.* Ed. Brian Swann and Roberta Hill. 4.2 (1979): 5–9. Rev. Swann, ed. *Smoothing the Ground.* 87–97.

Hymes, Dell. "Anthologies and Narrators." Swann and Krupat, *Recovering the Word* 41–84.

———. *"In Vain I Tried to Tell You": Essays in Native American Ethnopoetics.* Conduct and Communication Ser. Studies in Native American Literature 1. Philadelphia: U of Pennsylvania P, 1981.

———. "Some North Pacific Coast Poems: A Problem in Anthropological Philology." *AA* 67.3 (1965): 316–41. *"In Vain I Tried to Tell You"* 35–64.

Jacobs, Melville. *Pattern in Cultural Anthropology.* Homewood: Dorsey, 1964.

Jahner, Elaine A. "Cognitive Style in Oral Literature." *Language and Style* 16 (1982): 32–51.

———. "Stone Boy: Persistent Hero." Swann, *Smoothing the Ground* 171–86.

Kaiser, Rudolf. "Chief Seattle's Speech(es): American Origins and European Reception." Swann and Krupat, *Recovering the Word* 497–536.

Kealiinohomoku, Joann W. "The Drama of the Hopi Ogres." Frisbie, *Southwestern Indian Ritual Drama* 37–69.

Kinkade, M. Dale. "Bluejay and His Sister." Swann and Krupat, *Recovering the Word* 255–96.

Kluckhohn, Clyde. "Recurrent Themes in Myths and Mythmaking." *Daedalus* 88 (1959): 268–79. Dundes, *The Study of Folklore* 158–68.

Köngäs-Miranda, Elii "The Earth-Diver." *Ethnohistory* 7 (1960): 151–80.

Kroeber, Karl. "Deconstructionist Criticism and American Indian Literature." *Boundary 2* 7 (1979): 73–89.

———. "Scarface vs. Scar-face: The Problem of Versions." *JFI* 18.2–3 (1981): 99–124. Commentary by Sandra K. D. Stahl, Elaine Jahner, Barbara Babcock, Barre Toelken, and Dell Hymes and rebuttal by Kroeber, 125–56.

———, ed. *Traditional Literatures of the American Indian: Texts and Interpretations.* Lincoln: U of Nebraska P, 1981.

———. "The Wolf Comes: Indian Poetry and Linguistic Criticism." Swann, *Smoothing the Ground* 98–111.

Krupat, Arnold. "Post-Structuralism and Oral Literature." Swann and Krupat, *Recovering the Word* 113–28.

Leach, Edmund. *Claude Lévi-Strauss.* Modern Masters. New York: Viking, 1970.

———, ed. *The Structural Study of Myth and Totemism.* London: Tavistock, 1967.

Lévi-Strauss, Claude. "Four Winnebago Myths: A Structural Sketch." *Culture in History: Studies in Honor of Paul Radin.* Ed. Stanley Diamond. 1960. New York: Octagon, 1981. 351–62.

———. *From Honey to Ashes: Introduction to a Science of Mythology.* Vol. 2. 1966. Trans. John Weightman and Doreen Weightman. 1973. Chicago: U of Chicago P, 1983.

———. *The Origin of Table Manners.* Vol. 3. 1968. Trans. John Weightman and Doreen Weightman. New York: Harper, 1978.

———. *The Raw and the Cooked.* Vol. 1. 1964. Trans. John Weightman and Doreen Weightman. 1969. New York: Octagon, 1979.

———. "The Story of Asdiwal." Leach, *Structural Study of Myth and Totemism* 1–47.

———. *Structural Anthropology.* Trans. C. Jacobsen and B. G. Schoef. 1967. Chicago: U of Chicago P, 1983.

Lowie, Robert H. "The Test Theme in North American Mythology." *JAF* 21 (1908): 97–148.

Malotki, Ekkehart. "The Story of the 'Tsimonmanant' or Jimson Weed Girls: A Hopi Narrative Featuring the Motif of the Vagina Dentata." Swann, *Smoothing the Ground* 204–20.

Mattina, Anthony. "North American Indian Mythography: Editing Texts for the Printed Page." Swann and Krupat, *Recovering the Word* 129–48.

McAllester, David P. *Enemy Way Music: A Study of the Social and Esthetic Values as Seen in Navaho Music.* Archaeological and Ethnological Papers 41.3. Cambridge: Peabody Museum-Harvard UP, 1954.

——, ed. *Readings in Ethnomusicology.* New York: Johnson, 1971.

McGrath, Robin Gedalof. *Canadian Inuit Literature: The Development of a Tradition.* National Museum of Man, Mercury Ser. Canadian Ethnology Service Paper 94. Ottawa: National Museum of Man, 1984.

Merriam, Alan P. *Ethnomusicology of the Flathead Indians.* Viking Fund Pub. in Anthropology 44. New York: Werner Gren Foundation, 1967.

Moon, Sheila. *Changing Woman and Her Sisters: Feminine Aspects of Selves and Deities.* San Francisco: Guild for Psychological Studies, 1984.

——. *A Magic Dwells: A Poetic and Psychological Study of the Navaho Emergence Myth.* Middletown: Wesleyan UP, 1970.

Nettl, Bruno. *Blackfoot Musical Thought: Comparative Perspectives.* World Musics. Kent: Kent State UP, 1989.

——. *North American Indian Musical Styles.* Memoirs of the American Folklore Society 45 (1954).

——. "What Is Ethnomusicology?" McAllester, *Readings in Ethnomusicology* 3–14.

Norman, Howard A. "Wesucechak Becomes a Deer and Steals Language: An Anecdotal Linguistics Concerning the Swampy Cree Trickster." Swann and Krupat, *Recovering the Word* 402–21.

O'Bryan, Aileen. See sect. B.

Pope, Polly. "Toward a Structural Analysis of North American Trickster Tales." *SFQ* 31 (1967): 274–86.

Radin, Paul. *Literary Aspects of North American Mythology.* Canada Dept. of Mines. Museum Bull. 16. Anthropological Ser. 6. Ottawa: Govt. Printing Bur., 1915.

Ramsey, Jarold W. *Reading the Fire: Essays in the Traditional Indian Literatures of the Far West.* Lincoln: U of Nebraska P, 1983.

Reichard, Gladys A. "Literary Types and Dissemination of Myths." *JAF* 34 (1921): 269–307.

——. *Prayer: The Compulsive Word.* Monographs of the American Ethnographic Soc. 7 (1944). Seattle: U of Washington P, 1966.

Revard, Carter (Osage). "Traditional Osage Naming Ceremonies: Entering the Circle of Being." Swann and Krupat, *Recovering the Word* 446–66.

Rexroth, Kenneth. "American Indian Songs." Chapman, *Literature of the American Indians* 278–91.

Rice, Julian. "Encircling Ikto: Incest and Avoidance in *Dakota Texts.*" *South Dakota Review* 4 (1984): 92–103.

——. "How the Bird That Speaks Lakota Earned a Name." Swann and Krupat, *Recovering the Word* 422–45.

——. "An *Ohunkakan* Brings a Virgin Back to Camp." *AIQ* 7.4 (1983): 37–55.

——. Symbols: Meat for the Soul in Cheyenne Myth and Lakota Ritual." *WAL* 18 (1983): 105–32.

——. "Why the Lakota Still Have Their Own: Ella Deloria's *Dakota Texts.*" *WAL* 19 (1984): 205–17.

Rich, George W. "Rethinking the Star Husbands." *JAF* 84 (1971): 436–41.

Ricketts, Mac Linscott. "The North American Indian Trickster." *History of Religions* 5 (1966): 327–50.

Rooth, Anna Birgitta. "The Creation Myths of the North American Indians." *Anthropos* 52 (1957): 497–508.

Rothenberg, Jerome. "Total Translation: An Experiment in the Presentation of

American Indian Poetry." Chapman, *Literature of the American Indians* 292–307.

Sands, Kathleen Mullen, and Emory Sekaquaptewa. "Four Hopi Lullabies: A Study in Method and Meaning." *AIQ* 4 (1978): 195–210.

———. "The Singing Tree: Dynamics of a Yaqui Myth." *American Quarterly* 35 (1983): 355–75.

Sevillano, Mando. "Interpreting Native American Literature: An Archetypal Approach." *AICRJ* 10.1 (1986): 1–12.

Sherzer, Joel, and Greg Urban, eds. *Native South American Discourse.* Berlin: Mouton, 1986.

Sherzer, Joel, and Anthony Woodbury, eds. *Native American Discourse: Poetics and Politics.* Studies in Oral and Literate Culture 13. Cambridge: Cambridge UP, 1987.

Spencer, Katharine. *Mythology and Values: An Analysis of Navaho Chantway Myths.* Memoirs of the Journal of American Folklore 48 (1957). Austin: U of Texas P, 1975.

———. *Reflections of Social Life in the Navaho Origin Myth.* Univ. of New Mexico Publications in Anthropology 3 (1947). Millwood: Krause, 1977.

Swann, Brian. "A Note on Translation, and Remarks on Collaboration." Swann and Krupat, *Recovering the Word* 247–54.

———, ed. *Smoothing the Ground: Essays on Native American Oral Literature.* Berkeley: U of California P, 1983.

Swanton, Guy E. "Orpheus and Star Husband: Meaning and the Structure of Myths." *Ethnology* 15 (1976): 115–33.

Tedlock, Barbara. "Songs of the Zuni Kachina Society: Composition, Rehearsal, and Performance." Frisbie, *Southwestern Indian Ritual Drama* 7–35.

———. "Zuni Sacred Theatre." *AIQ* 7 (1983): 93–110.

Tedlock, Dennis. "The Poetics of Verisimilitude." Orig. pub. as "Pueblo Literature: Style and Verisimilitude." *New Perspectives on the Pueblos.* Ed. Alfonso Ortiz. Albuquerque: U of New Mexico P, 1972. 219–42. Rev. *The Spoken Word* 159–77.

———. "On the Translation of Style in Oral Narrative." *JAF* 84 (1971): 114–33. Rev. *The Spoken Word* 31–61.

———. *The Spoken Word and the Work of Interpretation.* Conduct and Communication Ser. Philadelphia: U of Pennsylvania P, 1983.

Theisz, Ron D. "Song Texts and Their Performers: The Centerpiece of Contemporary Lakota Identity Formulation." *Plains Indian Cultures: Past and Present Meanings.* Spec. issue of *Great Plains Quarterly* 7.2 (Spring 1987): 116–24.

Thompson, Stith. *Narrative Motif-Analysis as a Folklore Method.* Folklore Fellows Communications 161. Helsinki: Suomalainen Tiedeakatemia, 1955.

———. "The Star Husband Tale." Dundes, *The Study of Folklore* 414–74.

Toelken, Barre. *The Dynamics of Folklore.* Boston: Houghton, 1979.

———. "Life and Death in the Navajo Coyote Tales." Swan and Krupat, *Recovering the Word* 388–401.

———. "The 'Pretty Languages' of Yellowman: Genre, Mode, Texture in Navaho Coyote Narratives." *Genre* 2 (1969): 211–35. Ben-Amos, *Folklore Genres* 145–70.

Toelken, Barre, with Tacheeni Scott (Navajo). "Poetic Retranslation and the 'Pretty

Languages' of Yellowman." Kroeber, *Traditional Literatures of the American Indian* 65–116.

Vander, Judith. "The Song Repertoire of Four Shoshone Women: A Reflection of Cultural Movements and Sex Roles." *Ethnomusicology* 26 (1982): 73–83.

Waterman, T[homas] T. "The Explanatory Element in the Folk-Tales of the North-American Indians." *JAF* 27 (1914): 1–54.

Wheeler-Voegelin, Ermine, and Remedios W. Moore. "The Emergence Myth in Native North America." *Studies in Folklore*. Ed. W. Edson Richmond. Indiana Folklore Ser. 9. Bloomington: Indiana UP, 1957. Westport, Greenwood, 1972. 66–91.

Wiget, Andrew O. "His Life in His Tail: The Native American Trickster and the Literature of Possibility." Ruoff and Ward, *Redefining American Literary History*.

———. "Sayatasha's Night Chant: A Literary Textual Analysis of a Zuni Ritual Poem." *AICRJ* 4 (1980): 99–140.

———. "Telling the Tale: A Performance Analysis of a Hopi Coyote Story." Swann and Krupat, *Recovering the Word* 297–336.

———. "Truth and the Hopi: An Historiographic Study of Documented Oral Tradition Concerning the Coming of the Spanish." *Ethnohistory* 29 (1982): 181–99.

Young, Frank W. "A Fifth Analysis of the Star Husband Tale." *Ethnology* 9 (1970): 389–413.

———. "Folktales and Social Structure: A Comparison of Three Analyses of the Star-Husband Tale." *JAF* 91 (1978): 691–99.

STUDIES OF LIFE HISTORIES AND AUTOBIOGRAPHIES

Bataille, Gretchen M., and Kathleen Mullen Sands. *American Indian Women: Telling Their Lives*. Lincoln: U of Nebraska P, 1984.

Brumble, H. David, III. *American Indian Autobiography*. Berkeley: U of California P, 1988.

Krupat, Arnold. *For Those Who Come After: A Study of Native American Autobiography*. Berkeley: U of California P, 1985.

O'Brien, Lynne Woods. *Plains Indian Autobiographies*. Western Writers 10. Boise: Boise State College Press, 1973.

Ruoff, A. LaVonne Brown. "Three Nineteenth-Century American Indian Autobiographers." Ruoff and Ward, *Redefining American Literary History*.

Sands, Kathleen Mullen. "Telling 'A Good One': Creating a Papago Autobiography." *MELUS* 10 (1983): 355–75.

Smith, William F., Jr. "American Indian Autobiographies." *AIQ* 2 (1975): 237–45.

GENERAL LITERARY STUDIES

The following section includes works that deal with both oral and written literatures or only with the latter.

Allen, Paula Gunn (Laguna/Sioux). *The Sacred Hoop*. See sect. F.

———, ed. *Studies in American Indian Literature: Critical Essays and Course Designs*. New York: MLA, 1983.

————. "This Wilderness in My Blood: Spiritual Foundations of the Poetry of Five American Indian Women." Schöler, *Coyote Was Here* 95–115. Joy Harjo (Creek), Linda Hogan (Chickasaw), Mary Tall Mountain (Athabascan), Wendy Rose (Hopi/Miwok), Carol Lee Sanchez (Laguna/Sioux), and Paula Gunn Allen.

————. " 'Whose Dream Is This Anyway?' Remythologizing and Self-Redefinitions of Contemporary American Indian Fiction." *Literature and the Visual Arts in Contemporary Society.* Ed. Suzanne Ferguson and Barbara Groselclose. Columbus: Ohio State UP, 1985. 95–122.

Antell, Judith A. "Momaday, Welch, and Silko: Expressing the Feminine Principle through Male Alienation." *AIQ* 12.3 (1988): 213–20.

"Barnes, Jim," *Contemporary Authors,* 1983 ed. 43–43.

Beidler, Peter G. "Animals and Human Development in the Contemporary American Indian Novel." *WAL* 14 (1979): 133–48.

Bevis, William. "Native American Novels: Homing In." Swann and Krupat, *Recovering the Word* 580–620.

Bruchac, Joseph (Abenaki), ed. *Survival This Way: Interviews with American Indian Poets.* Sun Tracks 15. Tucson: U of Arizona P, 1987. Interviews with Paula Gunn Allen (Laguna/Sioux), Peter Blue Cloud (Mohawk), Diane Burns (Ojibwa/Chemehuevi), Elizabeth Cook-Lynn (Sioux), Louise Erdrich (Ojibwa), Joy Harjo (Creek), Lance Henson (Cheyenne), Linda Hogan (Chickasaw), Karoniaktatie (Mohawk), Maurice Kenny (Mohawk), Harold Littlebird (Laguna/Santo Domingo), N. Scott Momaday (Kiowa), Duane Niatum (Klallam), Simon Ortiz (Acoma), Carter Revard (Osage), Wendy Rose (Hopi/Miwok), Luci Tapahonso (Navajo), Gerald Vizenor (Ojibwa), James Welch (Blackfeet/Gros Ventre), Roberta Hill Whiteman (Oneida), and Ray A. Young Bear (Mesquakie).

Castro, Michael. *Interpreting the Indian: Twentieth-Century Poets and the Native Americans.* Albuquerque: U of New Mexico P, 1983.

Chapman, Abraham, ed. *Literature of the American Indians: Views and Interpretations.* New York: NAL, 1975.

Coltelli, Laura, ed. *Native American Literature.* Pisa: U of Pisa P, 1989.

————, ed. *Winged Words: American Indian Writers Speak.* American Indian Lives. Lincoln: U of Nebraska P, 1990. Interviews with Paula Gunn Allen (Laguna/Sioux), Michael Dorris (Modoc), Louise Erdrich (Ojibwa), Joy Harjo (Creek), Linda Hogan (Chickasaw), N. Scott Momaday (Kiowa), Simon Ortiz (Acoma), Wendy Rose (Hopi/Miwok), Gerald Vizenor (Ojibwa), and James Welch (Blackfeet/Gros Ventre).

Hundley, Patrick D. *The Magic of Names: Three Native American Poets. Interviews with Norman H. Russell, Lance Henson, Jim Weaver Barnes.* Marvin: Blue Cloud, 1980.

Huntsman, Jeffrey. "Native American Theatre." *Ethnic Theatre in the United States.* Ed. Maxine Schwartz Seller. Westport: Greenwood: 1983. 355–85.

Jahner, Elaine. "A Critical Approach to American Indian Literature." Allen, *Studies in American Indian Literature* 211–24.

Kroeber, Karl. "Technology and Tribal Narrative." Vizenor, *Narrative Chance* 17–37.

Larson, Charles R. *American Indian Fiction.* Albuquerque: U of New Mexico P, 1978.

Liberty, Margot, ed. *American Indian Intellectuals.* 1976 Proceedings of the American Ethnological Soc. St. Paul: West, 1978.

Lincoln, Kenneth. *Native American Renaissance.* 1983. 2nd ed. rev. Los Angeles: U of California P, 1985.

Littlefield, Daniel F., Jr. (Cherokee), and James W. Parins. "Short Fiction Writers of the Indian Territory." *American Studies* 23.1 (1982): 23–48. William Jones (Sauk), Alexander Posey (Creek), John Oskison (Cherokee).

Lyon, Thomas, and J. Golden Taylor, eds. *A Literary History of the American West* Dallas: Texas Christian UP, 1987.

Momaday, N. Scott (Kiowa). "The Native Voice." *The Columbia Literary History of the United States*. Ed. Emory Elliott. New York: Columbia UP, 1988. 5–15.

Morris, Richard Joseph, ed. *Native American Press in Wisconsin and the Nation*. Madison: U of Wisconsin Library School, 1982.

Murphy, James E., and Sharon M. Murphy. *Let My People Know: American Indian Journalism, 1828–1978*. Norman: U of Oklahoma P, 1981.

Niatum, Duane. "History in the Colors of Song: A Few Words on Contemporary Native American Poetry." Schöler, *Coyote Was Here* 25–34.

———. "On Stereotypes." *Parnassus* 7 (1978): 160–66. Swann and Krupat, *Recovering the Word* 552–62.

Oaks, Priscilla. "The First Generation of Native American Novelists." *MELUS* 5 (1978): 57–65. John Joseph Mathews (Osage), D'Arcy McNickle (Cree/Salish), and John Milton Oskison (Cherokee).

Ramsey, Jarold W. "Thoreau's Last Words and America's First Literatures." Ruoff and Ward, *Redefining American Literary History*.

Roemer, Kenneth M. "Bear and Elk: The Nature(s) of Contemporary American Indian Poetry." Allen, *Studies in American Indian Literature* 178–91.

Rothenberg, Jerome, and Diane Rothenberg, eds. *Symposium of the Whole: A Range of Discourse toward an Ethnopoetics*. Berkeley: U of California P, 1983.

Ruoff, A. LaVonne Brown, ed. "Multicultural Literature, Part I. American Indian." Spec. issue of *Bulletin of the Association of Departments of English* 75 (1983).

———. "Old Traditions and New Forms." Allen, *Studies in American Indian Literature* 147–68.

———. "The Survival of Tradition: American Indian Oral and Written Narratives." *Ethnicity and Literature*. Spec. issue of *The Massachusetts Review* 27.2 (1986): 274–93.

Ruoff, A. LaVonne Brown, and Jerry W. Ward, Jr., eds. *Redefining American Literary History*. New York: MLA, 1990.

Ruppert, James. "Mediation and Multiple Narrative in Contemporary Native American Fiction." *Texas Studies in Literature and Language* 28.2 (1986): 209–25.

———. "Paula Gunn Allen and Joy Harjo: Closing the Distance between Personal and Mythic Space." *AIQ* 7 (1983): 27–40.

———. "The Uses of Oral Tradition in Six Contemporary Native American Poets." *AICRJ* 4 (1980): 87–110.

Sayre, Robert F. "Trickster." *NDQ* 53 (1985): 68–81.

Schöler, Bo, ed. *Coyote Was Here: Essays on Contemporary Native American Literary and Political Mobilization*. Spec. issue of *The Dolphin* 9 (1984).

Smith, Patricia Clark. "Ain't Seen You Since: Dissent among Female Relatives." Allen, *Studies in American Indian Literature* 108–26.

Smith, Patricia Clark, with Paula Gunn Allen (Laguna/Sioux). "Earthly Relations, Carnal Knowledge: Southwestern American Indian Writers and Landscape." *The Desert Is No Lady: Southwestern Landscapes in Women's Writing and Art*. Ed. Vera Norwood and Janice Monk. New Haven: Yale UP, 1987. 174–96. Luci Tapahonso (Navajo), Leslie Silko (Laguna), and Joy Harjo (Creek).

Standiford, Lester. "Worlds Made of Dawn: Characteristic Image and Incident in

Native American Imaginative Literature." *Ethnic Literatures since 1776: The Many Voices of America.* Eds. Wolodymyr T. Zyla and Wendell M. Aycock. Proceedings of the Comparative Literature Symposium 9. Lubbock: Texas Tech UP, 1978.

Swann, Brian, and Arnold Krupat, eds. *Recovering the Word: Essays on Native American Literature.* Berkeley: U of California P, 1987.

Velie, Alan R. *Four American Indian Literary Masters: N. Scott Momaday, James Welch, Leslie Marmon Silko, and Gerald Vizenor.* Norman: U of Oklahoma P, 1982.

Vizenor, Gerald (Ojibwa), ed. *Narrative Chance: Postmodern Discourse on Native American Indian Literatures.* Albuquerque: U of New Mexico P, 1989.

Wiget, Andrew O., ed. *Critical Essays on Native American Literature.* Philadelphia: Hall, 1985.

———. *Native American Literature.* Twayne's United States Authors 467. Boston: Twayne, 1985.

———. "Sending a Voice: The Emergence of Contemporary Native American Poetry." *CE* 46.6 (1984): 598–609.

STUDIES OF AMERICAN INDIAN AUTHORS

Allen, Paula Gunn (Laguna/Sioux)

Jahner, Elaine. "A Laddered, Rain-Bearing Rug: Paula Gunn Allen's Poetry." *Women and Western American Literature.* Ed. Helen Winter Stauffer and Susan J. Rosowski. Troy: Whitston, 1982. 311–26.

Apes, William (Pequot)

McQuaid, Kim. "William Apes, Pequot, an Indian Reformer in the Jackson Era." *New England Quarterly* 50 (1977): 605–25.

Black Elk (Sioux)

Castro, Michael. "Translating Indian Consciousness: Lew Sarett and John G. Neihardt." *Interpreting the Indian: Twentieth-Century Poets and the Native American.* By Castro. Albuquerque: U of New Mexico P, 1983. 71–97.

Couser, G. Thomas. "*Black Elk Speaks* with Forked Tongue." *Studies in Autobiography.* Ed. James Olney. New York: Oxford UP, 1988. 73–88.

Deloria, Vine, Jr. (Sioux), ed. *A Sender of Words: Essays in Memory of John G. Neihardt.* Salt Lake City: Howe, 1984.

DeMallie, Raymond J., ed. *The Sixth Grandfather: Black Elk's Teachings Given to John G. Neihardt.* Foreword Hilda Neihardt Petri. Lincoln: U of Nebraska P, 1984.

Rice, Julian. "*Akicita* of the Thunder: Horses in Black Elk's Vision." *Native American Literature.* Spec. issue of *MELUS* 12.1 (1985): 5–23.

Sayre, Robert. "Vision and Experience in *Black Elk Speaks.*" *CE* 32 (1971): 509–35.

Blowsnake, Sam (Winnebago)

Brumble, H. David, III. "Sam Blowsnake's Confessions: *Crashing Thunder* and the History of American Indian Autobiography." Swann and Krupat, *Recovering the Word* 537–51.

Carter, Forrest [Asa] (Cherokee)

Clayton, Lawrence. "Forrest Carter/Asa Carter and Politics." *WAL* 21.1 (1986): 19–26.

Copway, George (Ojibwa)

Knobel, Dale T. "Know-Nothings and Indians: Strange Bedfellows?" *Western Historical Quarterly* 15 (1984): 175–98.

Ruoff, A. LaVonne Brown. "George Copway: Nineteenth-Century American Indian Autobiographer." *Auto/Biography* 3.2 (1987): 6–17.

Smith, Donald B. "The Life of George Copway or Kah-ge-ga-gah-bowh (1818–1869)—and a Review of His Writings." *Journal of Canadian Studies* 23.3 (1988): 5–38.

Deloria, Ella C. (Sioux)

Medicine, Bea (Sioux). "Ella C. Deloria: The Emic Voice." *MELUS* 7.4 (1980): 23–30.

Eastman, Charles A. (Sioux)

Miller, David R. "Charles Alexander Eastman, the 'Winner': From Deep Woods to Civilization." Liberty, *American Indian Intellectuals* 61–73.

Stensland, Anna L. "Charles Alexander Eastman: Sioux Storyteller and Historian." *AIQ* 3 (1977): 199–208.

Wilson, Raymond. *Ohiyesa: Charles Eastman, Santee Sioux.* Urbana, U of Illinois P, 1983.

Erdrich, Louise (Ojibwa)

Brewington, Lillian, Normie Bullard, and Robert W. Reising, comps. "Writing in Love: An Annotated Bibliography of Critical Responses to the Poetry and Novels of Louise Erdrich and Michael Dorris." *AICRJ* 10.4 (1986): 81–86.

Gleason, William. " 'Her Laugh an Ace': The Function of Humor in Louise Erdrich's *Love Medicine.*" *AICRJ* 11.3 (1985): 51–73.

McKenzie, James. "Lipsha's Good Road Home: The Revival of Chippewa Culture in *Love Medicine.*" *AICRJ* 10.3 (1986): 53–63.

Silberman, Robert, "Opening the Text: *Love Medicine* and the Return of the Native American Woman." Vizenor, *Narrative Chance* 101–20.

Johnson, Emily Pauline (Mohawk)

Foster, Mrs. W. Garland (Anne). *The Mohawk Princess, Being Some Account of the Life of Teka-hion-wake (E. Pauline Johnson).* Vancouver: Lion's Gate, 1931.

Keller, Betty. *Pauline: A Biography of Pauline Johnson.* Vancouver: Douglas, 1981.

McRaye, Walter. *Pauline Johnson and Her Friends.* Toronto: Ryerson, 1947.

———. *Town Hall To-night.* Toronto: Ryerson, 1929.

La Flesche, Francis (Omaha)

Green, Norma Kidd. *Iron Eye's Family: The Children of Joseph La Flesche.* Lincoln: U of Nebraska P, 1969.

Liberty, Margot. "Francis La Flesche: The Osage Odyssey." Liberty, *American Indian Intellectuals* 45–59.

Long, Sylvester Clark [Long Lance] (Lumbee)

Smith, Donald B. "From Sylvester Long to Chief Buffalo Child Long Lance." Clifton, *Being and Becoming Indian* 183–203.

———. *Long Lance, the True Story of an Imposter.* Toronto: Macmillan, 1982; Lincoln: U of Nebraska P, 1983.

Mathews, John Joseph (Osage)

Hunter, Carol (Osage). "The Historical Context in John Joseph Mathews' *Sundown.*" *MELUS* 9 (1982): 61–72.

———. "The Protagonist as a Mixed-Blood in John Joseph Mathew's Novel *Sundown.*" *AIQ* 6 (1982): 319–37.

Ruoff, A. LaVonne Brown. "John Joseph Mathews's *Talking to the Moon*: Literary and Osage Contexts." *Essays in Multicultural Autobiography.* Ed. James Robert Payne. Knoxville: U of Tennessee P, forthcoming.

Wilson, Terry P. (Potawatomi). "Osage Oxonian: The Heritage of John Joseph Mathews." *CO* 59 (1981): 264–92.

McNickle, D'Arcy (Cree/Salish)

Owens, Louis (Cherokee). "The 'Map of the Mind': D'Arcy McNickle and the American Indian Novel." *WAL* 194 (1985): 275–83.

Ruppert, James. *D'Arcy McNickle.* Western Writers 83. Boise: Boise State UP, 1988.

———. "Politics and Culture in the Fiction of D'Arcy McNickle." *Rocky Mountain Review of Language and Literature* 42.4 (1988): 185–95.

———. "Textual Perspectives and the Reader in *The Surrounded.*" Vizenor, *Narrative Chance* 91–100.

Momaday, N. Scott (Kiowa)

Allen, Paula Gunn (Laguna/Sioux). "Bringing Home the Fact: Tradition and Continuity in the Imagination." Swann and Krupat, *Recovering the Word* 563–79.

Evers, Larry. "Words and Place: A Reading of *House Made of Dawn.*" *WAL* 11 (1977): 297–320. Wiget, *Critical Essays on Native American Literature* 211–30.

Hirsch, Bernard. "Self-Hatred and Spiritual Corruption in *House Made of Dawn.*" *WAL* 17 (1983): 307–20.

Hogan, Linda (Chickasaw). "Who Puts Together." Allen, *Studies in American Indian Literature* 169–77.

Lattin, Vernon E. "The Quest for Mythic Vision in Contemporary Native American and Chicano Fiction." *AL* 50 (1979): 625–40.

Lincoln, Kenneth. "Tai-Me to Rainy Mountain: The Makings of American Indian Literature." *AIQ* 10.2 (1986): 101–17.

McAllister, Harold S. "Incarnate Grace and the Paths of Salvation in *House Made of Dawn.*" *South Dakota Review* 12 (1974–75): 115–25.

Roemer, Kenneth M., ed. *Approaches to Teaching Momaday's* The Way to Rainy Mountain. New York: MLA, 1988.

Scarberry-Garcia, Susan. *Landmarks of Healing: A Study of* House Made of Dawn. Albuquerque: U of New Mexico P, 1990.

Schubnell, Matthias. *N. Scott Momaday: The Cultural and Literary Background.* Norman: U of Oklahoma P, 1985.

Trimble, Martha Scott. *N. Scott Momaday.* Western Writers 9. Boise: Boise State UP, 1973.

Watkins, Floyd. "Culture versus Anonymity in *House Made of Dawn.*" *Time and Place: Some Origins of American Fiction.* By Watkins. Athens: U of Georgia P, 1977. 133–71.

Woodard, Charles L. *Ancestral Voice: Conversations with N. Scott Momaday.* Lincoln: U of Nebraska P, 1989.

Montezuma, Carlos (Yavapai)

Iverson, Peter. *Carlos Montezuma and the Changing World of American Indians.* Albuquerque: U of New Mexico P, 1982.

Mourning Dove [Christine Quintasket] (Colville)

Brown, Alanna. "Mourning Dove's Voice in *Cogewea.*" *Wicazo Sa Review* 4.2 (1988): 2–15.

Dearborn, Mary. "Pocahontas's Sisters: A Case Study of American Indian Women

Writers." *Pocahontas's Daughters: Gender and Ethnicity in American Culture*. By Dearborn. New York: Oxford UP, 1986. 12–30.

Fisher, Dexter. "Introduction." *Cogewea, the Half-Blood: A Depiction of the Great Montana Cattle Range*. With notes and biographical sketch by Lucullus Virgil McWhorter. Lincoln: U of Nebraska P, 1981. v–xxix.

Miller, Jay. "Introduction." *Mourning Dove: A Salishan Autobiography*. American Indian Lives. Lincoln: U of Nebraska P, 1990.

———. "Mourning Dove: The Author as Cultural Mediator." Clifton, *Being and Becoming Indian* 160–82.

Occom, Samson (Mohegan)

Blodgett, Harold. *Samson Occom*. Dartmouth College Manuscript Ser. 3 Hanover: Dartmouth College Press, 1935.

Love, W. Deloss. *Samson Occom and the Christian Indians of New England*. Boston: Pilgrim, 1899.

Richardson, Leon Burr. *An Indian Preacher in England, Being Letters and Diaries Relating to the Mission of the Reverend Samson Occom and the Reverend Nathaniel Whitaker. . . .* Dartmouth College Manuscript Ser. 2. Hanover: Dartmouth College Press, 1938.

Ortiz, Simon J. (Acoma)

Gingerich, Willard. "The Old Voices of Acoma: Simon Ortiz's Mythic Indigenism." *Southwest Review* 64 (1979): 18–30.

Smith, Patricia. "Coyote Ortiz: *Canis latrans latrans* in the Poetry of Simon Ortiz." *Minority Voices* 3 (1979): 1–17.

Wiget, Andrew O. *Simon Ortiz*. Western Writers 74. Boise: Idaho State UP, 1986.

Pokagon, Simon (Potawatomi)

Buechner, Cecelia Bain. *The Pokagons*. 1933. Berrien Springs: Hardscrabble, 1976.

Clifton, James A. *The Pokagons, 1683–1983: Catholic Potawatomi of the St. Joseph River Valley*. Washington: Potawatomi Nation and UP of America, 1984.

———. "Simon Pokagon and the Sand-Bar Case: Michigan Potawatomi Claims to Chicago's Lake Front." *Michigan History* 71.5 (1987): 12–17.

Dickason, David H. "Chief Simon Pokagon: 'The Indian Longfellow.' " *Indiana Magazine of History* 57 (1971): 127–40.

Posey, Alexander (Creek)

Barnett, Leona G. (Creek). "*Este Cate Emunkv*: Red Man Always." *CO* 46 (1968): 20–40.

Callacombe, Doris. "Alexander Lawrence Posey." *CO* 11 (1933): 1011–18. Biographical sketch.

Dale, Edward Everett. "Journal of Alexander Lawrence Posey with Annotations." *CO* 45 (1967–68): 393–432.

Posey, Alexander L. "Journal of Creek Enrollment Field Party, 1905." *CO* 46 (1968): 2–19. Annotated by unidentified editor.

Ridge, John Rollin (Cherokee)

Debo, Angie. "John Rollin Ridge." *Southwest Review* 17 (1932): 59–71.

Foreman, Carolyn Thomas. "Edward W. Busyhead and John Rollin Ridge, Cherokee Editors in California." *CO* 14 (1936): 295–311.

Jackson, Joseph Henry. *Anybody's Gold: The Story of California's Mining Towns*. New York: Appleton, 1941.

Nadeau, Remi. *The Real Joaquín Murieta: Robin Hood Hero or Gold Rush Gangster?* Corona del Mar: Trans-Anglo Books, 1974.

Parins, James W. *John Rollin Ridge: His Life and Works.* American Indian Lives. Lincoln: U of Nebraska P, 1991.

Ranck, M. A. "John Rollin Ridge in California." *CO* 10 (1932): 560–69.

Walker, Franklin. *San Francisco's Literary Frontier.* 1939. Seattle: U of Washington P, 1969.

Riggs, [Rolla] Lynn (Cherokee)

Braunlich, Phyllis Cole. *Haunted by Home: The Life and Letters of Lynn Riggs.* Norman: U of Oklahoma P, 1988.

Erhard, Thomas. *Lynn Riggs, Southwest Playwright.* Austin: Steck-Vaughn, 1970.

Rogers, Will (Cherokee)

Alworth, E. Paul. *Will Rogers.* Twayne's United States Authors 236. Boston: Twayne, 1974.

Brown, William R. *The Imagemaker: Will Rogers and the American Dream.* Columbia: U of Missouri P, 1970.

Clark, Blue (Creek). "The Literary Will Rogers." *CO* 57 (1979): 385–94. Gibson, *Will Rogers* 133–42.

Day, Donald. *Will Rogers: A Biography.* New York: McKay, 1962.

Gibson, Arrell M., ed. *Will Rogers: A Centennial Tribute.* Oklahoma Ser. 12. Oklahoma City: Oklahoma Historical Soc., 1979. Also published as *CO* 57.3 (1979).

Rose, Wendy (Hopi/Miwok)

Lincoln, Kenneth. "Finding the Loss." *Parnassus* 10.1 (1982): 285–96.

Silko, Leslie Marmon (Laguna)

Allen, Paula Gunn (Laguna/Sioux). "The Psychological Landscape of *Ceremony.*" *AIQ* 5 (1979): 7–12.

Bell, Robert C. "Circular Design in *Ceremony.*" *AIQ* 5 (1979): 47–62.

Evers, Larry, and Denny Carr. "A Conversation with Leslie Marmon Silko." *Sun Tracks* 3 (1976): 28–33.

Danielson, Linda. "*Storyteller*: Grandmother Spider's Web." *Journal of the Southwest* 30.3 (1988): 325–55.

Fisher, Dexter. "Stories and Their Tellers: A Conversation with Leslie Marmon Silko." *The Third Woman: Minority Women Writers of the United States.* Ed. Fisher. Boston: Houghton, 1980. 18–23.

Jahner, Elaine. "An Act of Attention: Event Structure in *Ceremony.*" *AIQ* 5.1 (1979): 37–46.

———. "The Novel and Oral Tradition: An Interview with Leslie Marmon Silko." *Book Forum* 5 (1981): 383–88.

Krupat, Arnold. "The Dialogic of Silko's *Storyteller.*" Vizenor, *Narrative Chance* 55–68.

Nelson, Robert. "Place and Vision: The Function of Landscape in *Ceremony.*" *Journal of the Southwest* 30.3 (1988): 281–316.

Ruoff, A. LaVonne Brown. "Ritual and Renewal: Keres Traditions in the Short Fiction of Leslie Silko." *MELUS* 5 (1978): 2–17.

Ruppert, James. "The Reader's Lessons in *Ceremony.*" *Arizona Quarterly* 44.1 (1988): 78–85.

———. "Story Telling: The Fiction of Leslie Silko." *Journal of Ethnic Studies* 9 (1981): 53–58.

Sands, Kathleen Mullen, ed. *Leslie Marmon Silko's* Ceremony. Spec. issue of *AIQ* 5.1 (1979): 1–75.

Seyersted, Per. *Leslie Marmon Silko.* Western Writers 45. Boise: Boise State UP, 1980.

Swan, Edith. "Healing via the Sunwise Cycle in Silko's *Ceremony.*" *AIQ* 12.4 (1988): 313–28.

———. "Laguna Symbolic Geography and Silko's *Ceremony.*" *AIQ* 12.3 (1988): 229–49.

Vangen, Kathryn Shanley (Assiniboin). "The Devil's Domain: Leslie Silko's 'Storyteller.'" Schöler, *Coyote Was Here* 116–23.

Smith, Martin Cruz (Senecu del Sur/Yaqui)

Beidler, Peter G. "Indians in Martin Cruz Smith's *Nightwing*: A Review Article." *AIQ* 5 (1979): 155–59.

Vizenor, Gerald (Ojibwa)

Owens, Louis (Cherokee). " 'Ecstatic Strategies' : Gerald Vizenor's *Darkness in Saint Louis Bearheart.*" Vizenor, *Narrative Chance* 141–53.

Ruoff, A. LaVonne Brown. "Woodland Word Warrior: An Introduction to the Works of Gerald Vizenor." *MELUS* 13.1–2 (1986): 13–43.

Velie, Alan R. "The Trickster Novel." Vizenor, *Narrative Chance* 121–37.

Wilson, Terry P. (Potawatomi), and Robert Black, eds. *Gerald Vizenor Issue. AIQ* 9.1 (1985): 1–78.

Welch, James (Blackfeet/Gros Ventre)

Barry, Nora Baker. "*Winter in the Blood* as Elegy." *AIQ* 4 (1978): 149–57.

Beidler, Peter G., ed. *James Welch's* Winter in the Blood. Spec. issue of *AIQ* 4 (1978): 93–172.

McFarland, Ron, ed. *James Welch.* American Authors 1. Lewiston: Confluence, 1986.

Ruoff, A. LaVonne Brown. "Alienation and the Female Principle in *Winter in the Blood.*" *AIQ* 4 (1978): 107–22. Rev. McFarland, *James Welch* 59–82.

———. "The Influence of Emilio Vittorini's *In Sicily* on James Welch's *Winter in the Blood.*" Coltelli, *Native American Literature* 141–50.

Sands, Kathleen Mullen. "Alienation and Broken Narrative in *Winter in the Blood.*" *AIQ* 4.2 (1978): 97–105.

———. "*The Death of Jim Loney*: Indian or Not." McFarland, *James Welch* 147–58.

Thackeray, William. "Animal Allies and Transformers of *Winter in the Blood.*" *MELUS* 12 (1985): 37–64.

———. "Crying for Pity in *Winter in the Blood.*" *MELUS* 7 (1980): 61–78.

Velie, Alan R. "James Welch's Poetry." *AICRJ* 3.1 (1979): 19–38.

Wild, Peter. *James Welch.* Western Writers 57. Boise: Boise State UP, 1983.

Winnemucca, Sarah (Paiute)

Canfield, Gae Whitney. *Sarah Winnemucca of the Northern Paiutes.* Norman: U of Oklahoma P, 1983.

Fowler, Catharine S. "Sarah Winnemucca." Liberty, *American Indian Intellectuals* 33–42.

E. Teaching American Indian Literatures

Allen, Paula Gunn (Laguna/Sioux), ed. *Studies in American Indian Literature: Critical Essays and Course Designs.* New York: MLA, 1983.

Dorris, Michael A. (Modoc). "Native American Literature in an Ethnohistorical Context." *CE* 41.2 (1979): 147–62.

Evers, Larry. "Continuity and Change in American Indian Oral Literature." *ADE Bulletin* 75 (1983): 43–46.

———. "Native American Oral Literatures in the College English Classroom: An Omaha Example." *CE* 36 (1975) 649–62.

Ramsey, Jarold. "American Indian Literature and American Literature: An Overview." *ADE Bulletin* 75 (1983): 35–38.

———. "A Supplement to Michael Dorris's 'Native American Literature.'" *CE* 41.8 (1980): 933–35.

———. "The Teacher of Modern American Indian Writings as Ethnographer and Critic." *CE* 41.2 (1979): 163–69.

Ruoff, A. LaVonne Brown, ed. *Multicultural Literature I: American Indian.* Spec. issue of *ADE Bulletin* 75 (1983).

———. "Teaching American Indian Authors, 1772–1968." *ADE Bulletin* 75 (1983): 39–48.

F. Backgrounds

Albers, Patricia, and Beatrice Medicine (Sioux), eds. *The Hidden Half: Studies of Plains Indian Women.* Lanham: UP of America, 1983.

Allen, Paula Gunn (Laguna/Sioux). *The Sacred Hoop: Recovering the Feminine in American Indian Traditions.* Boston: Beacon, 1986.

Apes, William (Pequot). *Indian Nullification of the Unconstitutional Laws of Massachusetts, Relative to the Marshpee Tribe; or, The Pretended Riot Explained.* 1835. Foreword Jack Campisi. Stanfordville: Coleman, 1979.

Barnett, Louise K. *The Ignoble Savage: American Literary Racism, 1790–1890.* Westport: Greenwood, 1975.

Basso, Keith H. " 'To Give Up on Words': Silence in Western Apache Culture." *Southwestern Journal of Anthropology* 26 (1970): 312–30. Rpt. in *Apachean Culture History and Ethnology.* Ed. Basso and Morris E. Opler. Anthropological Papers of the Univ. of Arizona 21. Tucson: U of Arizona P, 1971. 151–61.

Bataille, Gretchen M., and Charles L. P. Silet, eds. *The Pretend Indians: Images of Native Americans in the Movies.* Foreword Vine Deloria, Jr. Ames: Iowa State UP, 1980.

Berkhofer, Robert F., Jr. *The White Man's Indian: Images of the American Indian from Columbus to the Present.* New York: Knopf, 1978. New York: Vintage, 1979.

Bieder, Robert. *Science Encounters the Indian, 1820–1880: The Early Years of American Ethnology.* Oklahoma: U of Oklahoma P, 1986.

Blackbird, Andrew J. [Mackawdegbenessy] (Ottawa). *History of the Ottawa and Chippewa Indians of Michigan; a Grammar of Theirr [sic] Language, and Personal and Family History of the Author.* 1887. Petosky: Little Traverse Regional History Soc., 1977.

Boas, Franz, ed. *Handbook of American Indian Languages.* 2 vols. BBAE 40 (1911).

Bright, William. See sect. D.

Bronson, Ruth Muskrat (Cherokee). *Indians Are People Too.* New York: Friendship, 1944.

Brown, Dee. *Bury My Heart at Wounded Knee: An Indian History of the American West.* New York: Holt, 1971. New York: Bantam, 1972.

Brown, Joseph Epes, ed. *The Sacred Pipe: Based on Black Elk's Account of the Seven Rites of the Oglala Sioux.* 1953. Civilization of the American Indian 36. Norman: U of Oklahoma P, 1961. Penguin Metaphysical Lib. Baltimore: Penguin, 1971.

Campbell, Lyle, and Marianne Mekun, eds. *The Languages of Native America: Historical and Comparative Assessment.* Austin: U of Texas P, 1979.

Capps, Walter Holden, ed. *Seeing with a Native Eye: Essays on Native American Religion.* New York: Harper, 1976.

Chiapelli, Fredi, Michael J. B. Allen, and Robert L. Benson, eds. *First Images of America: The Impact of the New World on the Old.* 2 vols. Berkeley: U of California P, 1976.

Clarke, Peter Dooyentate (Wyandot). *Origin and Traditional History of the Wyandotts, and Sketches of Other Indian Tribes of North America: True Traditional Stories of Tecumseh and His League, in the Years 1811 and 1812.* Toronto: Hunter, 1870.

Clifton, James A. "Alternate Identities and Cultural Frontiers." Clifton, *Being and Becoming Indian* 1–37.

———, ed. *Being and Becoming Indian: Biographical Studies of North American Frontiers.* Chicago: Dorsey, 1989.

Copway, George (Ojibwa). *The Traditional History and Characteristic Sketches of the Ojibway Nation.* London: Gilpin, 1850. Repub. as *Indian Life and Indian History, by an Indian Author, Embracing the Traditions of the North American Indian Tribes Regarding Themselves, Particularly of the Most Important of All the Tribes, the Ojibways.* 1858. New York: AMS, 1977.

Cusick, David (Tuscarora). *Sketches of Ancient History of the Six Nations. . . .* Lewiston: Author, 1827. 2nd ed. Lockport: Lathrop, 1828. 3rd ed. Lockport: Turner, 1848.

Debo, Angie. *And Still the Waters Run.* 1940. With new preface, "Thirty-Two Years After." Princeton: Princeton UP, 1972.

———. *A History of the Indians of the United States.* Civilization of the American Indian 106. Norman: U of Oklahoma P, 1970.

———. *The Rise and Fall of the Choctaw Republic.* 1934. 2nd ed. Civilization of the American Indian 6. Norman: U of Oklahoma P, 1961.

———. *The Road to Disappearance.* Civilization of the American Indian 22. Norman: U of Oklahoma P, 1941.

Deloria, Ella C. (Sioux). *Speaking of Indians.* Ed. Agnes Picotte (Sioux) and Paul N. Pavich. 1944. Vermillion: Dakota P, 1979.

Deloria, Vine, Jr., ed. (Sioux). *American Indian Policy in the Twentieth Century.* Norman: U of Oklahoma P, 1985.

———. *Behind the Trail of Broken Treaties: An Indian Declaration of Independence.* 1974. Austin: U of Texas P, 1985.

———. *God Is Red.* New York: Grosset, 1973. New York: Dell, 1973.

———. *The Metaphysics of Modern Existence.* New York: Harper, 1979.

———. *Of Utmost Good Faith.* San Francisco: Straight Arrow, 1971.

Deloria, Vine, Jr., and Clifford M. Lytle. *American Indians and American Justice.* Austin: U of Texas P, 1983.

———. *The Nations Within: The Past and Present Future of Indian Sovereignty.* New York: Pantheon, 1984.

Densmore, Frances. *Chippewa Customs.* BBAE 86 (1929). Introd. Nina Marchetti Archambal. St. Paul: Minnesota Historical Soc., 1979.

Dictionary of Indians of North America. 3 vols. St. Clair Shores: Scholarly, 1980.

Dobyns, Henry. *Their Number Become Thinned: Native American Population Dynamics in Eastern North America.* With an essay co-authored with William R. Swagerty. Native American Historic Demography. Knoxville: U of Tennessee P—Newberry Library Center for History of the American Indian, 1983.

Dockstader, Frederick J. (Oneida). Comp. *Great North American Indians: Profiles in Life and Leadership.* New York: Van Nostrand, 1977.

Dorris, Michael A. (Modoc). "The Grass Still Grows, the Rivers Still Flow: Contemporary Native Americans." *Daedalus* 110 (1981): 43–69.

Drake, Samuel G. *Indian Biography, Containing the Lives of More Than Two Hundred Chiefs. . . .* Boston: Drake, 1832.

Drinnon, Richard. *Facing West: The Metaphysics of Indian-Hating and Empire-Building.* Minneapolis: U of Minnesota P, 1980. New York: NAL, 1980.

Driver, Harold E. *Indians of North America.* 2nd ed. Chicago: U of Chicago P, 1969.

Eastman, Charles A. (Sioux). *Indian Heroes and Great Chieftains.* Boston: Little, 1918.

———. *The Indian To-day: The Past and Future of the First Americans.* 1915. New York: AMS, 1975.

———. *The Soul of the Indian: An Interpretation.* 1911. Lincoln: U of Nebraska P, 1980.

Edmunds, R. David (Cherokee), ed. *American Indian Leaders: Studies in Diversity.* Lincoln: U of Nebraska P, 1980.

Farb, Peter. *Man's Rise to Civilization: The Cultural Ascent of the Indians of North America.* 2nd ed. rev. New York: Dutton, 1978.

Fixico, Donald L. (Sauk/Fox/Creek/Seminole). *An Anthology of Western Great Lakes Indian History.* Milwaukee: U of Wisconsin, 1987.

Foreman, Carolyn Thomas. *Indian Women Chiefs.* Washington: Zenger, 1976.

Garbarino, Merwyn S. (Yuchi). *Native American Heritage.* Boston: Little, 1976. 2nd ed. Charlottesville: Teleprint, 1985.

Garfield, Viola E. "The Tsimshian and Their Neighbors." *The Tsimshian Indians and Their Arts.* Seattle: U of Washington Press, n.d. 5–37. Orig. pub. as parts 1 and 2 of *The Tsimshian: Their Arts and Music.* Ed. Marian W. Smith. PAES 18 (1952): 1–302.

Garter Snake (Gros Ventre). *The Seven Visions of Bull Lodge.* Comp. Fred P. Gone (Gros Ventre). Ed. George Horse Capture (Gros Ventre). Ann Arbor: Bearclaw, 1980.

Gibson, Arrell Morgan. *The American Indian: Prehistory to the Present.* Lexington: Heath, 1980.

Gill, Sam. *Mother Earth: An American Story.* Chicago: U of Chicago P, 1987.

———. *Native American Religions: An Introduction.* The Religious Life of Man. Belmont: Wadsworth, 1982.

———. *Native American Religious Action: A Performance Approach to Religion.* Columbia: U of South Carolina P, 1987.

———. *Sacred Words: A Study of Navajo Religion and Prayer.* Contributions in Intercultural and Comparative Studies. Westport: Greenwood, 1981.

Green, Rayna (Cherokee). "Native American Women: Review Essay." *Signs* 6 (1980): 248–67.

————. "The Pocahontas Perplex: The Image of Indian Women in American Culture." *Massachusetts Review* 4 (1978): 33–56.

Hagan, William T. *American Indians.* Rev. ed. Chicago History of American Civilization 8. Chicago: U of Chicago P, 1979.

Hoxie, Frederick E., ed. *Indians in American History.* Arlington Heights: Harlan Davidson, 1988.

Hultkrantz, Åke. *The Religions of the American Indians.* Trans. Monica Setterwall. Hermeneutics: Studies in the History of Religions. 1967. Berkeley: U of California P, 1979.

Hunter, Lois Marie (Shinnecock). *The Shinnecock Indians.* Islip: Buys, 1950.

Jennings, Francis. *The Invasion of America: Indians, Colonialism, and the Cant of Conquest.* Chapel Hill: U of North Carolina P, 1975. New York: Norton, 1976.

Johnson, Elias (Tuscarora). *Legends, Traditions and Laws, of the Iroquois, or Six Nations, and History of the Tuscarora Indians.* 1881. New York: AMS, 1977.

Jones, Eugene H. *Native Americans as Shown on the Stage, 1753–1916.* Metuchen: Scarecrow, 1988.

Jones, Peter [Kahkewaquonaby] (Ojibwa). *History of the Ojebway Indians, with Especial Reference to Their Conversion to Christianity. . . .* 1861. Freeport: Books for Libraries, 1970.

Josephy, Alvin M., Jr. *The Patriot Chiefs: A Chronicle of American Indian Resistance.* 1961. New York: Penguin, 1976.

Keiser, Albert. *The Indian in American Literature.* 1933. New York: Octagon, 1970.

La Barre, Weston. *The Peyote Cult.* 1959. 4th ed. enl. New York: Schocken, 1975.

Landes, Ruth. *Ojibwa Religion and the Midéwiwin.* Madison: U of Wisconsin P, 1968.

————. *The Ojibwa Woman.* CUCA 31 (1938). New York: Norton, 1971.

Liberty, Margot, ed. *American Indian Intellectuals.* 1976 Proceedings of the American Ethnological Soc. St. Paul: West, 1978.

Lurie, Nancy Oestreich. *North American Indian Lives.* Seattle: U of Washington P, 1985.

Mathews, John Joseph (Osage). *The Osages: Children of the Middle Waters.* Civilization of the American Indian 60. Norman: U of Oklahoma P, 1961.

McNickle, D'Arcy (Cree/Salish). *The Indian Tribes of the United States: Ethnic and Cultural Survival.* New York: Oxford UP, 1962.

————. *Native American Tribalism: Indian Survivals and Renewals.* New York: Oxford UP, 1973.

————. *They Came Here First: The Epic of the American Indian.* 1949. New York: Octagon, 1975.

McNickle, D'Arcy, and Harold E. Fey. *Indians and Other Americans: Two Ways of Life Meet.* New York: Harper, 1970.

Monkman, Leslie. *A Native Heritage: Images of the Indian in English Canadian Literature.* Toronto: U of Toronto P, 1981.

Mooney, James. *The Ghost Dance Religion and the Sioux Outbreak of 1890.* ARBAE 14.2 (1892–93). New York: Johnson, 1970. St. Clair Shores: Scholarly, 1970.

Moses, L. G., and Raymond Wilson, eds. *Indian Lives: Essays on Nineteenth and Twentieth Century Native American Leaders.* Albuquerque: U of New Mexico P, 1985.

Olsen, James S., and Raymond Wilson. *Native Americans in the Twentieth Century.* Urbana: U of Illinois P, 1987.

Ortiz, Alfonso (San Juan). *The Tewa World: Space, Time, Being, and Becoming in a Pueblo Society.* Chicago: U of Chicago P, 1969.

Oskison, John Milton (Cherokee). "Remaining Causes of Indian Discontent." 1907. Peyer, *The Elders Wrote* 152–58.

———. *Tecumseh and His Times: The Story of a Great Indian.* New York: Putnam, 1938.

Parsons, Elsie C. *Pueblo Indian Religion.* Chicago: U of Chicago P, 1939. Ethnology Ser. 2 vols. in 4. 1974.

Pearce, Roy H. *Savagism and Civilization: A Study of the Indian and the American Mind.* 1953. Foreword Arnold Krupat. Postscript by Pearce. Berkeley: U of California P, 1988. Orig. pub. as *The Savages of America.*

Porter, H. C. *The Inconstant Savage: England and the North American Indian, 1500–1660.* London: Duckworth, 1979.

Powell, John Wesley. "Indian Linguistic Families of America North of Mexico." ARBAE 7 (1891): 1–142.

Powell, Peter J. *Sweet Medicine: The Continuing Role of the Sacred Arrows, the Sun Dance, and the Sacred Buffalo Hut in Northern Cheyenne History.* 2 vols. Civilization of the American Indian 100. Norman: U of Oklahoma P, 1969.

Powers, Marla N. *Oglala Women: Myth, Ritual, and Reality.* Women in Culture and Society. Chicago: U of Chicago P, 1986.

Powers, William K. *Oglala Religion.* Lincoln: U of Nebraska P, 1975.

———. *Sacred Language: The Nature of Supernatural Discourse in Lakota.* Civilization of the American Indian 179. Norman: U of Oklahoma P, 1986.

———. *Yuwipi: Vision and Experience in Oglala Ritual.* Lincoln: U of Nebraska P, 1982.

Reichard, Gladys A. *Navaho Religion: A Study of Symbolism.* 1950. 2nd ed. Princeton: Princeton UP, 1963.

Ridge, John Rollin (Cherokee). *A Trumpet of Our Own: Yellow Bird's Essays on the North American Indian.* Comp. and ed. David Farmer and Rennard Strickland. San Francisco: Book Club of Calif., 1981.

Sahagun, Bernardino de. *General History of the Things of New Spain: Florentine Codex.* Monographs of the School of American Research 14. 13 vols in 12. Salt Lake City: U of Utah P, 1950–82.

Scheick, William J. *The Half-Blood: A Cultural Symbol in 19th Century American Fiction.* Lexington: U of Kentucky P, 1979.

Sebeok, Thomas, ed. *Native Languages of the Americas.* 2 vols. New York: Plenum, 1976.

Sheehan, Bernard W. *Savagism and Civility: Indians and Englishmen in Colonial Virginia.* Cambridge: Cambridge UP, 1980.

Slotkin, Richard. *Regeneration through Violence: The Mythology of the American Frontier, 1600–1860.* Middletown: Wesleyan UP, 1973.

Spencer, Robert F., Jesse D. Jennings, et al. *The Native Americans: Ethnology and Backgrounds of the North American Indians.* 2nd ed. New York: Harper, 1977.

Spicer, Edward H. *The American Indians.* Dimensions of Ethnicity. Boston: Harvard UP, 1982.

———. *Cycles of Conquest: The Impact of Spain, Mexico, and the United States on the Indians of the Southwest, 1533–1960.* Tucson: U of Arizona P, 1962.

Steward, Omer C. *Peyote Religion: A History.* Civilization of the American Indian 181. Norman: U of Oklahoma P, 1987.

Tanner, Helen Hornbeck. *Atlas of Great Lakes Indian History.* Civilization of the American Indian 174. Norman: U of Oklahoma P, 1987.

Tedlock, Dennis, and Barbara Tedlock, eds. *Teachings from the American Earth: Indian Religion and Philosophy.* New York: Liveright, 1975.

Thatcher, B. B. *Indian Biography: or, an Historical Account of Those Individuals Who Have Been Distinguished among the North American Natives.* . . . 2 vols. New York: Harper, 1832.

Thornton, Russell (Cherokee). *American Indian Holocaust and Survival: A Population History since 1942.* Civilization of the American Indian 186. Norman: U of Oklahoma P, 1987.

Turner, Frederick W., III. *Beyond Geography: The Western Spirit against the Wilderness.* 1980. New Brunswick: Rutgers UP, 1983.

Tyler, Hamilton. *Pueblo Animals and Myths.* Civilization of the American Indian 134. Norman: U of Oklahoma P, 1975.

———. *Pueblo Birds and Myths.* Civilization of the American Indian 147. Norman: U of Oklahoma P, 1979.

———. *Pueblo Gods and Myths.* Civilization of the American Indian 71. Norman: U of Oklahoma P, 1965.

Underhill, Ruth Murray. *Papago Indian Religion.* California Univ. Contributions to Anthropology 33 (1946). New York: AMS, 1969.

———. *Red Man's America: A History of Indians in the United States.* Rev. ed. Chicago: U of Chicago P, 1971.

———. *Red Man's Religion.* Chicago: U of Chicago P, 1965.

Vander, Judith. *Songprints: The Musical Experience of Five Shoshone Women.* Urbana: U of Illinois P, 1988.

Van Every, Dale. *Disinherited: The Lost Birthright of the American Indian.* New York: Morrow, 1966. New York: Avon, 1967.

Vaughn, A. T. "From White Man to Redskin: Changing Anglo-American Perceptions of the American Indian." *American Historical Review* 87 (1982): 917–53.

Vestal, Stanley. *Sitting Bull, Champion of the Sioux: A Biography.* Norman: U of Oklahoma P, 1957.

Walker, James R. *Lakota Belief and Ritual.* Ed. Raymond J. DeMallie and Elaine A. Jahner. Lincoln: U of Nebraska P, 1980.

Warren, William Whipple (Ojibwa). *History of the Ojibway, Based upon Traditions and Oral Statements.* Collections of the Minnesota Historical Soc. 5 (1885). Minneapolis: Ross and Haines, 1957. Introd. W. Roger Buffalohead (Ponca). Minneapolis: Minnesota Historical Soc., 1984.

Washburn, Wilcomb E., ed. *The Indian and the White Man.* Garden City: Doubleday, 1964.

———. *The Indian in America.* The New American Nation. New York: Harper, 1975.

Witherspoon, Gary. *Language and Art in the Navajo Universe.* Ann Arbor: U of Michigan P, 1977.

G. Films and Videotapes

Canadian Broadcasting Enterprise, 245 Park Ave., New York, NY 10167, has many films about Canadian Indian tribes.

Evers, Larry, prod., Denny Carr, dir. *Words and Place: Native Literature from the American Southwest.* Norman Ross, 1995 Broadway, New York, NY 10023. This excellent series includes the following programs: (1) "By This Song I Walk: Navajo Song." With Andrew Natonabah. (2) "Seyewailo: The Flower World." Yaqui Deer Songs. (3) "The Origin of the Crown Dance: An Apache Narrative" and "Ba'ts'oosee: An Apache Trickster Cycle." With Rudolph Kane. (4) "Iisaw: Hopi Coyote Stories." With Helen Sekaquaptewa. (5) "Natwaniwa: A Hopi Philosophical Statement." With George Nasoftie. (6) "Running on the Edge of the Rainbow: Laguna Stories and Poems." With Leslie Marmon Silko. (7) "Songs of My Hunter Heart: Laguna Songs and Poems." With Harold Littlebird. (8) "A Conversation with Vine Deloria, Jr." Available with transcripts, which include teaching guides and suggested background reading.

Ferrero, Pat, dir. *Hopi: Songs of the Fourth World.* Ferrero Films, 1259 Folsom St., San Francisco, CA 94103; New Day Films, 853 Broadway, Suite 1210, New York, NY 10003. Good documentary; sourcebook available.

Hilbert, Vi (Lushootseed), exec. prod., Crisca Bierwert, prod., and Pila Laronel, dir. *Sharing Legends at Upper Skagit.* Lushootseed Research, 10832 Desmoines Dr., South, Seattle, WA 98168. Elders from seven tribes tell stories at the Upper Skagit Tribal Center in 1985.

Masayesva, Victor (Hopi). *Hopi Clowns.* IS Productions, PO Box 747, Hotevilla, AZ 86030. Highly imaginative treatment.

———. *Itam Hakim Hopiit.* IS Productions, PO Box 747, Hotevilla, AZ 86030. Ross Macaya tells stories about the Hopi emergence and migration as well as the Pueblo Revolt of 1680. Hopi with English voiceover.

Native American Public Broadcasting Consortium, Inc., PO Box 83111, Lincoln, NE 68501, sells and rents films and videotapes about American Indians.

Vizenor, Gerald (Ojibwa). *Harold of Orange.* Film-in-the-Cities, 2388 University Ave., St. Paul, MN 55114. A modern Trickster story, featuring comedian Charlie Hill (Oneida) in the title role.

H. Journals and Small Presses

GENERAL JOURNALS

The following journals frequently publish works by American Indian and other minority authors and criticism of these literatures.

Alaska Quarterly Review. Dept. of English, Univ. of Alaska, Anchorage, 3221 Providence St., Anchorage, AL 99508.

Canadian Fiction Magazine. PO Box 946, Station F, Toronto, ON M4Y 2N9, Canada.

Contact II. PO Box 451, Bowling Green Sta., New York, NY 10004.

Dispatch. Newsletter of the Center for American Culture Studies,. Columbia Univ., 603 Lewisohn Hall, New York, NY 10027.

Journal of American Folklore. 1703 New Hampshire Ave., NW, Washington, DC 20009.

Journal of Ethnic Studies. Univ. of Western Washington., Bellingham, WA 98225.

Journal of the Southwest. Univ. of Arizona, Tucson, AZ 85719.

MELUS (Multi-Ethnic Literature of the United States). Dept. of English, Univ. of Massachusetts, Amherst, MA 01003.

NAIES. Newsletter of the National Assn. of Interdisciplinary Ethnic Studies. Ethnic Studies Dept., California State Polytechnic Univ., Pomona, CA 91768.

Puerto del Sol. Box 3E, New Mexico State Univ., Las Cruces, NM 88003. Southwestern literary magazine that often publishes American Indian authors.

Sinister Wisdom. PO Box 3252, Berkeley, CA 94703. Devoted to women's writing. Often publishes work by third-world women.

Yardbird Reader. Yardbird Publications, Inc., Box 2370, Sta. A, Berkeley, CA 94702. Literary magazine of third-world poetry.

AMERICAN INDIAN JOURNALS

American Indian Culture and Research Journal. American Indian Studies Center, 3220 Campbell Hall, Univ. of California, Los Angeles, CA 90024.

American Indian Quarterly. Native American Studies, Univ. of California, Berkeley, CA 94720.

ASAIL Notes. Dept. of English, Central Oregon Community Coll., 2600 NW College Way, Bend, OR 97701-5998.

Studies in American Indian Literatures. Department of English, University of Richmond, Richmond, VA 23173. Formerly published at Columbia University and briefly absorbed into *Dispatch*, this bulletin has been reactivated.

Wanbli Ho, PO Box 8, Sinte Gleska College, Mission, SD 57555.

Wicazo Sa Review. Indian Studies, Eastern Washington Univ., Cheney, WA 99004.

SELECTED SMALL PRESSES

The following small presses, cited in the selected bibliographies and listed in current directories, publish works by and about American Indians. The addresses given here are the most recent listed.

Ahsahta Press, Dept. of English, Idaho State Univ., Boise, ID 83725.

Akwesasne Notes, Mohawk Nation via Rooseveltown, NY 13683.

Alexanderian Press, 700 Hansen Way, PO Box 10080, Palo Alto, CA 94303-0812.

American Indian Studies Center, 3220 Campbell Hall, Univ. of California, Los Angeles, CA 90024.

August House, PO Box 3223, Little Rock, AR 72203-3223.

Ayer, 382 Main St., PO Box 958, Salem, NH 03079.

Backstreet Editions, PO Box 555, Port Jefferson, NY 11777.

Blackberry Press, Chimney Farm, RR #1, PO Box 228, Nobleborrow, ME 04555.

Blue Cloud Quarterly, PO Box 98, Marvin, SD 57251.

Bookslinger Press, 2163 Ford Parkway, St. Paul, MN 55116.

Burning Deck Press, 71 Elmgrove Ave., Providence, RI 02906.

Center for Adirondack Studies, North Country Community College Press, 20 Winona Ave., Saranac Lake, NY 12983.

Chalatien Press, 5859 Woodleigh Dr., Carmichael, CA 95608.

Chalfant Press, PO Box 787, Bishop, CA 93514.

Coffee House Press, PO Box 10870, Minneapolis, MN 55458.

Contact II, PO Box 451, Bowling Green Sta., New York, NY 10004.

Crossing Press, 17 West Main St., Trumansburg, NY 14886.

Elizabeth Press, 103 Van Etten Blvd., New Rochelle, NY 10804.

Fiction Collective, English Dept., Brooklyn College, Brooklyn, NY 11210,. Dist. by
Sun & Moon Press, 6363 Wilshire Blvd., Suite 115, Los Angeles, CA 90048.

Firebrand Press, 141 The Commons, Ithaca, NY 14850.

Great Raven, Box 858, Lewiston, ME 04240.

Greenfield Review Press, 2 Middlegrove Rd., Greenfield Center, NY 12833.

Harlan Davidson, 3110 North Arlington Heights Rd., Arlington Heights, IL 60004.

Holy Cow! Press, PO Box 3170, Mount Royal Sta., Duluth, MN 55803.

Indian University Press, Bacone College, Muskogee, OK 74403.

Irografts Ltd., RR #2, Okswehen, ON N0A 1M0 Canada.

Malki Museum, Morongo Indian Reservation, Banning, CA 92220.

Milkweed Editions, PO Box 3226, Minneapolis, MN 55403.

Navajo Community College Press, Tsaile, AZ 86556.

Nodin Press, c/o The Bookmen, Inc., 525 N. Third St., Minneapolis, MN 55401.

Norman Ross, 1995 Broadway, New York, NY 10023.

Northland Books, PO Box N, Flagstaff, AZ 86002.

Oyate Press, 2701 Mathews St., Berkeley, CA 94707.

Pemmican Publications, 504 Main St., Room 411, Winnipeg, MB R3B 1B8 Canada.

Point Riders Press, PO Box 2731, Norman, OK 73070.

I. Reed Books, Suite D, 1446 Sixth St., Berkeley, CA 94704.

Seklos, Dept. of English, Univ. of Aarhus, 800 Aarhus C, Denmark.

Spinster's Inc., PO Box 410687, San Francisco, CA 94107.

Straight Arrow Books, PO Box 1068, Coronado, CA 92118-1068.

Strawberry Press, PO Box 456, Bowling Green Sta., New York, NY 10004.

Sun Tracks Series, Univ. of Arizona, Tucson, AZ 85721.

Swift Kick Press, 1711 Amherst St., Buffalo, NY 14214.

Taurean Horn, 920 Levenworth St., #401, San Francisco, CA 94109.

Tejas Art Press, 207 Terrel Rd., San Antonio, TX 78209.

Theytus Books Ltd., PO Box 218, Penticton, BC V2A 6K3 Canada.

Thunder's Mouth Press, 93–99 Greene St., New York, NY 10012.

Tooth of Time Press, 634 Garcia St., Sante Fe, NM 87501.

Turtle Island Foundation, 2845 Buena Vista Way, Berkeley, CA 94708.

West End Press, PO Box 27334, Albuquerque, NM 87125.

White Pine Press, 76 Center St., Fredonia, NY 14063.

Important Dates in American Indian History, 1500 to the Present

c. 1500	Formation of the Iroquois Confederacy.
1535	Cartier arrives in St. Lawrence Valley.
1540	Coronado arrives in New Mexico and de Soto comes to the Southeast.
1598	Oñate establishes a Spanish colony in New Mexico.
1607	Settlement at Jamestown.
1620	Settlement at Plymouth Colony.
1622	Opechancanough's first uprising against Jamestown.
1637	Pequot War in New England.
1644	Opechancanough's last uprising in Virginia.
1672–76	King Philip's (Metacomet) War in New England.
1680	Pueblo Revolt.
1729	Destruction of the Natchez by French of New Orleans.
1754–63	French and Indian War.
1763	Pontiac's Rebellion against the British.
1772	Publication of Samson Occom's *Sermon Preached at the Execution of Moses Paul*, the first Indian best seller.
1775–83	American Revolution.
1799	Founding of the Handsome Lake religion among the Seneca.
1810–13	Tecumseh and Tenskwatawa try to control Indiana and establish an intertribal army.
1812	War of 1812.
1813–14	Creek War.
1824	Bureau of Indian Affairs established.
1827	Publication of David Cusick's *Sketches of Ancient History of the Six Nations*, earliest history published by an Indian.
1829	Publication of William Apes's *A Son of the Forest*, the first autobiography written by an Indian to be published.
1830	Removal Bill.
1832	Office of Commissioner of Indian Affairs created.
1833	Publication of *Black Hawk, an Autobiography*, the first narrated autobiography to gain widespread popularity.
1835–42	Seminole War.
1835	Publication of William Apes's *Indian Nullification of the Unconstitutional Laws of Massachusetts*, one of the first protest books published by an Indian.

1847	Opening of the Oregon Trail.
	Publication of George Copway's *The Life, History, and Travels of Kah-ge-ga-gah-bowh (George Copway)*, an autobiography.
1848	Treaty of Guadalupe Hidalgo brings southwestern and California tribes under U.S. control.
	Publication of Maungwudaus's *Account of the Ojibway Indians*, the earliest travel pamphlet written by an Indian to be published.
1849	Discovery of gold in California.
	Office of Indian Affairs transferred to Interior Department.
1851	Publication of George Copway's *Running Sketches of Men and Places*, the first full-length travel book by an Indian.
1854	Publication of John Rollin Ridge's *Life and Adventures of Joaquín Murieta*, the first novel by an Indian.
1861–65	United States Civil War.
1862	Minnesota Sioux uprising.
1863–64	Kit Carson's campaign against the Navajos and Apaches.
1864	Massacre at Sand Creek, Colorado, of the Cheyenne, November 28.
1867	Board of Indian Commissioners established.
1868	Posthumous publication of John Rollin Ridge's *Poems*, the first poetry book by an Indian.
1871	Negotiations of treaties with Indians abandoned by the United States.
1872	Modoc War.
1874–75	Red River War.
1876	Custer's Battle at the Little Big Horn, June 26.
1877	Chief Joseph leads the Nez Perce outbreak.
1882	Indian Rights Association founded.
1883	Publication of Sarah Winnemucca's *Life among the Piutes*, the first autobiography written by an American Indian woman.
1885	Last buffalo herd exterminated.
1886	Geronimo and his band of Apaches surrender.
1887	General Allotment Act (Dawes Act)
c. 1889	Ghost Dance religion spreads across the Plains.
1890	Massacre at Wounded Knee, Pine Ridge Reservation, South Dakota, December 29.
1895	Publication of Emily Pauline Johnson's *White Wampum*, the first book of poetry published by an Indian woman.
1902	Publication of Charles A. Eastman's *Indian Boyhood*, one of the first autobiographies by an Indian written for children.
	Alexander Posey purchases the *Indian Journal* in Eufaula, Oklahoma, and begins to write the "Fus Fixico Letters."
1910	Posthumous publication of *The Poems of Alexander Lawrence Posey*, one of the earliest such volumes by an Indian author.
1913	Publication of Johnson's *Moccasin Maker* and *Shagganappi*, the first books of short fiction and essays by an Indian woman.
1916	Publication of Charles A. Eastman's *From the Deep Woods to Civilization*.
1919	Publication of Will Rogers's *Rogers-isms: The Cowboy Philosopher on*

	the Peace Conference and *Rogers-isms: The Cowboy Philosopher on Prohibition*, the first of that author's many books.
1924	Congress awards citizenship to all Indians.
1927	Publication of Mourning Dove's *Cogewea*, the first novel written by an Indian woman.
1928	Meriam Report published, criticizing the government's treatment of Indians.
1931	Publication of Lynn Riggs's *Green Grow the Lilacs*, the original source of the hit musical *Oklahoma!* and the biggest Broadway success by an Indian playwright.
1932	Publication of John Joseph Mathews's *Wah'Kon-Tah*, the first book by an Indian author to be honored as a Book-of-the-Month selection.
1934	Wheeler-Howard Indian Reorganization Act.
1941	National Congress of American Indians established.
1953	House Concurrent Resolution 108 passed, instituting the policy of termination of the federal role in Indian affairs.
1961	American Indian Chicago Conference.
	Foundation of National Indian Youth Council.
1968	American Indian Movement founded.
	Passage of Indian Civil Rights Act.
	Publication of N. Scott Momaday's *House Made of Dawn*, the first book by an Indian author to win the Pulitzer Prize.
1969	Indians occupy Alcatraz Island.
	Publication of Momaday's *Way to Rainy Mountain*. The appearance of Momaday's two books ushers in a renaissance of American Indian literature.
1971	Alaska Native Claims Settlement Act passed.
1972	Indians occupy the Bureau of Indian Affairs headquarters in Washington, DC.
1973	Occupation at Wounded Knee, South Dakota.
1978	Passage of American Indian Religious Freedom Act and Indian Child Welfare Act.
1988	Supreme Court decision permits the Forest Service to build a road through land sacred to the Yurok, Karok, and Tolowa tribes of California, who claimed such an action deprived them of their First Amendment rights to free exercise of religion.
1989	Federal judge upholds off-reservation fishing rights of Wisconsin Chippewa, guaranteed by treaties in 1837 and 1842.

Index

The index lists persons, organizations, important bills and acts, events, and a few relevant topics about American Indians. Tribes of authors and scholars are given where known. Additional authors, scholars, and works are listed in "A Selected Bibliography."

Brown, Dee, 141
Brown, Joseph Epes, 143
Brown, William R., 137
Bruchac, Joseph (Abenaki), 13, 85, 92, 113, 117, 132
Brumble, H. David, iii, 117, 130
Buechner, Cecelia Bain, 136
Buffalo Bill. *See* Cody, William F.
Bullard, Normie, 134
Bullchild, Percy (Blackfeet), 122
Buller, Galen, 127–28
Bunzel, Ruth L., 20, 37–38, 120, 125
Bureau of Indian Affairs (U.S. Govt.), 5, 72, 85
Burns, Diane (Ojibwa/Chemehuevi), 113
Burns, Robert, 68
Bush, Barney (Shawnee/Cayuga), 106–07
Bushyhead, Edward W. (Cherokee), 136
Byler, Mary Gloyne (Cherokee), 116, 117, 140

Callacombe, Doris, 136
Canfield, Gae Whitney, 138
Capps, Walter Holden, 142
Carr, Denny, 9, 122–23
Carr, Pat, 128
Carson, Kit, 3, 106
Castro, Michael, 133
Chapman, Abraham, 118
Chief Eagle, Dallas (Sioux), 92
Chivington, J. M., 3
Chona, Maria (Papago), 61
Civil War, 3
Clark, Blue (Creek), 137
Clarke, Peter Dooyentate (Wyandot), 64, 141
Clements, William M., 116
Clifton, James A., 66, 136, 139–40
Clutesi, George (Tlingit), 122
Cody, William F. [Buffalo Bill], 57
Cole, Nat King, 109
Collier, John, 72
Colonnese, Tom, 117
Coltelli, Laura, 131, 132
Committee on the Literatures and Languages of America, MLA, viii
Condolence, Ritual of (Iroquois), 22–24
Conrad, Joseph, 89
Cook-Lynn, Elizabeth (Sioux), 113, 131
Copway, Elizabeth Howell, 54
Copway, George (Ojibwa), 11, 35, 39, 54–55, 63–64, 119, 130, 133, 141
Cornplanter, Jesse (Seneca), 42, 45, 122
Cortés, Hernan, 94
Count, Earl W., 126
Courlander, Harold, 11, 121
Couser, G. Thomas, 133
Cronyn, George W., 119

Cruikshank, Julie, 130
Curtin, Jeremiah, 126
Curtis, Natalie Burlin, 119
Cushing, Frank, 16
Cusick, David (Tuscarora), 63, 141
Custer, George Armstrong, 3, 61, 92, 114, 144
Custer Battle [Battle of the Little Big Horn], 61, 92

Dale, Edward Everett, 136
Danielson, Linda, 138
Dauenhauer, Nora (Tlingit), 118
Dauenhauer, Richard, 118
Dawes, Henry L., 3
Dawes Act. *See* General Allotment Act
Day, A. Grove, 29, 31, 119
Day, Donald, 137
Dearborn, Mary, 136
Debo, Angie, 136, 140, 141
Deloria, Ella C. (Sioux), 10–11, 75, 121
Deloria, Vine, Jr. (Sioux), 114, 133, 141, 142–43, 144
DeMallie, Raymond J., 61, 133
Densmore, Frances, 16–17, 19, 24, 26, 27, 28–29, 35, 36, 42, 84, 120, 122
Derrida, Jacques, 131
Dickason, David H., 136
Dickinson, Emily, 97
Dinesen, Isak, 60
Dixon, Roland, 46
Dobyns, Henry, 140
Dockstader, Frederick J. (Oneida), 139
Dorris, Adam, 89
Dorris, Michael A. (Modoc), ix, 85, 88–89, 116, 117, 134, 139, 140, 141
Dorsey, George A., 120
Dorsey, J. Owen, 57–58
Double-face (Crow), 50–51
Downes, Jerome, 84
Downing, [George] Todd (Choctaw), 75
Drake, Samuel G., 139
Drinnon, Richard, 144
Duncan, Annie Patsy (Klallam), 103
Dundes, Alan, 126, 127, 128
Dunne, Finley Peter, 68

Eastman, Charles A. [Ohiyesa] (Sioux), 3, 13, 41, 56–57, 69, 122, 130, 133–34, 139, 141, 142
Eastman, Elaine Goodale, 41, 56, 69, 122
Eastman, Jacob [Many Lightnings] (Sioux), 56
Eastman, Seth, 56
Edmunds, R. David (Cherokee), 139
Egge, Marion F., 117
Emerson, Ralph Waldo, 56